FabJob Guide to
Become a
Florist

ALISA GORDANEER

FABJOB GUIDE TO BECOME A FLORIST
by Alisa Gordaneer

ISBN 978-1-894638-62-3

Library and Archives Canada Cataloguing in Publication

Gordaneer, Alisa
FabJob Guide to become a florist / by Alisa Gordaneer.

Accompanied by CD-ROM.
Includes bibliographical references.
ISBN 978-1-894638-62-3

1. Florists—Vocational guidance. I. Title. II. Title: Florist.
SB443.G67 2005   745.92'023   C2004-905742-1

FabJob Inc.
19 Horizon View Court
Calgary, Alberta, Canada T3Z 3M5

FabJob Inc.
4616 25th Avenue NE, #224
Seattle, Washington, USA 98105

To order books in bulk phone 403-949-2039
To arrange a media interview phone 403-949-4980

www.FabJob.com

Contents

About the Author

Alisa Gordaneer started working with flowers at the age of 10, when her mother bought a shop called The Bay Fresh Flower Shop. She was pulled into the thick of the business several years later, with the takeover of Daisy Chain Florists Ltd (**www.daisychainflorists.com**).

Alisa graduated from scrubbing buckets and sweeping floors to processing flowers and helping customers, and then moved on to arranging flowers and managing the shop. She worked on the floral design and production team for the 1994 Commonwealth Games, during which she had the honor of delivering flowers to the private chamber of Queen Elizabeth II.

After visiting FTD for its 75th Anniversary celebrations in Southfield, Michigan, she returned to the state to attend florist training sessions, and eventually to live. In Michigan, Alisa developed her passion for gardening, and made extensive visits to floral and garden centers to increase her knowledge about indoor and outdoor plants and trends in floral design.

Alisa now works as a full-time editor and writer, and is a mother of two. She has written for several florist trade magazines, and has contributed essays, fiction and poetry to the books *Women Who Eat: A New Generation on the Glory of Food* (Seal Press, 2003); *Breeder: Real-Life Stories from the New Generation of Mothers* (Seal Press, 2001); *Love and Pomegranates* (Sono Nis, 2000); and *Threshold: Six Women, Six Poets* (Sono Nis, 1998). She is currently working on a novel.

In the busy weeks leading up to every major florist holiday, she still finds herself arranging flowers late into the night in the family shop.

Acknowledgement

The floral arrangements featured on the color pages in this book were done by FTD Master Designer **Miria Gordaneer**. Miria is the owner of Daisy Chain Florists, and has been designing flowers since 1979.

1. Introduction

Floristry is an exciting and challenging business — one that is quite literally growing with potential and blooming with opportunity. As a florist, you'll be surrounded by an endless supply of beauty.

Whether it's an arrangement for someone's birthday, a vase of flowers for a co-worker's desk, or a grandiose display for a gala party, you will be behind some of the most significant moments in people's lives. It's an honor that few other professions share. You will discover how to get started and succeed in this career in the *FabJob Guide to Become a Florist*.

As a floral designer, you'll find a world of creative challenges, artistic opportunities and personal relations that will keep you inspired and intrigued for years to come. In this chapter, you'll explore your role as a florist in people's everyday lives and discover some of the benefits of this fabulous career.

1.1 Welcome to the Florist Industry

Floristry is an unusual and rewarding profession in that it combines a diverse variety of skills and abilities. It offers daily challenges and a wide range of possibilities — from employment in a fast-paced, production-oriented store to running your own flower shop (or shops).

As a business, it combines stability with a wide range of exciting possibilities that run the gamut from fast cash-and-carry retail to intensive customer service as you work with clients to plan the flowers for their wedding or gala event.

You don't need any special training to get your first job in a flower shop, because many of the daily tasks required can be learned as you go, beginning with caring for customers and flowers. However, if you want to jump right in and be hired as a full-fledged floral designer, you'll want to get some training first, which we will cover in Chapter 2.

As a florist, you'll have a unique window into the cycles of life. No matter what the occasion, there are flowers to go with it. Florists make arrangements of delicate pink and blue flowers to help customers welcome new babies into the world. They make colorful table centerpieces for everything from birthdays and anniversaries to homecomings and holidays. Christmas wouldn't be the same without showy poinsettia plants or sweet-smelling pine wreaths, and a basket of flowers at Easter helps remind us that spring is near.

You'll help customers honor their mothers with flowers and plants at Mother's Day, and you'll prepare elegant boxes of long-stemmed roses for Valentine's gifts. You'll reflect a bride's personality and taste with custom-designed wedding bouquets, and help people honor their loved ones by creating beautiful floral funeral tributes.

1.2 Benefits of a Career in Floristry

Florists enjoy many benefits, but the first one you might notice when you walk into a flower shop is the incredible access to fresh flowers! Every day, you're surrounded by the beautiful colors and heady scents of fresh flowers, the shine of ribbons, the graceful lines of vases, and the lush foliage of tropical plants. Here are more benefits you'll enjoy as a florist:

Outlet for Creativity

As a florist, you have the opportunity to use your creativity in marketing, display, and production. You will create stunning floral arrangements and window displays that catch customers' eyes. If you enjoy crafts – especially three-dimensional ones like papier-mâché or modeling – you will likely excel at floristry. You will have a hands-on job that gives you a sense of satisfaction with the product of your work.

Variety

While the basics — flowers, plants, giftware, customer service — provide a stable framework for your days, the possible variations on these themes are endless. It's a job that changes from day to day, and season to season, always allowing you to test your fresh ideas and get excited about your new approach.

Fast-Paced Environment

Being a florist requires excellent organization and a sharp sense of timing — after all, when someone needs a bouquet of roses to appear at the table when they're in the middle of a romantic dinner, there's no excuse for getting the flowers there after the check has already arrived. You will exercise your ability to think fast, respond to changing circumstances ("She's decided to wear blue instead — so we'll need to change the color of her flowers."), and improvise solutions using your creative abilities and knowledge.

Making People Happy

Nothing is as satisfying as the smile on someone's face when they see the flowers you've arranged for them. Florists make people happy by providing them with something beautiful. Each customer who walks through the doors of a flower shop is there to fulfill a unique need to brighten someone's day. Your job will be to suggest the best arrangements that will please the lucky recipient.

Learning New Skills

While there are a variety of basic flower arrangements, there are always new arrangements to learn. You will have opportunities to focus on one set of skills (floral design is a highly regarded and easily transferable specialty that will allow you to find work in any professional florist shop) or to work on a range of abilities as you enter the exciting realm of running your own business.

Community Involvement

Being a florist allows you to participate in your community by providing clients with the products of your own creativity. You are among the first they turn to when they are happy, excited, or grieving — giving you a finger on the pulse of the community.

In my time as a florist, I've done flowers for the Lieutenant-Governor of British Columbia and sent an order that was to be delivered to Cuban president Fidel Castro. Being a florist helps you feel like you're part of the world at large and helping history along, one petal at a time.

Going New Places

You can take your skills far and wide and access worlds that would otherwise be closed to you. A florist I know has done work for Queen Juliana of the Netherlands and has made numerous trips to Europe to further her design studies. I have made arrangements for world-class athletes and seen my handiwork displayed in the hands of gold-medal winners on TV. I have delivered flowers to the room that would be the private chamber of Her Royal Highness, Queen Elizabeth II.

Meeting New People

Another former florist I know got a glimpse into a whole other world when she made the funeral sprays for a member of a motorcycle gang. His friends played tag in the parking lot on their motorcycles and picked up the black spray-painted arrangements while still playing tag in the flower shop. You'll meet many other interesting and exciting people at crucial points in their lives. You may witness a courtship through bouquets you prepare, and then provide the flower arrangements for the wedding. A few years later, you may find yourself making a bouquet for their new baby.

Ongoing Appreciation

In addition, knowing how to arrange flowers is a skill that will last you a lifetime and that has many applications outside your work as well. Your home will always look pleasing, thanks to your ability to make the simplest garden daisies – or the most elaborate holiday display of fir garlands and spicy carnations – look absolutely stunning. You'll be honored to make wedding bouquets for family, friends, and acquaintances. And you'll always have beauty on hand.

Financial Rewards

There are financial rewards to being a florist, too. If you choose to run your own business, you will find that the more effort you put in, the more you are rewarded with loyal customers, established accounts, and reciprocal orders from out-of-town florists. While a floral designer working at a flower shop is likely to make anywhere from $25,000 to $50,000 and more each year, a successful florist business can gross upwards of a million dollars annually.

1.3 Inside This Guide

This guide is meant to help you get started in the florist industry. After reading it thoroughly, you should have a good technical understanding of design, the functions of the florist industry, and the day-to-day workings of a typical flower shop. You will also gain the essential knowledge of how to start your own business and make it a success.

In Chapter 2 ("Creating Floral Arrangements"), we'll teach you how to create floral arrangements and describe the variety of services florists offer. We'll cover the basics of color and design. You'll learn about the essential equipment, tools, and supplies that florists use, and find out about flowers, greens and how to look after them in the store. Plus, you'll find out about the most frequently used flower shop plants. Then – the best part – you'll learn step-by-step techniques for making a wide variety of flower arrangements. We'll also talk about providing flowers for weddings and funerals.

Chapter 3 ("Preparing for Your Career") will lay out the skills you'll need as a florist. We'll talk about sales, organization, and creativity. We'll cover possible formal educational options, plus several informal ways to gain knowledge, like conducting information interviews or reading books and trade magazines. We'll also begin to look at ways for you to get your foot in the door at a flower shop as an intern, and what professional accreditations are available.

Once you've got some background in the industry, Chapter 4 ("Getting Hired") will discuss ways of getting your first fabulous job as a florist, and the types of positions you might try. We'll talk about finding a position, preparing for your interview, and making a good impression when you meet with your future employer.

In Chapter 5 ("Starting Your Own Flower Shop"), we'll explore how to open your own floral business. You'll learn about how to get started, how to set up your shop, and how to keep track of your finances. We'll also look at creating in-store displays and maintaining your new florist shop. We'll also talk about dealing with wholesalers and suppliers and how to hire help.

Then, in Chapter 6 ("Getting and Keeping Customers"), we'll talk about how to make your own shop a success. Here you'll learn how to attract and keep consumer and corporate customers. We'll discuss how to market and promote your store, and explore several promotional tools you can use. And you'll learn about how florists send out-of-area orders to people around the world.

Finally, Chapter 7 ("Resources") contains a list of professional associations you can turn to for further information and ongoing learning opportunities.

So read on to get prepared for an exciting career as a florist!

2. Creating Floral Arrangements

Whether you decide to take a part-time or full-time job as a florist or open up your own shop, you'll need to know the basics of creating floral arrangements. In this chapter, we will look at the different services florists provide and describe the many varieties of flowers and plants you will be working with.

Once you have a good foundation in basic floral design, you'll be ready to create your own arrangements. In this chapter you'll find step-by-step instructions for creating a variety of types of arrangements. Full-color photos of many common types of arrangements are included in the color section of this book.

2.1 Services Provided by a Florist

Florists sell, arrange, deliver, and send flowers. They sell indoor plants, permanent floral décor, giftware, and more. They provide wedding flowers, funeral tributes, and even special floral decorations and installations for special events. Here is an overview of the types of services a florist may provide.

Fresh Cut Flowers

Fresh cut flowers are the simplest, most economical way for most people to buy flowers. Priced by the stem, customers can choose as many or as few as they wish. Customers enjoy being able to select their own, and it is your role to assist them with their choices.

There are few rules when selecting a bouquet from the array of flowers available in a flower shop. It is best to let your customers take the lead, while you encourage them with suggestions and questions. Have them point to the flowers they like best so you can carefully ease the flowers from their containers. When they've chosen as many as they want, it is customary to add a spray of filler flower (like baby's breath) and greens (such as tree fern or leatherleaf fern).

Fresh cut flowers are then wrapped in paper or clear cellophane, which should be tied with ribbon around the stems of the flowers. This is a more festive touch and is often done for bouquets that will be used for dramatic presentations — a diva taking curtain calls at the end of an opera will be happier with a gorgeous bouquet she can show off without having to unwrap it!

Sometimes, fresh cut flowers are put together into small bouquets that are ready for customers to take home. These are called "cash-and-carry" bouquets and are typically displayed outside the store's main area, priced for impulse purchases.

Arrangements

There are two basic types of flower arrangements. One is the vase arrangement, in which fresh cut flowers are arranged in a glass, ceramic or plastic vase filled with water. This is a casual way of arranging flowers, though it requires greater skill to ensure the flowers stay in place. (Don't worry, we'll get to the secrets of how to do it later in this chapter.) The advantage of this method is that the flower stems are placed directly in water, which means the flowers may last longer this way. This is the way roses are traditionally presented.

The other way of arranging flowers, called the container arrangement, uses a floral foam – a plastic foam that easily absorbs and holds water, and into which stems are placed – that is anchored in a bowl, vase, lined basket or other container. The advantage of this method is that flowers stay exactly where they're placed, so you can have more creative control over the final look of the arrangement.

In addition to flowers, most arrangements include greens (either ferns, broadleaf evergreens, needled evergreens or a combination of those) and some sort of filler flower — often baby's breath, statice or waxflower, to name just a few. Sometimes they are accented by ribbons or other decorative items. This is particularly common for holiday arrangements.

While florists are always finding new ways to play with the endless combinations possible in flower arrangements – new color combinations, new flower mixes, bold use of shape and line – they follow a few basic design specifics. We'll look at those in section 2.4.2.

There are also standardized arrangements that are easy to duplicate, which are used for mass orders or out-of-area orders to ensure a uniform product. If a customer in Detroit admires a standardized arrangement and sends one to their mother in Vancouver, the florist in Vancouver will have the same container available and will prepare an arrangement to match the one the customer first saw in Detroit. This way, customer satisfaction can be guaranteed no matter where the flowers are arranged.

Wedding Bouquets and Décor

Florists have the honor of being crucial contributors to any wedding. They help the members of the wedding party choose the flowers they will wear and carry, the flowers they will use to decorate the reception, the cake table and the guests' tables, and the flowers they will send as thank-yous later.

Typically, wedding flowers consist of a showpiece bouquet for the bride and smaller bouquets for any attendants. The groom wears a boutonniere – a single flower prepared for wearing in his lapel – and the groom's attendants wear similar flowers. The mothers of the bride and groom wear corsages – clusters of flowers prepared for wearing – on their dresses or in their hair. Beyond that, the decorations are limited only by the client's taste and budget.

Some choose to have floral table centerpieces – oval-shaped arrangements that are long and low, occasionally serving as candleholders – to decorate the head table or all the guest tables. Others choose to go big and showy, walking through archways decorated in flowers, or more subtle, simply decorating their cake top with a small arrangement. The flowers can be formal and opulent, casual and understated, or anything in between.

Ultimately, wedding flowers should reflect the couple's taste and personalities. A florist can better understand what is needed by meeting with the members of the wedding party, asking them about the clothing they plan to wear, the location of the ceremony and reception, and the overall look the couple wishes to achieve.

Corsages and Boutonnieres

Nothing says "I'm special" like a flower to wear. That's why women wear corsages and men wear boutonnieres.

Typically accented with just a bit of greenery, a touch of baby's breath for contrast, and a few loops of ribbon, a corsage is worn by women for any occasion at which they are to be singled out, considered important, or honored. They are usually pinned on or worn on the wrist.

Boutonnieres, on the other hand, are usually a simple flower with a touch of greenery. In the 1980s Canadian Prime Minister Pierre Trudeau was famous for appearing with his signature red rose boutonniere.

Almost any type of flower can be made into a corsage, though some are more suited to the rigors of the task than others. Often, those special corsage-wearers will be hugged — and their flowers can't very well crumple at the first embrace.

Roses, carnations, miniature carnations and orchids are all common corsage and boutonniere flowers. Their stems are strengthened with a small piece of wire, and wrapped with green florists' tape (a sticky but non-adhesive tape) to create a natural look. The ends of the wire are often trimmed neatly or bent into a spiral or corkscrew. The florist provides a pin – safely tucked into the stem of the corsage or boutonniere – to assist the recipient in attaching the flowers to their clothes. Both are worn upwards, the same way the flower grows, and should never be worn pointing down.

Funeral Tributes

One florist I know says nothing makes her more sad than hearing the request "No flowers" at a funeral. She's not grieving for lost business — she's simply thinking about the loved ones sitting in the ceremony with nothing joyful or beautiful to look at. Funeral tributes vary according to region and tradition (remember the black spray-paint and the motorcycle gang), but are generally large-scale arrangements.

A funeral spray is an arrangement meant to be displayed on a wire easel next to the casket. A casket spray is meant to go on top of the casket. A wreath is usually displayed on an easel, while basket or container arrangements are meant to go on the floor or on podiums. Some arrangements take other shapes — a cross covered in a single color of flowers, for example, or a blanket made of numerous blossoms meant to cover the entire casket.

In any case, funeral flowers are meant to give the loved ones something to look at during the ceremony. They should evoke memories of the life of the deceased. A soldier, for example, would likely have the colors of the flag displayed in a funeral arrangement, while a gardener might have a vivid mix of colors and varieties of flowers.

Holiday Arrangements

The week or two preceding any of the major floral holidays is typically very busy for florists. These holidays are Valentine's Day, Easter, Mother's Day, and Christmas.

To make it easy for customers to order flowers for friends and family in other cities, order-gathering services (international florist networks) have developed standardized arrangements that are available in flower shops almost anywhere. For examples of some standardized arrangements, visit FTD's online selection guide. Go to **www.ftd.com** and click the "Flowers" option on the menu.

Usually, these arrangements are easy to mass-produce and are made in standardized containers available from the order-gathering service. Because florists must make many of them for each holiday, learning to do one or two seasonal special arrangements is a good way to practice arranging flowers.

Wreaths

There are three types of wreaths: Holiday, funeral, and decorative. All are circular arrangements of flowers, usually made on a frame or wreath form (a circle of floral foam). A holiday wreath typically incorporates evergreens, ribbons, and possibly some holiday ornaments. A funeral wreath typically is made mostly of flowers, usually of a single color. A decorative wreath is meant to adorn a front door, or an inside wall at any time of the year, and typically incorporates dried or artificial flowers, ribbons, and occasionally ornaments. It is usually made on a base of wicker, grapevine or other durable material.

Florists make holiday wreaths in advance of Christmas, funeral wreaths when required, and decorative wreaths during slow times in order to replenish the stock on hand. Visit **www.rockymountain wreaths.com** to find some examples of decorative wreaths.

Floral Décor

Like a decorative wreath, floral décor is meant to be enjoyed year-round. Florists will custom-design permanent arrangements to suit their customers' budget and tastes. Using dried and/or artificial flowers, florists can create stunning arrangements in vases or containers on hand, or even in a customer's own favorite container. These arrangements are meant to be used as accents in homes and offices and may remain in place for years.

Houseplants

Florists stock a variety of tropical plants meant to be kept indoors. Sold individually or arranged in groups, houseplants provide a longer-lasting alternative to cut or arranged flowers. A group of small plants still in their individual pots, but arranged together in a basket, is known as a basket garden or European garden. A similar group of small plants planted together in a bowl is known as a dish garden. If the plants are planted in a glass container with some sort of cover, it is known as a terrarium.

A website from Texas A&M University has a searchable database of the many varieties of houseplants available. The website is located at **http://horticulture.tamu.edu/interiorscape/search.html**.

Fruit Baskets

Florists don't just arrange flowers — many customers appreciate a gift they can eat! That is where fruit baskets come in. Typically florists make fruit baskets by taking a large, wide basket, padding it with tissue paper, excelsior (curly wood shavings) or Easter grass, and then filling it to overflowing with a variety of fresh fruit. The whole thing is wrapped in cellophane and topped with a ribbon, a small bouquet of flowers, or both.

Florists don't stop at fruit, though. A gourmet basket can include crackers, cheeses, nuts, chocolates, smoked meats and seafood in tins, small jars of jam or condiments, bottles of syrup, or even bottles of wine. Gift baskets of this sort can contain whatever the customer requests, but all are securely wrapped in cellophane and decorated.

Giftware

In addition to flowers and plants, many florists also carry vases, decorative items, stuffed toys, gift cards, candles, ornaments, and other items that may be added to flower arrangements or simply sold individually. They may also carry tools for caring for houseplants, such as watering cans, moisture meters (devices that tell if a plant's soil is too dry) and decorative pots.

Balloons and Balloon Bouquets

Many florists also offer latex and Mylar (shiny plastic) balloons. They are usually filled with helium and tied with thin, strong ribbon. Latex balloons, unless they're treated with a sealant, tend to last a day or two. Mylar balloons can keep floating as long as a month.

A bunch of balloons is called a balloon bouquet, and can include as many colors or styles as the customer wants. Latex balloons filled with helium typically sell for about a dollar or two each. Mylar balloons can sell for up to five dollars apiece.

You can find helium suppliers by looking in your local Yellow Pages for party planning services, party suppliers and balloon suppliers. You can also visit the websites for companies like Cylinder Central and SKIL Enterprises to learn about their helium delivery programs.

- *Cylinder Central*
  www.cylindercentral.com
  Phone: 800-421-5070

- *SKIL Enterprises*
  www.heliumsupplies.com
  Phone: 800-329-0010

Florists also make large-scale constructions, such as balloon arches, to decorate for special events. In this case, the balloons aren't filled with helium, but may be inflated with an air pump. They are then tied or twisted onto a thin wire framework until they cover the frame. This is often done on-site, as it is difficult to deliver one of these unwieldy constructions.

2.2   How to Process, Store and Maintain Flowers

Flowers are the mainstay of any florist business. They are also extremely fragile and perishable, and must be treated properly in order to keep them fresh and saleable for as long as possible. Different flowers have different preparation and storage needs, different lengths of time they can be expected to last, and different uses.

When flowers arrive from a supplier, they are either dry-shipped or in water. Dry-shipped means the flowers have been packed in wrapped bundles in a cardboard box and their stems have not been put in water. If flowers arrive in buckets, they have been shipped (still wrapped in bundles) with their stems in water, which means their stems have, at the very least, been cut once.

When a shipment of flowers arrives, it is important to prioritize them — that is, determine the order in which they will be prepared for sale. The procedure of preparing the flowers is known as processing. While processing basically involves removing extra leaves, cutting the stems and placing the flowers in a vase or bucket of water, how you do this is dictated by the individual flower type.

Prioritizing

The first flowers to process are the most delicate ones in the shipment

— usually roses and Dutch flowers. Once you have taken care of them, process dry-shipped flowers first, then process the ones shipped in water.

Bucket Preparation

For each variety of flower you process, prepare a bucket of water to which you have added the recommended amount of flower preservative or flower food. Large or long-stemmed flowers demand large, sturdy buckets or pails, while smaller, shorter-stemmed flowers require smaller buckets or vases. The pail should be between half and two-thirds the height of the flowers in order to ensure the bucket doesn't tip when it's full.

You will group the flowers in buckets according to variety. Roses will go together with roses, carnations with carnations, daffodils with daffodils, etc. If there are different types of one flower, such as long-stemmed red roses, medium-stemmed pink roses, and yellow spray roses (with many small flowers on one stem), each type should have its own bucket. If there are many colors of one variety of flower, they may all share a bucket.

In any case, the bucket should be wide enough at the mouth to allow the flowers in it to fit comfortably without crowding (which can cause bruised or broken petals) and without being too loose (which can also cause breakage).

The water in the bucket should be slightly warmer than room temperature, but not so warm as to feel warm to your hand. Specific temperature requirements are usually noted along with the description of the flowers in your shipment.

Flower Foods and Preservatives

To make sure flowers last as long as possible, it is important to use the recommended amount of flower food (also called "preservative") mixed with the water.

Flower foods contain a nutrient (usually some form of sugar), a citric acid and a fungicide. Some also contain an ingredient that keeps vase water clear. Flower foods come in liquid and powdered forms, both in large containers for commercial use and in small packets meant for individual customer use. Some brand names are Floralife, FloraNova (made by General Hydroponics), and Crystal Clear.

Spray-on preservatives are meant to be sprayed directly onto flower blooms and work by sealing the flower's pores to prevent evaporation. Some brand names are Crowning Glory (used for flowers), Pixie Sparkle (used for greens and evergreens) and Hawaiian Mist (used on whole arrangements after they are prepared).

Quick Dip is a flower hydration solution, which ensures that the flower stem's pores remain open to take in water. The cut ends of flower stems are dipped into a container of Quick Dip immediately before placing them into their bucket or vase.

Stripping, Grooming and Cutting

Stripping

Stripping is the process of removing from stems all leaves that will be below the water line in a bucket. It is important for prolonging the life of cut flowers, because leaves left in the water will rapidly deteriorate, contaminating the water. In addition, a flower stem will continue to nourish each leaf that is attached to it, which detracts from the nourishment received by the bloom.

To remove leaves, you may pull them off by hand. Grasp the stem below the bloom with one hand, making a loose fist around the stem with the other. Draw the fisted hand down over the leaves, pulling them off in a clump. You may also use a knife to draw down the stem.

Besides their leaves, roses must also be stripped of their thorns, either by hand or with a rose stripper, which is a metal or plastic device that slides over the stem to pull off leaves and break off the points of the thorns. It is important to remove just the sharp point of the thorn, and not the whole thorn, as doing so will create openings through which moisture can be lost. You can use shears or a knife to trim the sharp points from large, sturdy thorns. It is easier to maneuver stems and knives with bare hands, but some florists prefer to use heavy work gloves when processing roses.

Grooming

Grooming refers to the process of removing imperfect or damaged petals from an individual flower. On roses, for example, the outermost petals are called guard petals, and are usually removed. Some flowers, like chrysanthemums, can easily have one or two damaged petals removed and still be fit for sale.

Other flowers, like five-petaled orchids, should not have entire petals removed. If these types of flowers are damaged, they are not fit for sale and should be returned to the supplier if they arrived damaged, or disposed of if they were damaged in the store.

Cutting

Immediately before placing flowers in a bucket or an arrangement, you should cut the stems with a sharp knife, secateurs or shears. It is ideal to cut stems on an angle instead of straight across, because an angled cut allows a wider area for water to be absorbed by the stem. Some florists prefer to make these cuts underwater, but there is no evidence that doing so makes flowers last any longer.

2.3 Flowers, Greens, and Plants

As a florist, you'll be working with many different kinds of plant life. In this section, you'll learn more about the most commonly used flowers and greens you'll encounter on the job, plus you'll learn about some common household plants that customers may look to you for advice for.

2.3.1 Popular Flowers

The flower summaries in the following section are organized as follows:

- *Description:* Here the flower will be described, including how the petals and blossoms appear and what varieties are available.

- *Color:* Here you'll find out what colors are available.

- *Uses:* This section will explain the ways the flower is arranged or sold to the customer.

- *Special needs:* Special instructions for processing and maintaining the flower will be explained here.

- *Storage:* Storage requirements, such as temperature requirements, will be found here.

- *Average vase life:* This will tell you how long the flower should be expected to remain fresh and saleable.

- *Retail cost:* This is the price you would sell the flower for. Retail cost per stem is based on a 300 percent mark-up over wholesale. Costs may vary depending on region, season and availability, so these prices are given only as a guide to the relative costs of flower varieties. Pricing will be discussed in detail later in this guide.

NOTE: The words *calyx* and *stamen* will be used several times in this section. The calyx is the protective outer layer of leaves on a bud. The stamen is the male reproductive organ of a flower.

If you're unfamiliar with any of the flowers described here, you can find detailed information as well as pictures of 2,500 varieties at Sierra Flower Finder: **http://sierraflowerfinder.com/default.asp**.

Common Flowers

Roses

Description:	Multi-petal blossoms that radiate from a single calyx. Blossoms may be one to a stem (single) or many to a stem (spray). Fragrant, familiar and classic.
Colors:	All colors except true blue and black.
Uses:	Sold individually; in bouquets of six or twelve; boxed; or arranged in a vase. Also, they can be used in mixed arrangements or dried for use in dry arrangements.

Petals are sometimes removed and used for strewing (tossing or spreading over the floor or other surface, as at weddings) or dried for fragrant potpourri.

Special needs: Thorns must be trimmed and guard (outer) petals removed. Must be cut immediately before placement into water.

Storage: Store in the cooler, and periodically re-cut stems and replace them into fresh warm water with new flower food.

Average vase life: Four to seven days is average; in cool conditions and with daily cutting, can last up to two weeks and more.

Retail cost: Depends on stem length and quality, can range from $1.00 to $6.00 per stem.

Carnation — Standard and Mini

Description: Multiple petals gathered together in a single, bell-shaped calyx. Standard carnations have one bloom per stem; mini carnations have as many as five or ten blooms per stem. Sturdy, spicy-scented and long-lasting.

Colors: All except blue, green and black (though they may be dyed any of these). Sometimes striped or *picotee* (edged) with one or more colors.

Uses: Arrangements; cash and carry bouquets; cut flowers.

Special needs: Mini carnations should have the lower, smaller blooms removed for use in arrangements, leaving the three to five most open blooms on the stem for use as a cut flower.

Storage: Should be kept in the cooler at night, but can be displayed on the sales floor during the day. Re-cut once a week.

| *Average vase life:* | One to two weeks. |
| *Retail cost:* | $1.00 to $2.00 per stem. |

Chrysanthemum

Description:	Multiple oblong, round-ended petals radiating from a button-shaped center (*daisies*) or from a cluster of shorter petals (*mums*). Also come as button-shaped smaller flowers and with starburst or snowflake tips on the petals. Blossoms are usually clustered several to a stem, although large *Fuji mums* (wide, spidery blossoms) and decorative mums (which look like large pompons) come one bloom per stem.
Colors:	White, yellow, purple, pink, bronze, orange, tan and burgundy.
Uses:	In arrangements; as filler in cut flower bouquets and vase arrangements.
Special needs:	None.
Storage:	On sales floor during the day, and in the cooler at night.
Average vase life:	Up to 14 days.
Retail cost:	$1.00 to $2.00 per stem.

Freesia

Description:	Five- or six-petal trumpet-shaped blossoms, radiating in a curve from a single stem. Opens the lowest flower first, followed by smaller flowers to the tip of the stem. Fragrant with a strong, spicy, floral scent.
Colors:	Yellow, white, rust, and purple.
Uses:	Vase arrangements; cut flowers; arrangements.

Special needs:	None.
Storage:	Keep in the cooler, though fragrance is enhanced by warmth. Remove spent lower blooms as needed.
Average vase life:	Up to seven days.
Retail cost:	$1.75 to $2.00 per stem.

Gerbera Daisy

Description:	Numerous oblong, rounded petals surrounding an "eye" of smaller petals in similar or contrasting color.
Colors:	White, peach, red, yellow, pink, orange, and bi-colors.
Uses:	As a cut flower; in vase arrangements and container arrangements.
Special needs:	It's essential to Quick Dip these flowers before placing them in lukewarm water. Some florists also use plastic straws to support the stems, which can easily droop with incorrect care. A better practice is to ensure that stems are cut enough (up to two inches off the ends) at initial processing, and re-cut every two or three days.
Storage:	Store in cooler, but can tolerate sales floor conditions during the day. Re-cut every two to three days.
Average vase life:	7 to 10 days.
Retail cost:	$1.50 to $3.00 per stem.

Gladiolus

Description:	Tall, strong stems with six to eight blooms, opening from the bottom first. Can be as long as 24" to 30".

Colors:	White, pink, yellow, cream, green, purple, peach, red and orange.
Uses:	Provide strong lines in arrangements, height in cut flower bouquets.
Special needs: None.	
Storage:	Store in cooler. Can tolerate sales floor during day. Re-cut periodically and remove spent lower blooms.
Average vase life:	Seven to ten days.
Retail cost:	$2.00 to $3.00 per stem.

Lilies

Description:	Several varieties of lily are commonly available. *Asiatic lilies* typically have large, fragrant, six-petaled, trumpet-shaped blooms, up to 6" in diameter. There are two to three blooms per stem, and they are extremely fragrant.
	Other lilies, such as *Casablanca* and *Stargazer*, have up to six smaller, five- or six-petaled trumpet-shaped blooms per stem. These open in sequence from bottom to top.
Colors:	White, pink, pink-throated, orange, yellow, and bronze.
Uses:	As cut flowers; in vase and container arrangements to provide mass and fragrance.
Special needs:	Because the stamens carry pollen that can cause stains, remove all visible stamens.
Storage:	Cooler at night, sales floor during the day. Re-cut every three to four days.
Average vase life:	Up to 14 days, if spent lower flowers are removed.
Retail cost:	$2.50 to $7.00 per stem, depending on variety.

Alstroemeria (Peruvian Lily)

Description: Four to six buds bloom on stems radiating from a central stalk that is usually 24″ to 36″ long. Each bloom looks like a miniature lily, with numerous freckles in the throat area.

Colors: Red, pink, peach, salmon, yellow, white, and purple.

Uses: To provide mass in arrangements, as cut flowers.

Special needs: None.

Storage: Cooler at night, sales floor during the day. Recut every three to four days.

Average vase life: Up to 14 days.

Retail cost: $1.75 to $2.50 per stem.

Liatris

Description: Tall stem covered with short feathery blossoms that open from the top downwards. Narrow, dark green glossy leaves.

Colors: Purple or white.

Uses: Provides a strong vertical line in arrangements; creates interest in cut flower bouquets.

Special needs: None.

Storage: Cooler or sales floor.

Average vase life: Up to 14 days.

Retail cost: $1.75 to $2.00 per stem.

Lisianthus

Description:	Four wide, ruffled petals create bell-shaped flowers on a thin stem.
Colors:	Pink, white, purple and bi-color.
Uses:	In vase arrangements, as cut flowers.
Special needs:	Add a small amount of sugar to the water along with the flower food.
Storage:	Should not go in cooler. Sales floor conditions are ideal.
Average vase life:	Up to 14 days.
Retail cost:	$2.00 to $3.00 per stem.

Spring/Dutch Flowers

Description:	*Florists' iris* come in blue and white. They have three tall petals and three lower petals (falls) with yellow throats.
	Tulips can come in almost any color except true blue, and usually have six to eight petals grouped in a cup shape around a central pistil and stamens.
	Daffodils and *narcissus* are combinations of yellow and white. A cluster of six petals radiates from a single trumpet of similar or contrasting color.
	Anemones have six to ten petals radiating from a central button-shaped eye.
Uses:	As cut flowers; in vase arrangements and container arrangements.
Special needs:	Should be placed in cool water, not lukewarm, after cutting and Quick Dipping.

Storage:	Keep as cool as possi ble. Tulips will "grow" and need to be re-cut in order to keep them from drooping.
Average vase life:	Three to five days.
Retail cost:	Seventy-five cents to $2.00 per stem, depending on season and supplier.

Exotic Flowers

Orchids

Description:	Orchids come in several types, but all have five outer petals surrounding an inner throat in a star shape. *Cymbidium orchids* have smooth petals. *Cattleya orchids* have frilly petals. *Paphiopedilum orchids* have deep, pouch-shaped throats, and insignificant petals. *Dendrobium orchids* have numerous wide-petaled, small-throated flowers on a single stem.
Colors:	White, pink, purple, green, yellow, brown, rust, burgundy, and bi-color.
Uses:	Single orchids are popular for corsages; orchid stems are used as cut flowers or in arrangements.
Special needs:	Single orchid flowers should be trimmed and placed into water piks filled with water and flower food. Orchid stems should be cut and placed in a vase.
Storage:	Single flowers should be stored in the cooler. Stems can tolerate sales floor temperatures. Re-cut every four to five days.
Average vase life:	Up to three weeks with proper care.
Retail cost:	$5.00 to $10.00 per single flower or stem.

Anthurium

Description:	A glossy heart-shaped leaf (or "bract") surrounding a single stamen.
Colors:	Red, white, pink and green.
Uses:	Tropical cut flowers; arrangements; bouquets.
Special needs:	None.
Storage:	Avoid the cooler.
Average vase life:	Up to three weeks.
Retail cost:	$5.00 to $8.00 per stem.

Gardenia

Description:	Five to six fragrant white petals radiate from a central cluster of petals.
Colors:	White.
Uses:	Wedding bouquets, corsages.
Special needs:	Mist hands and flowers with plain water before handling to avoid bruising the flowers. Single flowers are shipped in boxes of up to three blossoms and should just be misted.
Storage:	Keep in cooler, in shipment boxes, until ready to use.
Average vase life:	One to two days.
Retail cost:	$5.00 to $10.00 per stem, depending on season and availability.

Seasonal Availability

While it is possible to get almost any kind of flower at any time of year, the price of any flower is bound to be lower when it is at the peak of its growing season. Daffodils and tulips are most inexpensive in the springtime, while they may be outrageously expensive in the fall.

By the same token, some flowers and plants are in higher demand at certain seasons – think of red roses at Valentine's Day, or poinsettias at Christmas, for example – so the laws of supply and demand come into play and make the prices go up for the most popular items. A wise florist will order just enough of what they need of any seasonal flower or plant, but knowing how much that is can be tricky.

Using last year's records is often a good place to figure out how much to order. For example, if there were lots of poinsettias left over last year, order fewer for this year's season. If you ran out of roses before all the Valentine's orders were filled, plan on ordering a few more bundles this time. During your first year of business, you will have to play it by ear. But keep good records to help you know what to do next time.

2.3.2 Greens and Fillers

The term "greens" refers to any non-flowering plant material used by florists in arrangements or bouquets. Greens are added to provide a background against which to showcase flowers, and to enhance the flowers' natural beauty.

In arrangements, greens are used to provide a framework or base upon which the arrangement may be created. Greens are chosen for their shape and size, and more than one type of green may be used in any given arrangement.

Upon their arrival from suppliers, greens should all have their stem ends cut. Place the greens into buckets filled with lukewarm water, with flower food added. Greens are not usually sold individually, but may be included as complimentary gifts along with a purchase of fresh flowers.

Ferns

Tree fern is a tall, dark green feathery fern, usually used in cut flower bouquets or in vase arrangements.

Plumosa fern, or asparagus fern, is lacy and bright green with sharp hooks on the stem. It is used in vase arrangements and with cut flowers.

Sword fern is shaped like a sword blade, with dark green leaves making a flat ladder up either side of a single stem. It is used to provide a strong vertical line in arrangements.

Leatherleaf fern is dark green with numerous widely serrated leaves arranged in a flat triangular shape on a strong stem. It is used with cut flowers, in vase arrangements, and broken apart to create a base in container arrangements.

Broadleaf Evergreens

Any broadleaf evergreen can be used in flower arrangements.

Salal has wide, dark green oval-shaped leaves with pointed tips on sturdy branches. It is used in cut flower bouquets or in arrangements. Individual leaves may be used in corsages or glued to backgrounds.

Boxwood has tiny, dark green oval leaves on woody stems. It is used as a filler in arrangements.

Holly has sharp, prickly serrated leaves, in dark green or variegated (dark green with cream edges) varieties, both with red berries. It is used as an accent in arrangements, or on its own.

All should have their cut ends trimmed and placed in lukewarm water with flower food upon arrival.

Needle Evergreens

Cedar has fragrant, flat, scaled leaves on sturdy, flexible stems. *Juniper* has similar characteristics, with spikier leaves. *Pine* and *spruce* both have numerous needles clustered around strong central stems. All of these are used in Christmas arrangements, wreaths, and bouquets.

They should all have their cut ends placed in warm water upon arrival, though they can also live for several days without any processing. All have some degree of sticky sap (also called "pitch") which can be removed from hands with vegetable oil.

Filler Flowers

Filler flowers are small, usually clustering flowers used to fill in gaps between larger flowers in arrangements, or to accent cut flower bouquets. They are sold by the stem or included as complementary gifts along with cut flower purchases.

Baby's breath is a delicate, white-blossomed flower that looks like tiny puffballs on thin stems. It should be cut and placed into extremely hot water, to which some florists like to add a teaspoon of bleach in addition to flower food. It is the classic accompaniment to roses, and can be tucked into bouquets, arrangements and corsages to give a light, airy look.

Asters look like tiny daisies clustered around a central stem. They come in white and purple, and should be cut and placed in lukewarm water with flower food upon arrival. They are used in arrangements.

Waxflower is a small pink or white waxy-looking flower that grows on a sturdy, wooden branch covered in tiny green needles. It has a distinctive lemony fragrance when cut. It's used with cut flowers and in arrangements.

Goldenrod looks like plumes of yellow on tall stems of bright green leaves. It is also used in arrangements. Upon arrival, it should be cut and placed in lukewarm water.

Statice is a solid purple, yellow, blue, pink, or white flower clustered on the ends of thick, sturdy stems ridged with green leaves. These leaves should be cut off with a knife and the stem ends trimmed before placing in lukewarm water. They are used in arrangements to provide a dash of contrasting color.

2.3.3 Plants You Should Know

Florists do much of their business in green and flowering plants and are often the first places consumers turn to for information regarding the care and keeping of plants.

As a florist, you should have a solid basic knowledge of the types of plants available, both as "gifts" (usually flowering plants in beautiful full bloom) and as plants for customers to integrate into their living space (usually foliage plants of assorted types).

What follows is information about some of the most popular of the thousands of species of plants available. You can expect to encounter these in almost any flower shop.

Flowering Plants

Flowering plants are popular gifts because their blooms last longer than cut flowers. In addition, many varieties can be transplanted into gardens, offering an ongoing gift. They are usually presented "dressed" – that is, with their pots covered in foil, mylar, or plastic pot covers, or placed in wicker baskets – and adorned with ribbons in matching or complementary colors.

African Violets

Description: Fuzzy heart-shaped leaves and delicate, intensely hued, ruffled flowers make these familiar flowering plants a long-time favorite. They are easy to care for, relatively inexpensive (usually selling for between $3 and $10 a plant, depending on size and wholesale price), and familiar to consumers. They make nice additions to basket gardens, and look good massed together.

Colors: White, pink, purple, burgundy, yellow, and multicolor. Leaves may be dark green or variegated (green and white), and sometimes have a reddish tone on their undersides.

Moisture: Some prefer to let African Violets nearly dry out between thorough waterings; others recommend keeping their soil barely moist.

Light: Up to 16 hours of artificial light per day, or bright indirect sunlight.

Bloom period: Removing spent blooms at the stem base will encourage this plant to bloom nearly continuously.

Special care:	Remove old blooms. Keep leaves dry when watering plant — if necessary, set the base of the pot in a dish of water rather than risk soaking leaves with a stream of water. If leaves start to yellow, remove them at their stem base. African violets can be propagated from a single healthy leaf placed with its stem in a pot of soil.

Azaleas

Description:	A small broadleaf evergreen shrub. Azaleas in full bloom are one of the most popular flowering plants. Their numerous rose-shaped flowers against small, dark-green oval leaves, make a stunning gift that can be transferred to the garden, where they will bloom again year after year.
Colors:	Pink, red, coral, orange, white, purple, and bi-color (pink/white).
Moisture:	Evenly moist, not wet.
Light:	Indirect sunlight.
Bloom period:	Available year-round, blooms for two to four weeks.
Special care:	Pinch off dead or wilted flowers regularly. Keep leaves and flowers dry when watering.

Begonias

Description:	Rieger begonias (small bright fleshy flowers up to one inch wide) and wax begonias (round, shiny leaves, mainly used for outdoor bedding plants) are classified as *fibrous-root begonias*.

Begonias grown for their showy elephant ear-shaped leaves (rex begonias, iron cross begonias) are classified as *rhizomatous begonias*. These are all suitable indoor plants, while *tuberous begonias*, with large, rose-shaped flowers, are most happy outdoors. |

Colors:	Red, yellow, white, pink, coral, orange, peach, or bi-color.
Moisture:	Allow the top inch of soil to dry between thorough waterings.
Light:	Bright indirect light.
Bloom period:	Several weeks; longer if spent flowers are regularly removed.
Special care:	Protect from mid-day sun; fertilize in summer months with all-purpose plant food.

Chrysanthemums

Description:	Also called "mums" or "daisies" (because some varieties have daisy-shaped blooms), these are popular plants both at Mother's Day and in the fall, when their warmer colors add a special glow to autumn arrangements. They have round, daisy, or pompon-shaped blooms at the ends of sturdy stalks covered in toothed leaves.
	Small plants (in 4" or 6" pots) make good additions to basket gardens, while larger plants are presented on their own. In warmer climates, these can be transplanted outdoors and will bloom every year.
Colors:	White, yellow, pink, purple, mauve, bronze, rust, orange, or red.
Moisture:	Keep evenly moist, and do not allow to dry out. Watering every two days is recommended.
Light:	Bright but indirect sunlight.
Bloom period:	Available year-round. Blooms for two to three weeks.
Special care:	Do not allow to dry out. Direct sunlight can harm flowers.

Cyclamen

Description: A pretty plant characterized by fleshy, heart-shaped leaves and inverted flowers on tall stems. Their petals point upwards from a down-turned center. The leaves may be dark green, delicately patterned or variegated in tones of green, silver and white.

Colors: White, pink, red, purple, or bi-color.

Moisture: Keep evenly moist, allow to absorb water by standing pot in a shallow dish of water. Remove from dish when soil is moist.

Light: Bright indirect light.

Bloom period: Each flower lasts about 10 days, and new ones appear from the center of the plant as old ones are removed.

Special care: Pull old flowers and leaves from the plant by grasping at the very base of their stems and pulling upwards.

Gerbera Daisies

Description: Long, green-toothed, slightly hairy leaves resembling dandelion leaves. Come with large (4") or miniature (2") daisy-shaped flowers growing from the center of a rosette of leaves. Available year-round, but best in summertime. Can be transplanted into gardens in moderate climates, and are perennial if winter temperatures stay above freezing.

Colors: White, pink, yellow, orange, peach, purple, or red.

Moisture: Evenly moist but not wet.

Light: Bright.

Bloom period: Flowers last two to three weeks before going to seed in a puffball shape (much like a dandelion).

Special care: Colors stay more intense with bright light.

Geranium

Description:	Round, scallop-edged leaves and clusters of five-petal flowers on slender stems. Leaves may be pale green, dark green or variegated (green and white). Some may be ivy-shaped (ivy geranium). Martha Washington geraniums (or Pelargonium) are a showier variety with clusters of pansy-shaped flowers and round leaves with serrated edges.
Colors:	White, red, pink, peach, coral, orange, purple, or mauve.
Moisture:	Can tolerate dryness.
Light:	Bright, can tolerate indirect light.
Bloom period:	If faded flowers are regularly removed, will continue to bloom and retain overall shape for several months.
Special care:	Can be easily propagated by cuttings. For larger blooms, feed with all-purpose plant food.

Gloxinia

Description:	Related to the African Violet, gloxinias have broad, round, hairy leaves and large upturned bell-shaped flowers in vibrant velvety colors with ruffled edges. Available year-round.
Colors:	Red, purple, pink, white and bi-color.
Moisture:	Medium to dry.
Light:	Bright indirect light.
Bloom period:	Buds keep coming up from the center of the plant if faded blooms are removed. Plants last two to three months before going into a period of dormancy lasting two to five months.

Special care:	Will die if over-watered. Can be brought back from dormancy with bright light, warmth and sparing amounts of water.

Hydrangea

Description:	Hydrangeas have woody stems, large dark-green heart-shaped leaves with serrated edges, and round clusters of tiny four-petal blossoms that resemble large pompons 4" to 6" wide. Their pastel colors and ball-shaped flower clusters make them popular gifts for Easter and Mother's Day. Transplanted to the garden, hydrangeas are a popular perennial shrub in many climate zones.
Colors:	White, pink, lavender, and blue.
Moisture:	Evenly moist but not wet.
Light:	Indirect but bright light is best.
Bloom period:	While garden hydrangeas actually bloom in the late summer, these are a popular springtime plant for florists. Their blooms last two to four weeks.
Special care:	Do not let stand in water.

Kalanchoe

Description:	Kalanchoes (pronounced *ka-lan-KO-ees*) have round, dark green leaves with a fleshy, shiny appearance, and clusters of small, four-petal flowers that rise above the leaves on slender stalks. A durable, hardy plant, these can tolerate drought and neglect, but not extreme cold. Can be used as an annual bedding plant in dry areas.
Colors:	Red, yellow, pink, white, coral, peach, and orange.
Moisture:	Allow to dry between waterings. Do not let stand in water.

Light:	Bright indirect light. Flowers stay more vibrant with at least four hours of bright light each day.
Bloom period:	Flowers can last four to eight weeks. Remove faded flowers as needed.
Special care:	After flowering is finished, cut off flower stems at their base and allow soil to dry almost completely. Then water thoroughly with all-purpose plant food, keep moist, and a new crop of flowers should appear in a few weeks.

Poinsettia

Description:	The bright poinsettia is a popular gift plant around the Christmas season, though it can last year-round. The flowers are actually small and yellow and look like tiny buds in the centers of showy colored leaves, called bracts. Once thought to be poisonous, it has now been widely proven that poinsettias are actually non-toxic.
	Small poinsettias come in pots as tiny as 2" wide, while large ones can be in pots as wide as 18 to 24". These large plants tend to actually be several smaller plants in one container. You can tell the quality of a poinsettia by counting the number of blooms — the better the plant, the more "heads" it will have.
Colors:	White, yellow, red, pink, peach, marbled or varie-gated (red and maroon, pink and white), or speck-led (white speckles on red, for instance).
Moisture:	Allow surface of soil to dry before watering thoroughly. Do not let stand in water.
Light:	Bright, indirect sunlight is best.
Bloom period:	Most poinsettias stay in bloom far longer than their owners care to look at them. Two or three months is not uncommon.

Special care:	Be careful not to break off branches or leaves, which ooze a sticky white sap when broken. A period of two months of complete darkness each fall is said to encourage poinsettia plants to bloom again in December, though most people prefer to purchase new plants each holiday season.

Zygocactus

Description:	Known as the Christmas cactus or Easter cactus (named after the blooming season of different varieties), these are colorful flowering plants that bloom year after year with little care. Their leaves are inch-long, waxy and dark green, forming toothed chains that can be up to 24" long. The multi-petal, trumpet-shaped flowers hang down from the ends of the stems.
Colors:	White, pink, red, lavender, and bi-color.
Moisture:	Keep soil evenly moist.
Light:	Bright, indirect light.
Bloom period:	Two to four weeks. Remove faded flowers as needed.
Special care:	Do not expose to night temperatures below 55 degrees Fahrenheit. Feed all-purpose plant food every two weeks when in bloom.

Foliage Plants

Studies have shown that indoor plants improve the air quality in homes and offices, and many people enjoy looking after green plants indoors. But their success has less to do with green thumbs and more to do with putting the right plant in the right place.

When recommending foliage plants to your customers, one of the most important considerations is where they plan to keep the plant. In a sunny window or sunroom? Or in a relatively dark north-facing study?

By determining the light available where the plant is to be placed, you can determine the variety of plant to give them the best results. No matter how much attention they lavish on a light-loving areca palm, if it's kept in a dark room, it won't survive for long. Your knowledge of plant varieties will help your customers be satisfied with their choice of indoor plants.

To determine the light conditions of an area, ask your customer about its location. If they are at home, they can put a sheet of white paper on the spot where the plant will be displayed, and then hold their hand 12 inches above the paper. If there is no shadow, this is a low-light spot.

Other indications of low light include being more than three feet away from a north-facing window, or more than 10 feet away from a south-facing window.

If the plant's chosen spot is directly in front of a north window, near a west or east-facing window, or more than five feet away from a south-facing window, it is a moderate light spot. If the plant is to be placed directly in a west or east-facing window, or within five feet of a south-facing window, this is a high light spot.

There are thousands of varieties of foliage plants available; what follows are some suggestions for low, moderate and high light conditions. Because common names can vary from region to region, the unvarying botanical or Latin name is given first, followed by the common name.

Low Light-Loving Plants

Any of the following will be happy in a low-light spot:

- *Aglaonema* (Chinese evergreen) forms clumps of narrow sword-shaped leaves. Can tolerate little water and even less light.

- *Spathiphyllum* (peace lily) has long, broad, dark green sword-shaped leaves and white flowers that look like a single oval leaf behind a finger-shaped spath.

- *Nephrolepis* (sword fern, Boston fern) need well-drained soil and indirect light. Feed monthly with all-purpose plant food, and mist when conditions are dry (such as in winter).

- *Philodendron* has wide, shiny, heart-shaped leaves and a tendency to vine.

- *Sansevieria* (snake plant) can tolerate dry conditions as well as low light.

Visit the University of Illinois Extension's website at **www.urbanext. uiuc.edu/houseplants/types_low.html** to learn more about plants for low-light conditions.

Moderate Light-Loving Plants

Any of the following will be happy in a medium-light spot:

- *Asparagus densiflorus "sprengeri"* (asparagus fern) is a delicate, lacy plant with long stems and fine, inch-long leaves. It likes moderate humidity, so mist when conditions are dry.

- *Chlorophytum* (spider plant) is an easy-care plant with long, strap-like leaves in dark green or variegated green and white stripes. Sends off "babies" that look like spiders; these can be planted to produce new plants.

- *Dieffenbachia* (dumb cane) has broad heart-shaped leaves radiating from a tall stalk. Its sap can burn mouths, hence the name.

- *Dracaena fragrans* (corn plant) has tall woody stalks with long, broad leaves resembling those of corn. Stems of the smaller varieties are sold as the popular "lucky bamboo."

- *Dracaena marginata* (red-edge dracaena, Madagascar dragon tree) has tall, woody stems with narrow, pointed strap-like leaves radiating from the stem. Leaves can be dark green or striped red and green. Easy to care for.

- *Ficus benjamina* (weeping fig) has small, pointed, dark green oval-shaped leaves and a tall, woody stem. It can't tolerate drafts or chills and must be frequently misted.

- *Ficus elastica* (rubber plant) has large, broad, dark green oval-shaped leaves with a shiny, leathery look to them. They radiate from sturdy trunks. They are slow-growing, but can reach five to ten feet eventually.

- *Pothos* (devil's ivy) is a long, vining plant with small (2") heart-shaped leaves (green or variegated). Needs little care, and can tolerate periods of drought.

- *Schefflera* (umbrella plant) has tall stalks with clusters of dark green oval leaves that resemble the spines in an umbrella.

Visit **www.urbanext.uiuc.edu/houseplants/types_medium.html** to learn more about plants for medium-light conditions.

High Light-Loving Plants

Any of the following will be happy in a bright-light spot:

- *Araucaria heterophylla* (Norfolk island pine) has long, flexible, spiny branches that resemble evergreen branches radiating from a spiky trunk. May be used as a live indoor Christmas tree, but if so, care should be taken to avoid burning the delicate branches with the heat of lights.

- *Calathea zebrina* (zebra plant) has oval leaves up to two feet long, with bars of pale and dark green. These need high humidity, which can be provided by frequent misting.

- *Chrysalidocarpus lutescens* (areca palm) has long, feathery, strappy leaves resembling a grassy palm tree. Needs frequent misting and should not be allowed to dry out.

- *Codiaeum varigatum* (croton) has large, leathery, glossy leaves with bright stripes of green, yellow, purple, red and pink. Needs plenty of water.

You can find out more about plants for bright-light conditions at **www.urbanext.uiuc.edu/houseplants/types_high.html**.

Cacti and Succulents

Customers who don't have time to look after plants or who have areas in their homes that get hot and dry may want to consider the many varieties of cacti and succulent plants. Cacti are characterized by their spines, which can be long and sharp as needles, or tiny and fuzzy-looking (but intensely painful if touched). All cacti are succulent plants (which store water in their tissues to ensure they survive over a period of drought), but not all succulent plants are cacti. Many varieties have no spines at all.

When handling cacti, it is wise to wear thick leather gloves or wrap the plant in a few sheets of newspaper before trying to move it. The University of Nebraska has an excellent guide to caring for cactus in the home at **www.ianr.unl.edu/pubs/Horticulture/g187.htm**.

The word "succulent" refers to any plant that has thick, fleshy leaves. Kalanchoes are a type of succulent, as are zygocactus. As a rule, they require little water because they evolved in desert and dry conditions to take advantage of small amounts of water when available. Allowing this type of plant to dry thoroughly between waterings mimics its natural habitat.

You can find out more about succulent plants at The Succulent Plant Page (**www.succulent-plant.com**).

Novelty Plants: Venus Fly Trap And More

Plant-buying customers can always have their interest piqued by a new variety of plant, and novelty plants are often sold for that very purpose. Some, like the *Venus Fly Trap*, have specific, finicky needs, and tend not to last as long as the more hardy varieties of indoor plants. But they are lots of fun. Others, like *bonsai* or *orchids*, can inspire enormous collections of their many types. Some varieties to try:

Amaryllis

This is a spectacular flower that has large, trumpet-shaped flowers and long, strappy green leaves. It is grown from a large bulb, and "amaryllis kits" with bulb, growing medium and pot all included make popular gifts.

Bonsai

While true bonsai is an ancient art requiring many years of training and patience, commercially available bonsai refers to any miniature plant that's been made to resemble traditional bonsai.

Usually presented in a small ceramic dish, sometimes with an ornament such as a ceramic pagoda or bridge, the miniature trees (some popular ones are juniper and ficus) are twisted and gnarled to make them look ancient and weathered.

Dionaea muscipula (Venus Fly Trap)

Native to the southeastern United States, these unusual plants are named because they derive their nutrients from the insects that unluckily venture into their up-to-one-inch-long "traps" — clamshell-shaped lobes at the ends of broad triangular leaves.

When the insect touches a sensitive hair on the inside of the clamshell-shaped trap, the trap closes, with the bug inside. They are great fun to watch and can be triggered by touching the sensitive hairs, but if the plant is triggered too often, it dies. Once the traps are closed, they do not re-open.

Mimosa pudica (Sensitive Plant)

With their delicate, feathery leaves, these small (about 8" to 12" high) plants are beautiful in their own right. But they are also entertaining — with the slightest touch, they wilt downwards, only to recover in about 15 minutes.

Orchids

There are more than 15,000 varieties of orchid in the world, but the ones most often seen at flower shops are the Phalaenopsis (with wide, butterfly-shaped blooms in white, mauve, purple or bi-color).

They have clusters of up to 12 blooms on a single stem rising from a cluster of three to five oblong, leathery leaves. The flowers last up to six weeks, and when they are finished, the stem should be cut off at its base. With regular watering, occasional doses of all-purpose plant food, and relatively high humidity, they will bloom again in about a year.

You can see an excellent collection of photographs of the many orchid varieties at **http://ourworld.cs.com/cycadite/orchidtable.html**.

Paperwhites

Sold in the fall as bulbs, these are easily "forced" to encourage them to bloom at the holiday season. Force these bulbs by placing them, rounded end down, in a low dish filled with small stones. Keep the stones covered in water. They will sprout and bloom in two to four weeks, displaying their fragrant white star-shaped flowers.

Seedman.com (**www.seedman.com**) offers a vast selection of the more familiar as well as exotic seeds to the home gardener, universities and research facilities. Their website features illustrations of each type of plant whose seeds they offer. Scroll down to the "Seeds" section to find everything from acacias to ylang ylang trees.

2.4 Elements and Principles of Design

Floral design is, of course, at the heart of any florist's business. The arrangements you make become your shop's signature, and your skill in arranging flowers is something you can become not just known for, but internationally recognized for.

Some of the world's top flower designers, like Hitomi Gilliam, still operate their own flower shops and practice their art every day. Gilliam operates Satsuki's in Mission, BC., but conducts workshops across North America. Check out her personal page at **www.hitomi-art.com**.

Others, like Steve Rittner, operate flower design schools, sharing their expertise with aspiring floral designers. Rittner runs Rittners School of Floral Design in Boston, Massachusetts (**www.floralschool.com**).

It takes many years of hands-on practice to reach the level of these accomplished individuals. But the good news is, in every case, they apply the same universal principles of design to their award-winning creations as you will apply to your first flower arrangement. And those universal design concepts can be easily learned.

2.4.1 Color and Design

Color is intrinsic to floral design, and one of the first considerations when you're making an arrangement. What color does the customer want? Are they fond of bright colors or pastels? Would they like a mixed arrangement using many different colors? And if so, how can you make that arrangement look harmonious with all the different colors you could include?

Fortunately, there's a simple tool that you can use to ensure that your color combinations are always perfect. It's called the color wheel, and you may have already encountered one in art class, in the interior paint section at your favorite hardware store, or in many other places where there's the need to combine different colors for a pleasing effect.

You don't need to have an actual color wheel on hand, and you don't need to match the colors of flowers exactly to the colors on the wheel. But it provides a guide. Your own eyes will take you the rest of the way, telling you what combinations are most pleasing to you.

You can get a color wheel at an art supplies or craft store, or buy one online for as little as $4 from The Color Wheel Company. Visit **www. colorwheelco.com** or phone 541-929-7526 to order one.

The Color Wheel

If you imagine all of the colors of the rainbow bent into the shape of a pie, you have a good idea of the color wheel. Each color blends into the next, offering a wide range of colors to choose from when you make floral arrangements.

The color wheel includes the three primary, or pure, colors: red, yellow, and blue. It also includes the secondary colors which are equal combinations of two primary colors:

red + blue = purple

red + yellow = orange

blue + yellow = green

Intermediate (also known as tertiary) colors are an equal combination of a primary color and a secondary color next to it on the ring. For example, blue (a primary color) and purple (a secondary color) combine to make blue-purple. The six intermediate colors are: blue-purple, blue-green, yellow-green, yellow-orange, red-orange, and red-purple.

In addition, colors have different values — a term that refers to the lightness or darkness of each color. Colors can be made brighter by the addition of white — these are called hues. Pastel colors – such as pink, which is a lighter shade of red – are tints. If black is added, colors are made darker. These are called shades. Navy blue, for example, is a shade of blue. Black, white and grey are considered to be neutral.

The colors on the red-yellow-orange side of the color wheel are considered to be warm, energizing colors, while blues, purples and greens are considered to be cool and relaxing colors. Most flowers are to be found in the warm range, while greens and filler flowers (such as statice) can be found in the cool range.

Warm, stimulating, or intense colors attract the eye, while cool pastel colors provide a more restful place for the eye to wander. This is useful to remember, as it allows you a way to control where a viewer looks, and the way they perceive your design.

Color Schemes

There are numerous ways to combine colors to achieve beautiful results. Some florists say that all flowers go together, regardless of color — and in nature, this is certainly true. If you're aiming for a natural look, you may want to toss all rules to the wind. However, if you want stunning arrangements that make the best use of color, then sticking to color schemes – groupings of colors that are pleasing together – is the sure way to success.

Monochromatic Color Scheme

A monochromatic color scheme takes advantage of the many tints and shades of one color. For example, by combining all the different colors of red flowers available, you would be able to make a strong statement about warmth and energy.

Analogous Color Scheme

This color scheme uses hues found next to each other on the color wheel — yellow, orange and red, for example. There should be at least three colors, and you may include tints and shades of each hue, but no more than one primary color.

Complementary Color Scheme

A complementary color scheme uses two colors that are opposite or near-opposite on the color wheel, such as red and green, or blue and orange. A split complementary color scheme uses three colors, equally apart on the color wheel, such as red, yellow and blue.

Contrasting Color Scheme

This scheme uses colors that have strong differences between them. Black and white is an obvious one, as is bright red and soft blue. You can also use contrast in texture (such as shiny and dull) or in size (large and small) to create contrast in an arrangement.

2.4.2 Design Basics

When florists talk about flower arrangements, they often refer to their shape, form, line and texture. These are all elements of design — the building blocks, as it were, that are used in each arrangement.

With regards to actual materials, keep in mind the terms "hardware," which refers to the container, filler, tape and other materials used in an arrangement, and "mechanics," which refers to the structures and techniques whereby the arrangement is held in place, such as wires and tape. The "materials" are the plant products you use to make the arrangement.

Elements of Design

Shape and Form

All flower arrangements can be described with the same basic shapes you already know — square, rectangle, circle, triangle, etc. In addition, there are curved "C" and "S" shapes, and arrangements can be vertical or horizontal.

A designer considers the total space available for the arrangement and the spaces created by the flowers themselves. *Positive space* is space filled with material, while *negative space* is the shape of the space around and between the flowers. Both are important considerations in a design. In all cases, however, the space in an arrangement is planned, and flowers are placed precisely to highlight that space.

Form refers to the three-dimensional object that all flower arrangements become. It may be closed (compact and solid) or it may be open (loose, spreading and airy).

Closed forms appear heavier than open forms. Forms may also be regular – a round daisy, for example – or irregular, like a serrated leaf. Overlapping materials can contribute to depth — the illusion that something is actually more dimensional than it really is.

Line

The line of an arrangement outlines its basic structure and is the path the eye should follow when looking at an arrangement. Line can be vertical, diagonal, curved, or horizontal, and it can have its own characteristics, such as thin, thick, short or long. Curved lines can evoke movement and informality, while straight lines can evoke formality.

You may use flowers or stems to follow the line of an arrangement, or you may emphasize the line by repeated shapes, flowers, textures, or forms that are placed along the imagined line.

Mass or Size

The size of individual flowers should be taken into consideration when you make any arrangement. A large flower is out of place in a tiny vase, as is a delicate flower in an enormous wedding arrangement. For each flower to be appreciated, and its full value realized, it should be used in the appropriate context.

The density of a flower – for example, if it is a tight, compact shape like a carnation – should also be taken into consideration. A compact flower will have greater mass than an irregularly shaped flower, like an alstroemeria or orchid.

Texture

Smooth or rough, soft or hard, dull or glossy, the surface of a material is described by its texture. Smooth textures appear larger. Rough ones look smaller than they actually are. Color can also be affected by texture, as rough textures will make a color look more dull than the same color on a smooth material.

Principles of Design

When florists make arrangements, they use a number of principles to ensure the arrangement looks good. These include considerations such as the focal point of an arrangement, the scale and proportion of the flowers in it, and the way the flowers work together to create visual balance, rhythm and harmony.

Proportion and Scale

The rule of thumb used to determine proportion is called the Golden Mean, which is a ratio of 1 to 1.6. It is the ideal size of one thing in proportion to another. In other words, if one flower in a corsage is one inch across, the ideal proportion for the other flower in the corsage would be 1.6 inches across. However, this is not a hard and fast rule. Proportion is determined largely by visual weight, and hence it is subject to the types of flowers, containers, and other materials used.

Balance

Balance, or the appearance of weight, can be symmetrical or asymmetrical. Even though the laws of gravity may not necessarily apply, the human eye is pleased when things that appear heavier (solid, darker colored objects) are lower in an arrangement than things that appear lighter. Note that this has to do with perception, not actual balance.

Rhythm

This is not rhythm as in music, but like music, it suggests motion. By the use of repetition (similar shapes or colors used more than once) or gradation (in which larger units are placed next to smaller units, next to even smaller units), you can achieve rhythm that makes your design seem exciting and visually alive.

Contrast

By putting different or opposite elements next to each other, you are able to create contrast. Each of the elements must be somehow related in order to contrast — that is, smooth and rough textures could contrast, as could light and dark colors, or large and small shapes.

Focal Point

The focal point of any arrangement is the largest, most visually dominant area. It may be achieved by placing a large flower, a bright color, or an interesting shape in the area where you want the viewer to look first. In every case, the focal point draws attention, and it is the point which the other lines of the design should move towards or from.

Harmony

This is the successful combination of all of the rules of design in one arrangement. You know you have achieved harmony when the arrangement appears "right" or "done." All the visual elements are in place.

2.5 How to Make Arrangements

Now it's time to have fun! Hands-on practice is the best way to learn the art of arranging flowers. Try at least a few of these types of arrangements and take pictures of each of them when you're finished so you have a lasting record of your achievements and something to refer to once the flowers have faded.

When you go to a flower shop to buy the flowers you will use for practice, you will also be able to buy floral foam and basic containers. Explain to the florist why you need these items, and ask what they recommend. If you go in at a quiet time when the florist isn't busy with orders or customers, you may also be able to watch them work for a while. This is invaluable and could lead to further instruction, tips or even job leads.

2.5.1 How to Make a Container Arrangement

You Will Need:

- A container

- Floral foam

- Greens

- Flowers

- Waterproof tape

- Knife

Directions:

First, cut a block of floral foam to fit the container. Trim any sharp edges to create more surface area. On a square block of foam, for example, you would cut off the corners. Insert the foam into the container, and secure it with waterproof tape if needed.

Add water, mixed with floral preservative or flower food, until the container is full of water and the foam is thoroughly saturated. Insert greens into the foam, beginning at the lowest point of the arrangement, and insert the stem ends of greens at evenly spaced points. For an all-around arrangement, for example, picture a compass. Put the first four stems of greens into the arrangement at each of the compass points. Then put the next four in between. Continue to insert greens until they are evenly spaced over the whole block of foam.

Next, take the largest flowers you will be using in the arrangement. These are the primary flowers. Cut the stem end of each flower just before inserting it into the arrangement. Place them according to the style of arrangement you are making (see the color section between pages 56 and 57 for examples). It is better to leave the stem a bit too long than to cut it too short.

Once the primary flowers are in place, take the next-smallest flowers you will be using. Insert them according to the design of the arrangement. Continue with the next smallest flowers, and then move on to filler flowers. Insert the filler flowers wherever they are needed, in places where there are obvious gaps or holes.

2.5.2 How to Make a Vase Arrangement

You Will Need:

- A wide-necked vase

- Three, five or seven stems of greens

- At least 12 stems of flowers

- Filler flowers

- A wired bow

Directions:

Begin with a clean vase filled to the neck with lukewarm water and flower food. Cut three to five stems of greenery to no higher than one and a half times the height of the vase.

Insert the stems of greenery into the vase so they "weave" or interlace together. If you are using three, imagine the stems forming a triangle. If you are using five, imagine the stems making a five-pointed star. If you are using seven, insert the last two vertically in the center of the star.

With a knife, cut the longest one so that its top will be no higher than two and a half times as high as the vase. Insert it into the center of the vase. Continue cutting and inserting the same variety of flower, each one slightly shorter than the next.

Move on to the next variety of flower. As you did with the container arrangement, insert each one in between the main flowers already there. You will work downwards – with slightly shorter stems each time – and around in a circle, placing the flowers at equal distances from each other.

Continue with the next variety, and the next, and the next. When you have inserted all your main flowers, add your filler flowers to fill in any gaps in between stems. Use no more than three or four stems of filler flower.

Tie a ribbon around the neck of the vase, and attach a bow by tying it on with the loose ends of the ribbon, or make a bow held with wire and insert the wire into the vase as though it were a flower.

Using a narrower "bud" vase follows essentially the same principle, though with fewer flowers. You can arrange a single rose in a bud vase by cutting it so it's no taller than one and a half times the height of the vase, placing it in the water-filled vase and adding one or two stems of greens, and one or two stems of baby's breath. Finish with a bow.

How to Tie a Bow

You will need:

- A roll of ribbon (one inch wide is a good size to learn with)

- Florists' wire (medium gauge)

- Scissors

Start with the loose end of a roll of ribbon, in order to ensure you have enough ribbon available to make a satisfying bow.

Examine the ribbon to determine the inside and the outside. The inside will be dull or matte, while the outside will be shiny, patterned or flocked (as in the case of velvet ribbon). Some types of ribbons are equally shiny on both sides, which is beautiful, but not as easy to learn with.

Unroll about 12 inches of ribbon and pinch the loose end between your thumb and forefinger, a few inches from the end. Twist it halfway around, so the ribbon is pleated at the point you've chosen. Hold it at the pleat between your thumb and forefinger.

While pinching the pleat in one hand, use the other hand to draw out four or five inches of ribbon, which you will form into a loop, twisting it to ensure the outside of the ribbon is on the outside of the loop. Bring the bottom of the loop down to the first pinch and pinch it together with the first pleat, holding the two pleats tightly together. Picture the ribbon traveling in a series of figure 8s.

Still holding the two pleats pinched together, twist the ribbon halfway around and make another loop of the same size, in the opposite direction. (The twist ensures the outside of the ribbon remains visible.) Pinch the base of the loop along with the other pleats (the middle of the 8). At this point, you should have a complete figure 8, with a tail at one side and the ribbon still attached to the spool at the other.

Twist the ribbon and make another, slightly smaller loop, in the direction of the very first loop you made. Pinch it at the base, and make another loop of the same size, pinching that too. Now you should have two figure 8s pinched between your fingers.

You may be satisfied with four loops, or if you want to make a fuller bow, you may continue to add loops, each pair of slightly smaller size, until you have six or even eight loops.

When you have sufficient loops, make one final loop that forms a complete circle over the center of the 8 — instead of having the roll-end of the ribbon extending towards the top or the bottom of the 8, you will have it extending in the opposite direction from the tail (the loose end). Pinch that into the center of the 8, too.

While still holding the pinched pleats, cut the ribbon from the roll, allowing a tail of at least as long as the tail you began with. With your free hand, take a length of florists' wire, and slide it through the final circular loop. Bend it down over the pinched pleats, so that it is folded over either side of them. Push the pinched pleats tightly together into the fold of the wire.

Grasp the wire ends with your free hand and twist them tightly together so that the pinched pleats of the ribbon are held securely. Adjust the bow by straightening out any pleats that hide the ribbon's outside surface, and by "fluffing" it up.

You're done! You can use the wire to put the bow into a vase arrangement or onto a flowering plant. If you need a bow for a bouquet of cut flowers or a box of flowers, you may use a length (usually at least 24") of narrower ribbon instead of the wire. This can be used to tie the bow to a package or bouquet.

Visit **www.save-on-crafts.com/makflorbow.html** for a visual demonstration of bow-tying.

2.5.3 How to Make a Hand-Tied Bouquet

You Will Need:

- At least 12 stems of flowers

- String, raffia (palm fibers used for decorating) or ribbon

- Shears or secateurs

Directions:

Start with your center flower — the one with the longest, most sturdy stem. Hold it firmly in your left (non-dominant) hand, about half-way between the end of the stem and the bloom.

Take your next flower (any variety) and place its stem alongside the first stem, with its bloom next to the first. Hold the two stems firmly together. This is called the binding point.

Take the third flower, and place its stem alongside the second stem, with its bloom next to the second. Hold all three tightly. Continue in this manner, in effect surrounding the center stem with the stems of the other flowers. They should tilt at a slight angle, so that they lean diagonally on each other, and are all held tightly at the binding point. Do this until all flowers are used.

Bind the flowers tightly with ribbon, raffia or string at the binding point (where your left hand is holding onto them). The bouquet should be rounded on top, with a group of diagonally-slanted stems below.

With a pair of shears or secateurs, cut the bottoms of the stems straight across so that the bottom of the stems and the top of the blooms are the same distance from the binding point. After cutting, the stem ends should form a flat plane, allowing you to stand the bouquet on its own. Trim individual ends as needed to achieve this effect.

Attach a bow to the binding point, or place the bouquet on a large square of cellophane. Draw the corners of the cellophane up around the bouquet, grasp the bouquet's binding point through the cellophane, and tie a ribbon around the outside of the cellophane to secure it. This will form a "bag" around the stems, and if the cellophane is tied on tightly enough, you may even add water to this bag to keep the flowers fresh. For an added touch, gather the corners of the cellophane above the blooms and tie them together with a smaller ribbon.

2.5.4 How to Make a Corsage or Boutonniere

You Will Need:

- Several flowers with shorter stems

- Greens

- Filler flowers

- Medium- and fine-gauge florists' wire

- Stem tape

- Ribbon

- Wire cutters

- Scissors

Directions:

Begin with the flowers you will use. In this case, we will make a classic corsage using three roses of varying degrees of openness. We will choose shorter-stemmed roses, as they are less expensive to use.

Cut the flowers, leaving about half an inch of stem below the calyx. Insert a half-length of medium-gauge florists' wire into the widest part of the calyx, piercing it. Slide the wire halfway through the calyx and bend both sides of the wire downwards, towards the stem end. Grasp the wire and twist the flower gently to wind the wire around the stem.

Unroll an inch or two of stem tape and begin wrapping it tightly around the calyx. The easiest way to do this is to hold the tape firmly over your forefinger and twist the flower. Tug gently at the tape as you twist, stretching the tape down over the length of the stem. When you have reached the bottom of the stem, pull sharply on the tape to detach it. Repeat these steps with the rest of the flowers to be used.

Once you have all three flowers wired and taped, hold the largest one by the stem, and place the one with the next largest bloom just above it. Twist the wired stems together and tape them. Then, add the smallest bloom just above the medium one, and twist that stem onto the first two. Tape them all together.

Using the same technique, you may tape individual leaves (like ivy, leatherleaf fern, plumosa fern, or salal) or clusters of filler flower (like baby's breath, wax flower, or statice) directly onto the stems, tucking them between the main flowers. Alternately, some florists attach the filler flowers around each individual main flower first, and assemble them with the filler flowers already attached.

Some florists also like to roll individual loose petals into tubes, which they wire with fine florists' wire, then tape and attach onto the corsage as though these were flowers.

Once the corsage is assembled, bend the flowers into position (so they're facing outwards), and make a bow out of narrow ribbon. It should be proportionate to the flowers and never more than one-third the size of the corsage. Wrap the wire of the bow around the corsage stem, and wrap the stem with one more layer of stem tape to hide the wire.

Trim the ragged ends of the stem by cutting them with wire cutters or secateurs. Twist the trimmed end around a pencil to create a cork-screw, or simply bend it back upon itself. Insert a corsage pin into the stem, or attach to a wristlet (small circles of elastic or plastic fitted with a metal prong) if making a wrist corsage. Place in a corsage box. Mist well and store in the cooler until pickup or delivery.

Boutonnieres follow essentially the same procedure, though they usually only require one main flower, and don't have bows unless requested.

Arrangements You Need to Know

On the next few pages, you will find photos and descriptions of some of the more common types of floral arrangements.

Posy/Country/Colonial/ Tussy Mussy/Victorian/ Millefiori/All-Around *(below)*

There are many names for this very popular style of arrange-ment, but they all come down to one basic shape: round. Meant to be viewed from all sides, this circular-shaped arrangement should be symmetrical and form a loose half-globe shape. They may be arranged in containers or in handled baskets. **Millefiori** refers to a style that includes more flowers than greens or filler flowers. A **table center-piece** is a low, elongated posy, often with candles included in the center of the oval.

One-Sided *(above)*

One-sided arrangements are usually used in situations where they will be viewed from the front only — funeral arrangements or flowers for a mantle piece, for example. They are usually shaped like triangles — either equilateral, or a right triangle (facing left or right) — or like fans, in which all the stems appear to radiate from a single point low in the arrangement. They may be arranged in containers, vases, or baskets (often with handles that arch over and among the flowers).

Hand-Tied *(below left)*

A bouquet of cut flowers tied together at a binding point partway down their stems. The stems may be angled or spiraled, allowing the arrangement to stand up on its own, or they may be bound together with ribbon to form a handle for the bouquet. A ribbon bow is usually tied on at the binding point.

Bud Vase *(right)*

A bud vase is a narrow or narrow-necked vase that can accommodate only a few stems, and "bud vase" is also the name for the type of arrangement that is made in one of these vases. Meant to be viewed from all sides, they focus on a single flower or a few individual flowers, and are accented with small amounts of greens and filler flowers, occasionally ribbons and sometimes sticks or grasses to add height.

Vase Arrangement

Refers to any group of flowers arranged in a vase. These are meant to be viewed from all angles. A mixed vase arrangement would include several types of flowers, while a rose vase arrangement would include just the requested number of roses (usually 6, 12, 18 or 24) and plenty of greens and filler flowers.

Design Styles You Need to Know

The arrangements on the previous two pages can be influenced by and created in a variety of design styles. Here are the major styles.

Formal Linear *(right)*

Line is essential to this design style. You should be able to visually identify the beginning and end of each line in the arrangement. The AIFD (American Institute of Floral Designers) defines this style as "an asymmetrical balanced design of few materials, usually placed in groups, that emphasizes forms and lines. Generous use of space accentuates the individual flowers, leaves, stem angles, colors and textures."

Crescent *(left)*

As its name suggests, this arrangement takes a C shape, whether it is an upright C or one that is slightly leaning backwards, like a crescent moon. The viewer's eyes are drawn from the top of the crescent downwards to the bottom. Usually prepared in a container or basket, it is meant to be viewed from the front.

Biedermeier *(left)*

Dating from the early 1800s, this design style is a tight, circular style of flower arrangement constructed with either concentric circles or spirals of floral material in contrasting colors and textures. Each line is distinct and closely placed beside the next. May be hand-tied or arranged in a container.

Western Line *(right)*

Any arrangement with asymmetrical lines radiating from a single focal point, and a loose L-shaped form, is considered to be in the Western Line style. The vertical part of the L may be slightly off-center, and the horizontal part may be almost diagonal. Usually prepared in a container (though may also be arranged in a vase), this is meant to be viewed mainly from the front.

Horizontal

A long, low arrangement, usually taking the shape of a rectangle or oval. Horizontal arrangements are useful for table center pieces, casket sprays and mantle piece arrangements in particular. Meant to be viewed from all sides, and above. Prepared in containers, often oblong ones.

Hogarth Curve *(left)*

Named after the 18th-century English painter William Hogarth, this is a graceful S-shaped curving arrangement. It is prepared in an unobtrusive container to allow the form to be dominant, and is sometimes displayed on a pedestal to allow the shape to be fully appreciated. The S may be made with many blooms arranged into the shape, or may be simply suggested by twigs or stems. This is a formal style of arrangement.

Ikebana *(right)*

It takes many years to master the ancient Japanese art of ikebana, but ikebana principles of simplicity and grace can be applied to floral design with pleasing results. Essentially, there should be three main parts to an ikebana design — a focal point, which is often placed low in the arrangement; a middle point, which is slightly higher; and a top point, which is about twice as high as the middle point. These points may be made with flowers, twigs, or other natural materials, and the arrangement is usually made in a low container with minimal mechanics. In general, ikebana is characterized by sparse lines and a focus on the individual beauty of each piece of material used.

Landscape *(right)*

Meant to be an interpretation of nature rather than an imitation of it, the landscape style makes use of natural materials such as leaves, twigs, sticks and stones, and it may focus more on greens than on flowers. It can be prepared in a container (though it should be a natural-looking one) or basket. Meant to be viewed from all sides, this is an informal design style.

New Convention *(left)*

This design style is characterized by vertical and horizontal lines intersecting to form right (90 degree) angles. There may be a base of flowers or greenery placed low on the arrangement to form a pillow-like clump from which the vertical or horizontal stems emerge. The vertical and horizontal lines are repeated in clusters of similar materials (i.e. a clump of liatris placed vertically and another horizontally, then a clump of larkspur placed vertically and another horizontally). It is meant to be viewed from all sides, so care should be taken to ensure angles are maintained.

Vegetative *(left)*

This design style mimics nature in that it provides clusters of flowers that are (or might be) found together in nature. It can use parallel lines (clusters of flowers placed next to each other but not touching) or radial lines that make the flowers appear as though they are growing from one central plant. It's meant to be viewed from all sides, and usually it is prepared in containers (long and low in the case of the parallel style, and round in the case of the radial style).

Parallel Systems *(right)*

The parallel systems style of arrangement is relatively uncommon, but can be striking. It uses groups of flowers, usually with long stems, though not necessarily, to create clusters of parallel lines that do not cross or touch. The negative space between the flower clusters is as important as the clusters themselves. Parallel systems may be vertical or horizontal, though vertical is more common. (Note: While the arrangement in this photo may appear the same as the New Convention arrangement on the previous page, all flowers in this arrangement are parallel, while the New Convention style also has horizontal materials at a 90-degree angle).

Vertical *(below)*

A tall, sometimes skinny, up-and-down arrangement in which the materials are one and a half to two times the height of the container, but the side-to-side measurements of the materials do not exceed the side-to-side measurements of the container.

Waterfall or Cascade *(above)*

While this is a popular style for wedding bouquets, it is also very pleasing as an arrangement. It can be prepared in a vase, in which the flowers appear to be spilling out of the vase and down one side, or in a container, usually meant to be placed on a pedestal or mantle piece to allow the flowers to hang gracefully. In addition to appearing to spill over the edge of the container, the materials are layered over each other, sometimes with longer materials over shorter ones, to emphasize texture. It's meant to be viewed from at least three sides.

2.5.5 How to Make a Wedding Bouquet

You Will Need:

- Flowers according to choice or recipe

- Greens

- Filler flowers

- Bouquet holder

- Medium-gauge florists' wire

- Stem tape

- Ribbon

- Any desired accessories (like strings of beads, for example)

Directions:

In some ways, a wedding bouquet is like a big corsage, though it is often made with the added benefit of a floral foam-filled bouquet holder. There are also hand-tied wedding bouquets, which follow the same procedure as that of hand-tied bouquets, though instead of letting the stems splay outwards, they are usually bound tightly by wrapping them with ribbon to form a handle. In this case, let's look at making a traditional wedding bouquet in a holder.

Soak the bouquet holder and its foam in warm water and cut flower food. Place the handle of the holder into a wire bouquet stand, or in the mouth of a sturdy, narrow vase.

Attach any complicated greenery or decorations – such as a cascade of ivy, beads or ribbon – to the holder by wiring the stems together and twisting the wire onto the cage of the bouquet holder. Trim the ends and tuck them out of sight into the foam.

Add the greenery, using the same procedure as described in the "container arrangements" section (section 2.5.1). Follow the general shape that the finished bouquet is to take. For example, if it's a cascade, use longer stems of greenery towards the bottom of the bouquet.

Insert the main focal point flowers, ensuring they are secure in their place. Insert the next smallest flowers, following the shape of the bouquet or at least ensuring they are equally spaced.

Continue with the next smallest flowers, and the next. Once you have inserted all the flowers, add filler flowers. You may also extend the shape of the bouquet, if needed, by wiring and taping stems to the proper length and inserting them into the foam. Finish with a bow, in a matching color, tied onto the base of the holder.

2.5.6 How to Make a Funeral Wreath

You Will Need:

- Flowers of choice

- Greens

- One prepared wreath form

- Ribbon

- Scissors

- Hot glue in a pot

Directions:

Begin by placing the wreath form flat on your workspace, and preparing your greens by cutting them into short lengths or individual stemmed leaves (such as with ivy or salal). If the wreath form is made of floral foam, you may insert the greens directly into the foam; if it is made of a wire frame stuffed with sphagnum moss and wrapped with plastic strips, you may insert the stems beneath the edges of the plastic strips. You may also use small lengths of wire bent into "U" shapes to pin greens into place.

In either case, point the leaves all in the same direction and layer the leaves over each other so that the effect is of shingles. Continue until the entire wreath is covered in greens.

If the wreath design requires the whole thing to be covered in flowers, cut the stems short and insert them in the same way as you did the leaves. If this is the case, an all-floral foam wreath is best.

You may also use hot glue to attach the flowers. Dip the calyx of each flower into the glue pot and place them on top of the greens. Keep in mind that glued flowers will not last as long and must be sprayed with a preservative such as Hawaiian Mist or Crowning Glory to prevent dehydration.

If there are to be one or two clusters of flowers on the wreath, you may either tape or glue a small foam holder or a piece of floral foam to the points on the wreath where the clusters are to be placed. Insert greens into these pieces of foam just as you would with any arrangement, and then insert your flowers according to the design of the wreath.

Attach any ribbon required either with wire or glue. If you use glue, be sure that the end of the ribbon is attached to a spot where it will not be seen, as glue tends to soak through ribbon and look messy.

2.5.7 How to Make a Basket Garden

You Will Need:

- Basket

- Plants in pots

- Sphagnum moss

- Wired bow

- Decorative pik

Directions:

Choose a wide, low basket or container that is big enough to accommodate several small plants (no larger than 6"), and that is as deep as the tallest plant pot.

If the basket is not lined with a plastic liner, line it with a piece of cellophane or florists foil (cellophane is preferred). Place the plants, with their pots, into the basket so that the best side of each plant faces outwards, with the tallest plant in the center or at the back. Pretend that you're organizing them for a portrait, and want to make sure each one can be seen.

Cover the soil in the plant pots with wads of sphagnum moss, Easter grass or other light, decorative material. Add a bow on a wire, a decorative pik, or both, by inserting them into the soil of one of the pots.

2.5.8 How to Make a Fruit Basket

You Will Need:

- Fruit of choice in groups of three

- Basket

- Tissue paper

- Easter grass or excelsior

- Cellophane

- Ribbon

Directions:

Place the fruit so that it's in easy reach. Make sure all pieces are free of bruises and blemishes, and that bananas are slightly under-ripe. Choose a wide, low basket, with or without a handle. Place the basket in the center of a piece of cellophane large enough to draw up over the basket and extend for at least 24 to 30 inches.

Ball up several sheets of tissue paper and use them to line the basket. If you like, you may also add a few handfuls of Easter grass or other light decorative material (except moss) at this point.

Select pieces of fruit in groups of three (i.e. three oranges, three apples, three pears) and arrange them in the basket, sturdiest on the bottom. If you are using a large fruit such as a melon or pineapple, place this in the basket first and arrange the other fruits evenly around it.

Neatly trim the ends of banana stems and use bananas to help hold rounder fruit in place. As with flower arrangements, work from the largest fruits to the smallest. Continue piling the fruit on top of itself until you've used all your pieces.

Carefully draw the corners of the cellophane up over the top of the fruit pile, holding them together above the fruit. Gather the cellophane into a bunch over the top of the fruit and bind it with a thin ribbon or tape. Fold and tuck the edges of cellophane over each other and seal them with small, unobtrusive pieces of clear adhesive tape.

Tie a ribbon and attach a bow to the binding point of the cellophane. Trim the edges of the cellophane with scissors, if needed.

2.5.9 How to Dress a Plant

You Will Need:

- One plant in a plastic pot

- Florists' foil

- One wired bow

Directions:

Tear off a piece of florists' foil that is approximately three to four times as wide as the height of the plant pot. Place it silver side up, colored side down. Fold the edges of the foil inward to form flaps about one inch wide along each side. Place the plant pot in the center of the foil square.

Grasp two opposite sides of the foil and gently draw them up along the sides of the plant pot. Leaving the edge loose, gently tuck the foil into the top of the plant pot. Make a vertical fold in the foil on either side of the tuck, and tuck the folded part into the top of the pot as well. Turn the entire pot and repeat the above with the other two sides of the foil.

Press the foil into place around the pot, and adjust if necessary. Add a bow on a wire to the side of the pot by inserting the wire through the foil and into the soil.

You may also dress a plant with a Speed-Cover – a pre-folded mylar or plastic pouch – or with a circle of colored plastic drawn up over the edges of the pot and tied into place. Or you may place the entire pot into a wicker basket or other container that is slightly wider and deeper than the pot itself. Hide the soil with moss or other material, and add a bow to the side of the basket or container by inserting its wire into the soil of the plant pot.

2.6 Wedding Flowers

Wedding flowers are one of the biggest single floral purchases consumers will ever make. Contemporary brides have access to a wide range of design influences, from television weddings to current bridal magazines. There are no hard and fast rules about wedding flowers, but there are many long-standing traditions that may play into a bride's desires for her special day.

As such, it is your job as a florist to help your clients choose the flower ensemble that will suit their personality, taste and budget, and make their wedding a day to remember. Many different types of flower arrangements may be incorporated into a wedding, and it is up to you to suggest and design the best ones.

2.6.1 Meeting With Clients

Your first meeting with a bride is an opportunity for you to gather information about her needs, and for her to see the kind of work you can do for her. Some florists may charge a consultation fee, which will be applied to the cost of the final order. Others prefer to offer free consultations. Either is acceptable.

The Consultation

Set aside at least an hour for your initial consultation. Plan it at a time convenient to you and the bride — after the day's deliveries have gone out, for example, or when someone else is working at the shop to handle phone calls and walk-in customers. Have the bride bring a photo or drawing of her dress, samples of fabric from her bridesmaids' dresses, and a list of all members of the wedding party. If she has already determined her budget, she should have that in mind as well.

You can do a wedding consultation in any area of the shop. Sometimes florists have a special wedding area decorated with sample bouquets, corsages and other arrangements made of artificial flowers. They usually have a table and chairs set up so clients can be comfortable while they look at wedding flower portfolios and selection guides. However, any area of the store where you're out of the way of foot traffic works well. Have the following on hand:

- A pen

- Wedding order forms (see the sample form later in this section)

- A portfolio of any wedding work you or the shop's other designers have done (an album of photos is sufficient)

- Wedding flower selection guides and brochures (FTD and Teleflora both publish these materials for their members — see section 6.3 for more information on becoming a member)

- A calculator for adding up the cost of the flowers requested

- A calendar to mark the date of the wedding and note the date that the order should be confirmed by

ɔf Style

ɹu first meet with a bride-to-be, let her tell you about her
er dreams, the members of her wedding party, and the ideas
she h̬ɔ in mind for her flowers. Ask the following questions to determine her sense of style:

- What are her favorite flowers?

- What are her favorite colors?

- Does she consider herself a traditional person? An earthy person? A high-style person?

- Are there any flowers that have significance to her?

- Does she want to be able to preserve her wedding bouquet afterwards?

- What is her dress like?

- What will the bridesmaids wear? The groomsmen? The flower girl and ring bearer?

- Where will the wedding be held? The reception?

- What time of day is the wedding? (The later in the day the ceremony is held, the more formal the wedding is likely to be.)

- How many guests are invited?

- Will the dinner be sit-down, or buffet-style? Or will it be cocktails and hors d'oeuvres?

- What will the cake be like?

TIP: As a florist, you will find it beneficial to know about wedding traditions. A good way to read up on this subject is to check out the book *I Do! I Do!: From the Veil to the Vows — How Classic Wedding Traditions Came to Be*, by Susan Waggoner.

Working Within the Clients' Budget

When planning a wedding ensemble, it helps to know the clients' budget in advance. If their budget is small (under $300), you will know to suggest less expensive flowers in order to allow them to have as many arrangements as they want. If their budget is moderate ($500 to $1,000), you will be able to suggest more expensive flowers, such as orchids or roses, or encourage them to include more types of arrangements, such as cake-toppers or an arrangement for the guestbook table. If their budget is large ($1,000 and up), you will be able to help them visualize their wedding fantasies and make them come true.

In every case, though, you will need to bear in mind the cost of flowers and the cost of your labor for preparing the wedding. (For more on this topic, see section 5.7 on "Setting Prices.")

If the bride wants lilies of the valley, but is getting married in December, you will also need to take into account that the requested flowers will be more expensive than at other times of the year. (Or encourage her to substitute an equally beautiful, fragrant flower that is in season.) Generally, flowers that are in season or are easily available (such as carnations, chrysanthemums, and alstroemeria) are less expensive. Flowers that are in high demand for weddings (such as gardenias or stephanotis) or that are out of season tend to be more expensive. Guide your client toward decisions that fit within her budget.

Once you've calculated the price of all the items the client wants in her wedding ensemble, and she's agreed to that price, you need to stick with it. You may do so by ordering the more exotic flowers in advance to take advantage of better prices from your suppliers. You can also plan your time in order to ensure you will be able to prepare the arrangements without having to work overtime or hire extra help. A sample invoice for a flower order is included on the next two pages.

2.6.2 Flowers for Wedding Party Members

The Bride

The bride's bouquet is the focal point of any wedding flower ensemble. It sets the tone for the rest of the pieces, and at least some of the types of flowers included in the bride's bouquet are used in the groom's boutonniere and the bouquets of other wedding party members.

Sample Wedding Flower Order Form

Bride: _____   Groom: _____
Address: _____   Address: _____
          _____   _____
          _____   _____
Phone: _____   Phone: _____

Schedule

Date of Wedding:

Ceremony Location:
Delivery time: _____   *Pickup time:* _____

Reception Location:
Delivery time: _____   *Pickup time:* _____

Dinner Location:
Delivery time: _____   *Pickup time:* _____

Flowers Ordered

Bride   Total: $_____
Bouquet style: _____
Flowers to include: _____
Floral headpiece: _____

Honor Attendant   Total: $_____
Bouquet style: _____
Flowers to include: _____

Bridesmaids   Total: $_____
Number of bridesmaids: _____
Bouquet style: _____
Flowers to include: _____

Flower Girl   Total: $_____
Bouquet style: _____
Flowers to include: _____

Floral Headpieces   Total: $_____
Number of headpieces: _____

Boutonnieres   Total: $_____
Groom: _____
Best man: _____
Groomsmen/ushers: _____
Fathers: _____
Grandfathers: _____
Ring bearer: _____

Corsages   Total: $_____
Bride's mother: _____
Groom's mother: _____
Grandmothers: _____

Decorations for Ceremony   Total: $_____
Main altar: _____
Aisle and pew decorations: _____
Canopy: _____
Candelabra: _____
Altar arrangement: _____
Aisle runner: _____

Decorations for Reception   Total: $_____
Cake and cake table: _____
Centerpieces: _____

Decorations for Rehearsal Dinner   Total: $_____
Centerpieces: _____

Totals

Subtotal: _____   Deposit: _____
Sales tax: _____   Balance: _____
Total: _____

Paid by: ___ *Cash*   ___ *Check*
                ___ *Credit Card*   ___ *Debit Card*

A bridal bouquet can take many shapes:

- The round, or posy, style is circular, sometimes spherical.

- The teardrop is shaped like an inverted teardrop.

- The cascade is like a waterfall of flowers.

- The hand-tied bouquet looks like a natural gathering of flowers.

- The arm bouquet is a long, elegant arrangement that rests on the bride's forearm.

- The free-style bouquet uses contemporary design techniques to create a unique look as individual as the bride herself.

Other possibilities include an S-curve, a crescent or C-shape, a handled basket filled with flowers, a garland of flowers that can be worn like a boa or scarf, and a decorated fur or velvet muff (for Christmas or winter weddings).

A sense of proportion is important. A tall bride is able to carry a long, cascading bouquet more easily than a petite bride. However, if a petite bride has her heart set on a cascade-style bouquet, it is possible to use smaller flowers (such as spray roses and miniature carnations) to create a smaller bouquet to meet her wishes.

The bride's bouquet should complement the style of her dress. If she has chosen a lacy, elaborate dress, a simple bouquet will enhance it. If she has a simple dress, she will be able to choose a more elaborate bouquet.

Color schemes can be monochromatic (all one color, such as white or pink or red), complementary (using opposing colors on the color wheel) or multicolored.

Headpieces For the Bride

Whether or not they choose to wear a veil, many brides want to wear floral headpieces. A simple corsage attached to a comb will work for brides with longer hair, if they plan to wear it up. Short-haired brides may choose a wreath of flowers to encircle their heads, while others may prefer a ribbon adorned with flowers to tie into their hair. Still others opt for sprigs of baby's breath or individual blossoms to tuck into their hairstyle. These flowers should be prepared in advance so the bride can take them to the hairstylist with her on her wedding day.

The Bridesmaids

The bridesmaids' bouquets may be smaller versions of the bride's bouquet, they may be simple round or posy style bouquets, or they may be hand-tied. In any case, they take their cue from the bride's bouquet and should complement the bridesmaids' dresses. Bright, strong-colored dresses call for white or strong-colored bridesmaids' bouquets, while pastel dresses require a more neutral or pastel choice.

Often the bridesmaids' bouquets will have the same type of flower as in the bride's bouquet, but in a different color — such as white roses in the bride's bouquet and pink roses for the bridesmaids.

It is not necessary for each bridesmaid's bouquet to look exactly like the next. A maid of honor may have a slightly larger bouquet. Individual bridesmaids may also choose the color of their bouquets, so that there are variations within a theme. And, of course, bridesmaids may also want hairpieces, though these are usually less elaborate than the one chosen by the bride.

The Groom

The groom's important role should be designated by his boutonniere. Usually a single flower matching a variety of flower in the bride's bouquet, his boutonniere is complemented by a small piece of greenery and perhaps a tuft of baby's breath or other small flower. The color of the groom's boutonniere is chosen to complement the clothing he is wearing.

The Groomsmen

The groomsmen are outfitted with boutonnieres similar to the groom's, but these may be smaller or made with less significant flowers. For example, if the groom is wearing a rose boutonniere to go with the roses in the bride's bouquet, the groomsmen may wear miniature carnation boutonnieres to go with the smaller flowers in her bouquet.

The Flower Girl

The flower girl is a younger member of the wedding party. If she is older than 10 years, she may carry a small version of the bridesmaids' bouquets. She may also carry flowers arranged in a small, handled, basket. A younger flower girl may carry a miniature bouquet or a basket of flower petals, which she can sprinkle on the floor a few at a time as she leads the wedding procession.

The Ring Bearer

The ring bearer, usually a young boy, may wear a miniature boutonniere or may carry the rings on a small satin pillow decorated with flowers.

The Mothers and Grandmothers

It is traditional to identify the mothers, grandmothers, and sometimes other significant female guests with corsages. These are chosen to match the clothing they will wear and do not need to coordinate with the wedding bouquets. Sometimes they may choose hairpieces or wrist corsages in order to avoid crushing their flowers with lots of hugs!

The Fathers and Grandfathers

The fathers and grandfathers of the bride and groom are traditionally identified with boutonnieres, which may match the boutonnieres of the groomsmen or may be chosen to complement their clothing.

Special Friends or Siblings

While they may not be officially part of the wedding party, it is nice to identify important friends or siblings of the bride and groom. These individuals may wear boutonnieres, corsages and hairpieces as they choose, and their flowers should be chosen to complement their clothing, not to go with the wedding party's flowers.

A sister who will be taking the photographs, for example, would perhaps wear a hairpiece of flowers. A brother who will be playing an instrument might wear a boutonniere, or decorate the top of his guitar with a small appropriate flower. The possibilities are as varied as the many people who may be involved in the wedding.

2.6.3 Décor for the Ceremony and Reception

Décor for the ceremony depends on where the wedding is taking place. Some churches have rules about the types of flowers or decorations allowed — it is best to check first to ensure the flowers the bride has in mind are allowed in the place she has chosen for her wedding. Assuming flowers are allowed, there are several options for flowers for the wedding ceremony.

Altar arrangements are large, usually one-sided arrangements meant to stand on the floor or on podiums on either side of the altar in a church. Other parts of a church that may be decorated include:

- The pulpit — with a large arrangement on it or in front of it

- The stage — with large arrangements at either side or smaller ones (or garlands) placed along the front

- The pews — which may be decorated with small arrangements clipped onto their ends, or with ribbons and bows

A Jewish ceremony may have a flower-adorned chuppah, or wedding canopy. A non-denominational wedding, particularly one held in a location other than a place of worship, may have any type of décor, depending on the location.

Some ideas are:

- Ivy or flower garlands

- Flower-decorated archways

- Potted flowering plants

- Flower petals strewn on the path the procession will take

- Large arrangements where the ceremony will happen

Small touches are also nice. A flower-decorated pen for signing the marriage register is an option, as is a small flower arrangement for the table on which the register rests.

Décor for the Reception

The reception should have a festive, party-like feeling. Some popular options include:

- Flower or ivy garlands to decorate the head table

- Flower-decorated archways

- Table centerpieces incorporating candles

- Flower-decorated buffet tables

- Arrangement or garlands for the cake table

Some couples may choose to use the same arrangements for several different purposes. An archway of flowers at the ceremony can be moved to the reception to create a grand entranceway. Flowers destined for guests' tables can line the church aisle down which the bride walks. If your customers want to do this, plan the arrangements with their dual purpose in mind, and use sturdy flowers, simple designs and containers that can be easily moved.

Flowers for the Cake

One of the focal points of the reception is the wedding cake, and this can be enhanced by flowers in a variety of ways. Florists can make cake-topper arrangements in small plastic containers using small quantities of floral foam. These can be placed on the cake at the last minute. Edible flowers such as pansies, nasturtiums, rose petals and carnation petals can be placed on the cake just before it goes on display.

Ask the bride who her caterer is so you can coordinate the cake flowers if she chooses to have them. A small corsage-like arrangement can also be attached to the knife the couple will use to cut the cake. The table on which the cake is displayed can be decorated with an arrangement, a vase of flowers, garlands of flowers or scattered petals.

2.6.4 Making the Arrangements

Once you have booked the wedding – that is, the bride has agreed to your quoted price, and paid a deposit (usually 10 percent of the total) – you may begin to pre-plan the supplies you'll need. Set aside any hard goods (like bouquet holders, containers, vases, etc.) that you will need, and label them with your client's name and the date of the wedding.

A month or two in advance, check with your suppliers to determine their prices for the desired flowers. Place an advance order if you will need anything unusual to ensure you are able to get it when you need it.

When the flowers arrive from the supplier, put all the flowers you will need in a separate set of buckets, also labeled for the wedding. That way, nobody else at the shop makes the mistake of using the flowers you'll need for another arrangement.

We discussed the techniques used in making wedding arrangements in the previous section. However, there is a particular order in which you should make the flowers for a wedding, based on the fragility of the flowers and the fact that wedding orders tend to require a lot of preparation:

1. Make any arrangements first. Vase arrangements should be made before container arrangements. These may be made the day before, if necessary.

2. Make any large floral décor pieces, such as archways, pew markers or other pieces.

3. Make the cake arrangements if they are made in floral foam.

4. Make the bouquets. Spray them with floral preserving solution and place them in the cooler on bouquet stands.

5. Make the corsages, boutonnieres and headpieces. Spray them with floral preserving solution, place them in their delivery boxes or bags, and place them in the cooler.

6. Organize any loose cake flowers and place them in a plastic bag. Mist water (not floral preserving solution) into the plastic bag and place them in the cooler.

7. Fill baskets with flower petals.

2.6.5 Delivery or Pickup of Arrangements

While some clients may want their wedding flowers delivered, it is preferable for a friend, family member or member of the wedding party to pick them up. That way, you can explain any specific instructions for individual flowers and demonstrate how to hold the bouquets or wear the boutonnieres. (A sample instruction sheet is included on the next page.)

To prepare the flowers for pickup, it is especially important to anchor vase arrangements securely in low boxes and hold them in place with rings of crumpled newspaper, cellophane tape, or both. Arrangements should be sent with the instruction to "Add water upon arrival."

The wedding bouquets and bridesmaids' bouquets should be supported on rings of newspaper (placed around the handles) or have their handles hitched over the sides of tall cardboard boxes. The bouquets should be enclosed by the boxes, and the handles attached to the cardboard to ensure they don't move in transit. Corsages and boutonnieres should be transported in small plastic corsage boxes or bags and contained in a larger cardboard box. Everything should be misted with water just before pickup.

If there are particularly large arrangements going to a wedding, they should be delivered and set up by the shop's in-house driver, or delivered by the shop's regular delivery service and supervised by the designer in order to ensure they are placed correctly and that flowers are at their peak. (See section 5.8 for more information about how to set up your delivery service.)

The driver should have clear, accurate address information, including directions to the specific part of the location where the flowers must go. It is not acceptable to leave them at the door — the driver will need to carry the arrangements to the church sanctuary, the country club's dining room, or wherever else the members of the wedding party will be found. It is the florist's responsibility to confirm this information with someone in the wedding party the day before the wedding.

The flowers should be delivered no less than an hour before the ceremony and, preferably, no more than two hours before.

Sample Instruction Sheet for Wedding Flowers

Congratulations on your big day! We at Fabulous Florists know you're busy, but please make sure to follow these instructions to help your flowers look perfect:

- Check the name tags on the corsages and boutonnieres.

- Your corsages and boutonnieres are worn with the blossom end up — the way flowers grow.

- Pin your corsages or boutonnieres onto clothing by threading the pin through the material, over the corsage stem, and back through the material once more (under, over, under). The point of the pin will stick out a little.

- The bride's bouquet is the biggest, most beautiful one, of course. The attendants' names are on slips of paper attached to the handles of each of their bouquets.

- Carry your bouquet with a firm grip and your arms extended naturally, so that you feel comfortable. Your hands and the bouquet handle should be just below waist-level.

- Please have someone look at you holding the bouquet before you make your entrance, in order to make sure you look your best.

- The guest table arrangements should be placed in the center of each table.

- The head table arrangements should be placed towards the front of the table, usually in front of the bride and groom's places.

- The cake arrangement should be given to the caterer to place on the cake when it arrives.

Congratulations, and we wish you a happy day. If you have any questions about your flowers, please call us immediately at 222-3333, and we will be pleased to assist. Thank you for letting us be a part of your special day.

2.7 Funeral Flowers

Flowers at funerals are an ancient tradition. They are a symbol of life, and a way of easing the grief of those attending a funeral. They offer a splash of color in an otherwise mournful day, and allow family members of the deceased to pay tribute to their loved one. As such, there are many types of funeral flowers suited to many different types of service, religious beliefs and traditions. Also called sympathy flowers, they convey a sense of sadness and sympathy to those attending the service.

When a customer orders funeral flowers, they are often deeply upset by their loved one's passing. As a florist, it is your role to be sympathetic and understanding and to help the customer choose the type of floral tribute that will reflect their loved one's life as much as their own relationship with the deceased.

Typically, family members will provide the most elaborate or personal arrangements. The flowers that adorn a casket are almost always chosen by family members. Friends and family from other cities may send arrangements to the service, or flowers to be delivered after the service to the home of the family. Some religious traditions dictate that specific flowers be used. If there are specific needs, your customers will inform you, as long as you ask.

In every case, it is up to you to provide a tribute that will help your customer honor their loved one. It is also important to check with the church or funeral home to ensure you are providing flowers that will meet their traditions or requirements.

Types of Services

There are several types of funeral service, and each suggests a different type of flower arrangement. For this reason, it is appropriate to ask the customer what type of service is planned:

- A church service held at the deceased's church

- A graveside service held at the cemetery

- A family service held at a funeral home

- A cremation held at a funeral home

- A memorial service held at a funeral home, church or other location, usually within a month of the loved one's death

Types of Funeral Arrangements

There are many types of flower arrangements used for funerals. Their use is partly dictated by the wishes of the family, partly by their budget, and partly by the type of service planned:

- Funeral sprays or sheafs are large, flat arrangements that are placed on the casket, displayed on a stand, or placed on the floor or the gravesite. They often include wide ribbons and may have the name of the deceased written on the ribbon.

- Container arrangements are large, usually one-sided arrangements prepared in disposable containers.

- Hand-tied bouquets are simple arrangements, often sent to the family after the service or used at graveside services.

- A casket cover is a large, casket-sized spray meant to cover the entire casket. It is usually ordered by the immediate family.

- A blanket spray is a blanket of flowers, made by gluing individual blossoms onto a fabric backing that is meant to cover the entire casket. It is usually provided by the immediate family.

- Wreaths are circular arrangements meant to be displayed on stands or laid on the gravesite. They are a symbol of eternity and are often used at memorials and public ceremonies.

- Crosses are popular for Christian ceremonies. They are typically made by gluing individual blossoms to a cross-shaped framework.

- A heart shape is made by gluing individual blossoms to a heart-shaped form or inserting short stems into a heart-shaped piece of floral foam. A "broken heart" is created by using all white flowers, with a jagged line of red flowers down the center.

- Other symbols used include the anchor (symbolizes hope) and the Star of David (a symbol of Judaism).

- An arrangement may be made to surround or accent a cremation urn. This type of arrangement is usually placed on an altar or small table alongside the urn.

- Arrangements for memorial services can include floral adornments for picture frames, large vase or container arrangements, and wreaths.

Types of flowers commonly used in funeral arrangements include:

- Roses

- Lilies (calla and Asiatic)

- Carnations

- Chrysanthemums

- Gladiolus

- Stocks

- Tulips

A Note on Regional Variations

Funeral traditions are influenced by region, and what is considered appropriate in one part of the country may not be right in another part. This is especially important to keep in mind when you're helping a customer choose a funeral tribute from a selection guide to send to another part of the world. The customer may have a sense of what they want to send, but if not, it is wise to let the filling florist suggest options appropriate for their area.

3. Preparing For Your Career

One of the wonderful things about becoming a florist is that you likely already have many of the skills you need.

Many people have walked into flower shops, not knowing anything about the business, and landed themselves jobs simply because of their enthusiasm and pleasant nature, coupled with a willingness to learn as they go. You could do this, too, and at some point you may want to find a florist willing to let you intern with them (more on that in section 3.2.4). But you'll have a better edge over the competition if you develop some essential skills before you make that first leap.

You're already motivated to learn – that's why you're reading this guide – and whether you practice for months or jump into a work situation tomorrow, that willingness to try something new is essential. When you combine this motivation and the dedication to practice what you learn (in the case of floral design, regular practice is a must), you'll have the advantage both when it comes to getting hired, and in your first few weeks and months on the job.

In this chapter, we'll look at some of the skills you'll need. We'll help you determine which ones you already have and which you need to work on. We'll talk about the many ways you can learn more about floristry, from formal schooling to internship opportunities. We'll also provide you with a list of books and magazines that you can learn from throughout your career.

3.1 Essential Skills

As a florist, you will have the opportunity to use both sides of your brain. Your creative right brain will be engaged as you make arrangements and combine colors. Your analytical left brain will be put to work determining costs of arrangements and figuring out how to get them to the right place at the right time, along with several dozen other bouquets all needing preparation and delivery that day.

You will have the chance to meet people and help them make purchasing decisions — a place where your personality can really shine. You'll make arrangements, install displays, and prepare flowers and plants for sale.

You'll exercise your memory as you remember the names of plants and flowers, and you'll expand your knowledge of plant and flower varieties virtually every day. And you will use your imagination daily as you visualize how arrangements might look, describe them to customers, and put those ideas into reality.

There are some skills that you will naturally already possess, and some that you can learn and develop. This section outlines the most important ones to focus on in the process of preparing for your career.

3.1.1 Interpersonal Skills

Are you a people person? Do friends describe you as outgoing, a great listener, and a friendly individual? If so, you'll be right at home in the retail part of a flower shop. Here are essential interpersonal skills you'll need in a flower shop:

Listening Skills

Listening skills are important. You will need to listen to customers to determine their needs, and to your co-workers and supervisor to understand instructions. You can improve your listening skills by focusing fully on someone when they are speaking. Here are some ways to do that:

- Don't interrupt the other person. Hear them out.

- Keep listening to the other person, even if you think you know what they will say next. If you make assumptions, you may miss the point they're making.

- Ask questions in order to clarify what the other person has said. Take notes if necessary.

- Use paraphrasing. In other words, repeat back your understanding of the wishes of the client.

Verbal Communication

Clear communication is essential because you will need to explain care or display of the flowers to customers, and you'll need to describe what the customers have ordered to designers. Since many sales happen over the phone, it is important to have a pleasant telephone manner and be polite, clear and pleasant.

In section 6.1 you will learn what to say to customers to increase sales and customer satisfaction.

Neat Handwriting

This sounds simple, but it's extremely important. Whether you're writing down a customer's order or preparing a card or delivery label, you'll need to write it down unless your shop has an entirely automated system to do these things.

Teamwork

Working together is important in a flower shop, as sales floor workers must provide clear instructions to designers, who must in turn prepare arrangements that will satisfy customers' requests. Everyone must participate at busy times, and nobody gets out of the basic essentials of sweeping the floor and answering the phone!

You can take a survey to help you assess your team player style at **www.wmich.edu/engineer/webal/docs/t08-tm-player-survey.doc**.

3.1.2 Manual Dexterity

You can't learn manual dexterity from a book, but you probably already have a certain degree of hand-eye coordination and dexterity. Think about the things you've already done from the list below — these will all contribute to your ability to manipulate floral materials:

- Typing

- Playing the piano or another instrument

- Tying your shoes, a tie or a bow

- Wrapping gifts

- Folding origami

- Making things from clay

- Shuffling cards

- Cutting vegetables

- Peeling potatoes

- Braiding

- Knitting or crocheting

- Decorating a Christmas tree

The three most difficult tasks florists perform with their hands are bow-tying, making hand-tied bouquets, and making corsages. All of these skills come easily with practice.

You may want to invest in a few rolls of ribbon and some wire, and in a bunch of flowers (or even a bunch of sticks!) to practice the techniques that will be described in the following sections. Remember that you don't have to get it right the first time, or the tenth. But chances are good that by the fiftieth time you've done it, you'll be as good as any seasoned professional.

3.1.3 Math and Computer Skills

Math Skills

There are a variety of situations in which florists need to be able to do basic arithmetic. Florists need to be able to:

- Subtract the cost of a delivery from a total order amount

- Add up the cost of materials in any given arrangement

- Multiply the wholesale cost of materials by 200 to 400 percent to determine retail price

- Add or subtract any percentage to or from a dollar amount

- Add 30 to 40 percent to any amount to account for labor costs

- Add up the total amount of a purchase

- Make correct change

- Determine the correct amount to be paid for out-of-country orders, based on foreign exchange rates

- Multiply the amount of a purchase by the state, provincial, and federal sales taxes that apply in your area, and add the amount of tax owed to determine the total

Many flower shops have cash registers or computer systems that automatically calculate the total purchase amounts, the amount of tax owed, the amount of change a customer is due, and any discount applicable. Still, it is good to be able to do these things with nothing more than a calculator. A good resource for brushing up your math skills is the book *Everyday Math for Dummies*, by Charles Seiter.

Computer Skills

You won't need to write code or create enormous databases in the regular course of working in a flower shop, but the following computer skills are helpful:

- Keyboarding

- Basic understanding of the Windows or Mac operating system

- Basic understanding of e-mail

- Basic understanding of the Internet

In addition, there are some specialized floral industry software packages that larger shops may use. These software packages are designed to be extremely user-friendly. If you are able to use a computer, you'll have little trouble using these systems to record and send orders, keep track of inventory, do accounting and even print delivery labels. You can find out more about these packages in section 5.3.4.

3.1.4 Organizational Ability

The most important organizational abilities you will need in a flower shop involve categorizing and sorting, prioritizing, and time management. These are simple skills to learn, and their practical application comes as a matter of course. However, understanding their necessity in the florist business is essential.

Categorizing and Sorting

Categorizing and sorting go hand in hand. Categorizing refers to the process of determining which things logically go together – whether they're items of one color, one type, or one size – and sorting is the process by which you put things into their various categories or groups. Once they're in the groups, of course, you'll need to store or display them neatly.

Prioritizing

Prioritizing refers to the process of deciding the order in which you should perform a group of tasks. In the floral industry – a time-sensitive business that deals with lots of perishable products – prioritizing is essential. Otherwise, the fresh roses that just arrived could end up wilted because a florist decided today would be a perfect day to reorganize the display shelves. That would be an example of setting wrong priorities.

Time Management

In a flower shop, managing your time will be a top priority. Your most immediate concerns are the needs of your customers and deliveries that are scheduled to be made today.

While customers require different amounts of time spent with them (someone rushing in to buy a quick bouquet on their way to visit a friend will take less time than a bride planning her wedding flowers), you should be able to gauge the amount of time it takes you to prepare any given type of arrangement. If you have 10 arrangements that you can prepare in 10 minutes each, it will take you 100 minutes, or just over an hour and a half to do them — if you're uninterrupted, that is.

Some florists overcome the interruptions by dividing tasks between employees — one person will prepare arrangements while the other attends to customer needs. Teams like this may function more efficiently than situations in which one person must do it all at once.

Time management is another area in which your prioritizing skills can be used. Divide the day's tasks into the most urgent, the most challenging and the easiest. Make a list of each category's tasks, if you like. Then begin. Do the most urgent first, and then tackle the most challenging. If you get hung up on the challenging one, take a break and do some of the easy ones before returning to the one that challenges you. You'll get a lot more done than if you put off the challenging one until the end of the day when you would rather go home.

Time management is a skill that you become better at with experience. But while you're getting that experience, you can find some good tips to help you along the way at **www.soe.rutgers.edu/osd/MoI/TM_Article.doc**. You can also subscribe to Time Management Tips, a free e-mail list that provides you with regular time-management tips. Find out more at **www.topica.com/lists/timemanagement**.

3.1.5 Creativity

As with manual dexterity, creativity is a skill which develops through use. If you are drawn to the floral industry, you likely are already a creative individual. You already have inherent creative tendencies if you are interested in any of the following: crafts, dancing, drawing, gardening, music, painting, sculpting, or writing. You can increase your creativity just by dabbling in any of the above activities. Your creativity will also increase as you advance through your career as a florist.

Now that you know what skills you need, let's look at how you can actually learn to become a florist.

3.2 Ways To Learn Floristry

With a basic aptitude for art, customer service, and business, anyone can learn how to be a florist. There's an important tool you can use to ensure you will get the most out of your training — whether it's on the job as an intern or volunteer, or in theory and practice as a student in an applied horticultural program.

That tool is careful observation:

- Watch carefully whenever you see a florist at work.

- Ask questions, especially ones beginning with "why" or "how" — these will get you the best responses.

- Listen to the answers to your questions.

- Look at every flower arrangement you encounter. Think about how it was made. How you would do it differently?

In this section, we'll look at some of the ways you can get your foot in the door and gain some experience as a florist, including:

- Information interviews

- Hands-on experimentation

- Volunteer opportunities

- Part-time and seasonal jobs

- Internships

- Books

- Educational institutions

Which of these you choose depends on your own personal preference and the resources available to you.

If there is a college or floral design school near you, you may choose to enroll in a course first before you go about looking for even a part-time job. Or you may prefer to try it on your own, experimenting by making arrangements of flowers from your yard or your neighbor's garden flowers (or even with twigs!). Or you may walk into a flower shop one day and get to talking with the florist, who might just mention that they need some help during the holidays.

There are many doors into the florist industry, and no matter which one you choose, opening any door is the first step towards your new career.

3.2.1 Information Interviews

One way to meet florists in your area, find out about possible job leads, and perhaps make a good impression on a flower shop manager, is to schedule an information interview.

An information interview is not a job interview, and you shouldn't appear that you're in the market for a job offer. You should be curious and interested, but not pushy. At this point, you're simply gathering information — but if you do it in a polite, professional way that indicates you're informed about the business, you may be remembered when the flower shop's manager is looking for someone to fill that now-vacant position.

Phone several flower shops in your area and ask to speak with the manager or designer. Introduce yourself and explain that you are gathering information about becoming a florist. Ask politely if you might come to their shop and spend half an hour with them or someone on their staff asking questions related to the field. If they decline, thank them for their time and hang up. Explaining yourself or begging them to reconsider won't leave them with a good impression of you. Just call a different flower shop.

If they agree, ask them their name and when a good time would be for them. Write down the date and time in your calendar or day planner, and do not forget your appointment. Show up on time, on the right day. Florists are frequently busy, and they are doing you a favor by taking time out from their work to talk to you.

Dress for your information interview in clean, casual clothing. Flower shops tend to be messy places, and florists don't often dress to the nines. A tidy pair of slacks and a sweater or buttoned shirt is fine for both men and women. The key is to appear professional.

Bring a notebook with you to jot down comments, or a small tape recorder if you prefer. (Keep in mind that tape recorders may make some people feel self-conscious, and the florist might ask you not to use it.) A digital camera can also help if you want to record any particular design styles, but be sure to ask permission before taking any photographs.

Be prepared with a list of questions. This is your opportunity to have your curiosity satisfied, so before you go, think of all the questions you've been dying to ask, and write them down. Group your questions according to topic — it will be much easier for the florist to focus on the answers if you're not jumping from ribbons to delivery to designs all in a few minutes.

Questions to Ask at an Information Interview

Consider asking these questions at your interview:

- How did you become interested in this business?

- What training did you have?

- Would you recommend that route? Why or why not? What would be better?

- How did you find yourself at this flower shop?

- How do people usually find work at flower shops?

- What do you do on a typical day?

- What industry trends are you watching right now?

- How do you think they'll affect your work?

- What do you find most enjoyable about your work?

- What do you find most challenging?

- Where do you hope your career will take you?

- What types of arrangements do you do the most?

- Could you demonstrate an arrangement for me?

Take no more than 30 minutes, even if you're eager to stay longer. Keep an eye on the time, and when half an hour is up, thank the florist politely for helping you. Ask for their card, and ask if there are other people they might recommend you speak with. Ask if you can use their name when you call the other florists.

As soon as you are done with the interview, send them a thank you note. Mention the date of your interview, and a specific piece of information that you learned. Include your name, address and phone number in the note, as well as on the envelope. For example:

Sample Thank You Letter

Sonja Rahn
2000 Main Street
Prettytown, PA 33221

Dear Sonja,

Thank you for taking the time to speak with me about your work as a floral designer on Tuesday, August 2. I enjoyed meeting with you and was especially impressed with your skill at making hand-tied bouquets. Thank you for demonstrating that for me. I'll remember your help whenever I see a sonja-colored rose (now I know they're not just called "peach")!

Best wishes,

Penelope Chisholme
4321 Tulip Lane
Prettytown, PA 33221
Phone: (111) 222-3333

Just as important as knowing what to do is knowing what not to do. Here are some don'ts to keep in mind:

- Don't call during the three weeks before Valentine's Day, Easter or Mother's Day, or during the four weeks before Christmas.

- Don't be late.

- Don't forget your appointment.

- Don't show up without questions to ask.

- Don't give a resume without being asked for one.

- Don't ask for a job.

- Don't get in the way of work being done.

- Don't ask for free flowers to practice with.

- Don't compare this shop with the competitor you interviewed yesterday.

3.2.2 Experiment on Your Own

There's nothing like hands-on experience to give you a good sense of the art of floral design. Visit your local florist and buy several bouquets of flowers. (The cash-and-carry bouquets, usually displayed at the front of the shop, are generally the least expensive.) Also ask to buy a bundle of greens (Leatherleaf fern is easy to begin with) and a few stems of baby's breath or other filler flower.

You'll also need a few bricks of floral foam and several containers suitable for making a few different design styles. Plus, ask for any brochures that may be available; florists often have give-away literature promoting arrangements for upcoming holidays. Explain why you need these items, and ask the florist's advice. Take their suggestions seriously — this is another kind of information interview.

Once you're home with your materials and supplies, practice processing the flowers. Trim the stems with a sharp paring knife by holding the knife blade up, edge facing you, in your four fingers. The blade should be parallel with your raised thumb, and your whole hand should be rigid. With your other hand, grasp the stem of a flower, and slide the point you wish to cut against the knife blade by pulling the flower stem directly away from you. Make sure you slice the stem on an angle rather than just chopping it off at the end.

Place the flowers in a vase of warm water, and prepare your containers and floral foam according to the instructions given in Chapter 2 on making arrangements.

You should practice placing the stems of greens into the foam, placing flowers into foam, and making arrangements. You can also try to copy the placement of flowers and greens in the brochures.

> **TIP:** Make sure each flower's "face" – the spot where you can see the most of the flower – is facing outwards in your

arrangement. Imagine a central point in the container, and picture the stems radiating out from that point.

3.2.3 Volunteer Opportunities

Many organizations have a need for volunteer help with flower arranging. Churches often decorate for different seasons, as do community centers and schools — anywhere people gather, there's a good chance flower arrangements will be needed at some point.

Ask the organization's administrator about who makes their flower arrangements, and if they have any upcoming occasions that would benefit from floral décor. Retirement homes, hospitals, and long-term care facilities all welcome arrangements. To keep your costs down, you may ask these groups if they have a budget for materials and supplies that you might use.

Sporting events – such as marathons, cycling races, and skating and gymnastics events – often need bouquets of flowers to present to the winning athletes. Contact the organizers of the event and ask whether there's a flower committee. You can join this group in preparing bouquets for the winners.

Most cities have garden clubs and flower-arranging clubs. Look in your Yellow Pages under "clubs" or "associations," or ask at your community center, Chamber of Commerce or garden centers. You can join these clubs and learn from other members and have opportunities to practice making flower arrangements for the club events.

3.2.4 Internships

Most formal internships are organized through college and trade school courses, but it is also possible to set up your own internship with a florist whose work you admire, as long as the florist is willing to let you do so.

Address a letter to the owner or manager of the flower shop where you are interested in doing an internship. In the letter, introduce yourself and explain that you would like to undertake an internship in their flower shop. Be specific about the terms of the internship (full-time, part-time, etc.) and duration (how long you want it to last). Explain what you hope to gain from the internship, and conclude by stating when and how you will follow up on your letter.

Sample Internship Letter

Jane Withnall, Owner
Fabulous Flowers
1234 Another Street
Prettytown, PA 33221

Dear Ms. Withnall,

My name is George Hamley, and I am a recent graduate of Prettytown College's two-year business diploma program. I am currently working on gathering practical experience in the floral industry in order to fulfill my career goal of becoming a florist.

I am writing to ask if you would be willing to have me perform a one-month part-time internship in your flower shop. I would like to observe and participate in the daily operations of a successful florist business and would welcome the opportunity to help out wherever possible. I would not ask to be paid for any work I did in the course of this internship, as I would gain immeasurably from the experience.

I've included my resume with this letter, and I will stop by your shop at 2:00 p.m. on Saturday, September 7, to introduce myself in person. I look forward to meeting with you and discussing the possibility of an internship. In the meantime, if you have any questions for me, you may call me at (111) 222-0116.

Sincerely,

George Hamley
1128 Daisy Circle
Prettytown, PA 33221

Also include a resume outlining your previous work experience and other qualifications. For an in-depth look at creating a resume, see section 4.4.1. Don't expect to be paid for this work. You are being paid in knowledge and experience. Don't expect to pay for it, either — you are paying for it by offering free help to the florist.

Do's and Don'ts for Landing an Internship

Do:

- Include a resume with your letter.

- Arrive prepared to jump in and help out, just in case.

- Ask if there are other florists who might be willing to take you on.

- Offer to help out in the weeks before a big florist holiday.

- Expect to be asked to perform the most basic tasks.

- Be professional and polite.

- Express your enthusiasm and share your knowledge.

- Plan your follow-up visit for a less-busy time of day — usually afternoons are quieter in most flower shops.

Don't:

- Assume the florist will automatically want to take you on — they may have other interns, a small space, or other reasons why an internship won't work for them.

- Get discouraged if they say no.

- Pressure a florist to give you a chance. If you are pushy, you will only offend them.

Sometimes, a florist may not have considered the idea of an internship and may be surprised by your offer. When you arrive to introduce yourself (be sure to show up when you said you would), don't expect them to make a decision that day. Just explain what your career goals are, offer to help out, and leave the decision to them.

3.2.5 Books to Read

There are many books you can read on the subject of flower arrangement and design. Check your local library for books about flower arranging, floral design, applied horticulture and even craft projects involving flowers.

Here's a list to get you started. While some of them are out of print, they can still be purchased used or found at your library. They are listed alphabetically by title.

- *A Master Guide to the Art of Flower Arranging*, by Alisa De Jong-Stout

- *The Art of Floral Arranging*, by Eileen Johnson

- *Complete Guide to Flower Arranging*, by Jane Packer

- *Decorating With Herbs*, by Simon Lycett

- *Emyl Jenkins' Pleasures of the Garden*, by Emyl Jenkins

- *Florals for All Seasons*, by Krause Publications

- *Flowerworks: Decorative Ideas for Fresh Arrangements*, by Gilly Love

- *Flower Power: Fresh, Fabulous Arrangements*, by Rebecca Cole

- *Flowers, Flowers!: Inspired Arrangements for All Occasions*, by Paula Pryke

- *Flowers With a Flourish: Floral Designs for Every Season*, by Simon Lycett

- *Fresh Cuts: Unexpected Arrangements with Branches, Buds, and Blooms*, by Edwina Von Gal, et al.

- *Herbal Bouquets*, by Emelie Tolley and Chris Mead

- *Lee Bailey's Small Bouquets*, by Lee Bailey

- *Period Flowers: Designs for Today Inspired by Centuries of Floral Art*, by Jane Newdick

- *Sensational Bouquets by Christian Tortu: Arrangements by a Master Floral Designer*, by Sylvain Thomas and Corine Delahaye

- *Simple Floral Displays: Natural-Looking Arrangements Using Fresh and Artificial Flowers, Fruits and Foliage*, by Jenny Raworth

- *Simple Flowers: Arrangements and Floral Accents for the Home,* by Noriko Hayakawa

- *Simply Flowers: Practical Advice and Beautiful Ideas for Creating Flower-Filled Rooms,* by Barbara Milo Ohrbach

- *Souvenirs: Gifts From the Garden,* by Kathryn Kleinman

- *Teach Yourself Flower Arranging,* by Judith Blacklock

- *The Beginner's Guide to Floristry,* by Rosemary Batho

- *The Florist Manual,* by A.B. Bourne and H. Bourne

- *The Knot Book of Wedding Flowers,* by Carley Roney

- *Tricia Guild Flower Sense: The Art of Decorating with Bouquets, Flowers, and Floral Designs,* by Tricia Guild

- *Flower Arranging for the First Time,* by Ruby Begonia

3.2.6 Trade Magazines and Newsletters

While many of these publications are available by subscription only, it is worthwhile to subscribe to one or two. In addition, many of them post some free information on their websites each month.

Alternately, you might be able to make friends with a florist who has a subscription and borrow their old copies — a great way to make another contact!

Canadian Florist

Website:	**http://florist.hortport.com/Current_Issue.htm**
Publisher:	Annex Publishing
Address:	P.O. Box 530
	105 Donly Drive South
	Simcoe, ON N3Y 4N5
Phone:	866-790-6070
Frequency:	Bimonthly
Cost:	$43.77 at Amazon.com

Floral Finance

Website:	**www.myteleflora.com/DesignEducation/ LibraryMain.aspx**
Publisher:	Teleflora
Address:	P.O. Box 30130
	Los Angeles, CA 90030-0130
Phone:	800-421-2815
Frequency:	Monthly
Cost:	$70.00/year (U.S.) or $100.00/year (Canada);
	must be a member of Teleflora Florists to subscribe

Floral Management Magazine

Website:	**www.safnow.org/content/category/8/112/224/**
Address:	1601 Duke Street
	Alexandria, VA 22314
Phone:	800-336-4743
Fax:	703-836-8705
Cost:	Free if you're a member of the Society of American Florists (membership starts at $273.00/year, but you can view some articles free online)

Florists' Review

Website:	**www.floristsreview.com/main**
Publisher:	Florists Review Enterprises
Address:	P.O.Box 4368
	Topeka, KS 66604
Phone:	800-367-4708
Fax:	785-266-0333
Email:	frsub@floristsreview.com
Frequency:	Monthly
Cost:	$42.00/year (U.S.), $55/year (Canada)

Flowers&

Website:	**www.myteleflora.com/DesignEducation/ LibraryMain.aspx**
Publisher:	Teleflora
Address:	P.O. Box 30130
	Los Angeles, CA 90030-0130

Phone:	800-421-2815
Frequency:	Monthly
Cost:	$54/year (U.S.); $60/year (Canada); student rates available

Flowers and Profits

Website:	**www.myteleflora.com/DesignEducation/ LibraryMain.aspx**
Publisher:	Teleflora
Address:	P.O. Box 30130 Los Angeles, CA 90030-0130
Phone:	800-421-2815
Frequency:	Monthly
Cost:	$80.00/year (U.S.); $134.00/year (Canada)

FTD Newsletter

Website:	**www.ftdi.com/newsletter**
Publisher:	Florists Transworld Delivery
Address:	3113 Woodcreek Drive Downer's Grove, IL 60515
Phone:	630-719-7800
Email:	newsletter@ftdi.com
Frequency:	Monthly
Cost:	Available free online

Gifts and Tablewares

Website:	**www.gifts-and-tablewares.com**
Address:	12 Concorde Place Suite 800 Toronto, Ontario M3C 4J2 Canada
Phone:	800-268-7742 (Canada) 800-387-0273 (U.S.)
Frequency:	Seven issues/year
Cost:	$43.95/year (Canada); $49.95 (U.S.)

Michigan Florist

Website:	**www.michiganfloral.org**
Publisher:	Michigan Floral Association

Address:	PO Box 67
	Haslett, MI 48810
Phone:	517-575-0110
Fax:	517-575-0115
Email:	rcrittenden@michiganfloral.org
Frequency:	Bimonthly
Cost:	Free with membership; see the "Join MFA" section
	of the website for rates

Monday Morning News Bud

Website:	**http://flowerscanada.org/content/en/newsbud.htm**
Publisher:	Flowers Canada
Address:	99 Fifth Avenue, Suite #305
	Ottawa, ON K1S 5P5
Phone:	800-447-5147
Email:	flowers@flowerscanada.ca
Frequency:	Weekly
Cost:	Available free online

Retail Florist

Website:	**www.myteleflora.com/DesignEducation/**
	LibraryMain.aspx
Publisher:	Teleflora
Address:	P.O. Box 30130
	Los Angeles, CA 90030-0130
Phone:	800-421-2815
Frequency:	Monthly
Cost:	$70.00/year (U.S.); $100.00/year (Canada)

Super Floral Retailing

Website:	**www.superfloralretailing.com/currentissue.html**
Publisher:	Vance Publishing
Address:	Super Floral Retailing
	Attn: Circulation Dept.
	P.O. Box 4368
	Topeka, KS 66604-0386
Phone:	800-355-8086
Cost:	Contact the magazine subscription department (click
	on "Subscriptions") for rates and a free issue

3.3 Education

There are numerous places where you can attend training programs to become a florist, with varying types of courses to take. There are no state or provincial certifications and a degree or certificate is not required to work as a florist, but you may want to further your education as a way of improving your profile in the job market.

The Society of American Florists has compiled a list of schools across the U.S. and Canada that offer degrees in floristry, horticulture, and other related fields. The list is available at **www.safnow.org/images/ stories/Ind._News_and_Info/Careers/schoollisting.pdf**. At the schools listed, you can take everything from day-long workshops to four-year degree programs. What's better? That depends on you — how long you want to spend in school, how intensive a program of study you are prepared to undertake, and what resources you have available to consider doing so.

Your local community college may also offer courses in floral design. Many high schools and vocational schools offer night classes, and some florists conduct flower arranging classes in their shops.

3.4 Professional Accreditations

Some florist industry organizations and associations offer professional accreditation programs. By administering exams in which florists can demonstrate their knowledge, design abilities and general understanding of the floral industry, the associations work to ensure a high level of competence overall.

In both Canada and the United States, the exams and design tests are rigorous, intended to gauge the competence of experienced florists. Some college and university programs work towards these exams, but it is also possible to undergo them independently.

Flowers Canada (**www.flowerscanada.org**) is the Canadian association that offers professional accreditation. In the United States, professional accreditation is offered through the American Institute of Floral Designers (**www.aifd.org**).

See Chapter 7 to find contact information for these and other professional floristry organizations throughout the U.S. and Canada.

4. Getting Hired

So you know the difference between an azalea and an anemone, and you're ready to get out there and find a job. By reading this guide, you're already more prepared than many others. Now, to get the extra leg up, decide where you want to focus your efforts in order to find yourself doing the job you enjoy most, in the place that makes you happiest.

4.1 Finding Your Ideal Flower Shop

The best way to find your ideal flower shop is to visit plenty of them and observe. Are the flowers and plants fresh and well-cared for? Is there a steady stream of customers stopping in? Are there interesting designs in the cooler, appealing displays on the shelves and in the windows, and giftware that you enjoy looking at? Is the staff cheerful and pleasant, ready to help? If so, you've found what might be your future workplace.

Ask the staff members how they like working there. How long have they done so? How many people are on staff? Is it a fun place to work? Now's the time to be as curious as you can. Don't be shy about your intentions — you might feel strange telling a stranger that you'd like to work with them, but once you do so, they might just suggest you apply.

There are a number of different ways flower shops are set up, and many different places where people can buy flowers. You need to determine where your skills, experience and personality will best fit.

The Small or Family-Run Business

Many flower shops are operated independently, by individual entrepreneurs or members of a family. It's not unusual for a flower shop to be owned by Grandma, operated by Mom, and staffed by Cousin A and Cousin B — with Brother helping out with deliveries and Uncle doing the accounting.

But just because everyone there seems to already know each other doesn't mean outsiders aren't welcome. In fact, outsiders are sometimes even more welcome because they bring a fresh perspective.

In this kind of store, expect to find fewer than 10 employees, except perhaps at busy times. All employees are expected to do all tasks, or at least know how to do them. If you are comfortable with smaller groups, enjoy being included as part of a "family" at work, and want to work in an independent business, this is where you'll probably feel most at home.

The Chain Operation

Larger flower shops often have two or more outlets where they sell similar products. They use the advantage offered by economy of scale and often prepare arrangements in a central location before shipping them off to their destinations or to any of the chain's individual stores.

These businesses tend to be larger, often with a budget for marketing and advertising that outstrips those at smaller shops. They are usually regional operations, often based in larger urban areas. Employees may specialize in sales floor (customer service) or work-room (designing and arranging) areas.

Expect to find between 10 and 50 employees in an organization like this, depending on the number of outlets in the chain. If you are willing to work any shift at any outlet, like working with larger groups, or would prefer to design without having to speak with customers, this may be the type of place you'll enjoy working at.

The Wholesaler

While wholesalers sometimes employ designers to mass-produce arrangements or bouquets, they also need employees to do the hands-on work of getting flowers from the producers and growers to the flower shops, all on a timely basis.

Expect to find anywhere from a dozen to hundreds of employees at a wholesaler. Employees may make bouquets, pack flowers, deliver orders to florists, drive sales trucks, work with florists to ensure their orders are fulfilled, buy flowers from auctions or growers, order items from producers, or work at accounting and payroll procedures. If you are the type of person who enjoys early mornings, a casual rough-and-tumble atmosphere, and independent work, you might want to work at a wholesaler.

The Market/Grocery Store

Many grocery stores and department stores offer bouquets of fresh flowers for cash-and-carry sale. While some get these bouquets ready-made from wholesalers, others employ staff members to prepare bouquets from bundles of fresh flowers and to replenish buckets as items are sold.

If you are the type of person who enjoys making lots of bouquets (not usually arrangements), likes to keep things tidy and organized, and likes to work in the varied atmosphere of a grocery or department store, you might enjoy this type of work.

4.2 Types Of Positions

Small flower shops usually need staff members to be able to do all things, from making a corsage to helping a bride choose her wedding flowers to sweeping the floors at the end of the day. As such, there's rarely a dull moment in a flower shop.

But there are also specific tasks that define different positions. Here's a quick overview.

Front of Store

A good front-of-store employee is outgoing, friendly, organized and has a sense of humor. The front-of-store employee is responsible for:

- Customer service
- Maintenance of displays
- Telephone sales
- Inventory control and security
- Sales desk maintenance
- Pricing items for sale
- Transmitting, receiving and recording orders

Designer

A good designer keeps track of design styles and trends, and is innovative, creative, and efficient. The designer is responsible for:

- Preparing arrangements
- Maintaining arrangements
- Building and creating displays
- Keeping track of materials used
- Pricing arrangements

Flower/Plant Maintenance

Also called a care and handling specialist, this employee is the one who ensures all flowers and plants are properly cared for and maintained so that they'll be appealing to customers. This person has a good knowledge of flower and plant varieties and their specific needs.

Manager/Owner

A good manager is a people person who has attended business courses, understands the industry, and has a strong vision for a company's success. We'll talk more about the responsibilities of a flower shop owner in an upcoming section, but essentially, the owner is responsible for:

- Ongoing operations

- Hiring and training of staff

- Personnel management and supervision

- Accounting

- Advertising

- Ordering product

- Ensuring quality

- Maintaining an ongoing vision for the company

4.3 How To Find Job Openings

4.3.1 Advertised Positions

Florists will sometimes advertise in the classified section of the local newspaper. However, there are many other venues, both online and in trade magazines, for them to search for new staff.

On the Internet, you can check the following sites:

- *FloralJobs.com*
  www.floraljobs.com

- *FloraPersonnel*
  www.florapersonnel.com

- *Flowers Canada — Workfair*
  http://flowerscanada.org/content/en/workfair.htm

4.3.2 Unadvertised Positions

You'll find many unadvertised positions through word of mouth. Visit the flower shop where you've become a regular customer and ask if they know of any positions coming up. Call wholesalers to find out if there are florists who are in need of extra staff for the holidays.

Call your local flower delivery company, and ask them if they've heard of any shops needing help. They're in contact with many shops every day, and often hear about staff needs.

4.3.3 Part-Time Jobs and Seasonal Help

Sometimes florists who don't need extra staff may be willing to hire someone for a part-time position. Part-timers usually work less than 24 hours per week and don't enjoy benefits like health insurance, which means they cost employers less overall. But in return, they are able to work flexible hours – which is especially good if you are attending school or taking a floristry course – and usually have the first dibs on any full-time work that comes up.

Seasonal help is extremely important in the florist industry, as there are four major holidays that require many orders to be filled in a short amount of time. Even if you're working in a different day job, you can often find work at a flower shop during busy times, as they often work after-hours to prepare seasonal arrangements.

The major florist holidays are Valentine's Day, Easter, Mother's Day and Christmas. To find work for any of these holidays, it is best to approach a flower shop owner or manager well in advance. If you want to help out for Christmas, for example, try making contact in September or October, offering your services for seasonal help.

In a cover letter (see section 4.4.2 for more on cover letters), state the hours and dates that you will be available during the three or four weeks before the holiday. The more available you are, the better your chances of being asked.

4.3.4 How to Create a Job

You don't need to wait to find someone to hire you. You can create your own job by preparing a portfolio of materials (see section 4.4.3) and promoting yourself and your flower arranging skills to friends, family, and members of your community.

You can also develop a specific skill, such as holiday wreath-making or cash-and-carry bouquet-making, and market yourself to flower shops on a contract basis. In other words, they hire you to prepare X number of wreaths or bouquets for Y amount of money.

Market yourself to several flower shops — if one doesn't need anyone right now, another might. Be reliable, efficient, and provide good work, and you'll be the person called first when there's a vacancy on staff. Florists are busy, and if you make yourself available and useful, they'll quite often be glad to have you on board.

4.3.5 Shop Visits

Become a regular customer of the store or stores where you hope to one day work. Stop in frequently. Get to know the owner or manager, the designers, and the sales floor staff. Ask about the new varieties of flowers they have in. Buy a few for your practice arrangements. Ask about their care. Talk about your previous experiences with caring for flowers — if they lasted a long time, explain how you made them last. If they didn't, ask for tips for next time.

The more you get to know the people working in a shop, the more familiar you'll be to them, and the better your chances are of landing a job or hearing about any openings that might come up.

Don't just be a customer, be a friend. Remember people's names. Ask about their lives. If nothing else, you will gain a great resource in your job search, and your search might end right there.

4.4 Job Hunting Materials

A resume, cover letter and portfolio are all essential when trying to get a job as a floral designer. If you are applying for an entry-level job at a flower shop, you don't need to have a portfolio of arrangements. But a sketchbook of drawings or a portfolio of paintings wouldn't be out of place, because it demonstrates your artistic and creative abilities.

4.4.1 How to Prepare a Resume

A resume is basically a list of your education and work experience. It should be short and clearly written. In it, list any work you've done that is relevant to the position you're applying for, as well as any positions you've held that contribute to your expertise.

FabJob has compiled a list of resume-writing resources at **www.fabjob.com/advice.html#resume**. A sample resume appears on page 112.

4.4.2 How to Prepare a Cover Letter

Like a resume, a cover letter should include basic information about you, about why you're interested in the position you're applying for, and about any experience or expertise you possess that would make you a good candidate for the job. Two or three paragraphs should be plenty. Close your letter by providing your phone number and offering to meet with the employer in person.

Print your cover letter on plain, good quality paper. Use a basic business style, and don't let it go longer than a page. Be sure to sign your letter.

FabJob has an excellent list of sites devoted to successful cover letters. View the list at **www.fabjob.com/cover-letters.html**. A sample cover letter appears in the next section.

4.4.3 How to Prepare a Portfolio or Samples

When you are practicing arrangements, be sure to have a camera handy. Digital is great, 35mm is fine, and even an instant camera will work (though you may be less satisfied with the range of focus).

Place the arrangement on a table against a blank wall. Better yet, hang a drape of plain fabric or a wide, long piece of paper (taken from a roll of newsprint or plain matte wrapping paper) down the wall and over the table. This will create a seamless background for your work.

Set up several lights to shine on the arrangement from about three feet away (desk lamps work just fine). The idea is to illuminate it evenly, but not to get the lights in the picture.

Take several photographs of every arrangement you make. One should be a top view, one a side view, and one a front view. Don't get anything else in the picture, but make sure you have the whole arrangement showing.

If you are using a 35mm camera, you can get excellent results with 400 ASA film. If you are using a digital camera, be sure to hold it extremely steady. In both cases, you may want to place your camera on a tripod to ensure it doesn't move.

When you have your photographs ready, you may mount them with photo corners into a scrapbook or simply place them in a plain photo album. If you are particularly proud of any arrangements, you may want to enlarge the photos to 8" x 10" or 8" x 12" sizes. This isn't essential, but it does catch the eye. Label each photo with the type of arrangement.

Sample Resume

Tia Hopkiss
4321 Any Street
Prettytown, PA 33333
Phone: 111-222-3333

Career Objective

To work as a creative, well-rounded member of a progressive flower shop's sales and design team.

Education

- **Floral Design I and II**
  Pretty Community College
  Graduated 2007

- **University Preparation Courses**
  Pretty Community College
  Graduated 2004

Relevant Experience

- **Sales Clerk**
  May 2007 – July 2008
  Happy Fashions
  111 Dress Street, Prettytown
  Supervisor: Doreen Steele

- **Student Assistant**
  September 2004 – April 2007
  Pretty Community College Horticulture Program
  234 Campus Way, Prettytown
  Supervisor: Fred Wah

- **Volunteer Flower Arranger**
  July 2007
  Sunny Community Center Annual Banquet
  Organizer: Vera Brown

References and portfolio available on request.

Sample Cover Letter

Tia Hopkiss
4321 Any Street
Prettytown, PA 33333
Phone: 111-222-3333

Jane Withnall, Owner
Fabulous Flowers
1234 Another Street
Prettytown, PA 33334

Dear Ms. Withnall,

I'm writing to introduce myself to you as a potential candidate for a position in your flower shop.

I am familiar with all aspects of the retail florist business. I have taken the introduction to floral design courses at Prettytown College, where I earned top marks for my corsages and container arrangements.

I volunteered to make the flower arrangements for my community center's Christmas banquet, which gave me the opportunity to perfect my skills in making table centerpieces and one-sided arrangements, and also allowed me to practice decorating Christmas trees.

My interest in the floral industry stems from my love of plants and flowers (I have a collection of nearly 50 houseplants) and my background in retail, working as a clerk in gift and clothing stores. I would welcome the opportunity to bring my skills and interests together. I can assure you I am a dedicated worker and an eager learner.

I look forward to showing you my portfolio. Please call me at 111-222-3333 at your earliest convenience.

Sincerely,
Tia Hopkiss

Prepare a cover page for your portfolio. It should be simple and to the point. A printed page with your name, address, phone number and e-mail address is sufficient, though you may wish to also include the heading "Portfolio" at the top of the page. This page should be the first thing a reader sees after opening the inside cover.

It is unusual to prepare samples for a florist interview unless you are specifically asked to do so. More likely, you will be invited to the flower shop to demonstrate your skills by making a few basic arrangements.

If this happens, be sure to show up on time, listen carefully to instructions, and prepare the types of arrangements you are asked to make. You may, however, be asked to make an arrangement of your choice. Do the most sophisticated type that you feel confident doing. Be mindful of material costs, and ask the florist if there are certain budgets they would like you to work within.

Even if you're given free rein, remember that you're working with someone else's flowers. Now's not the time to demonstrate that hundred-rose cascade you've always wanted to try! Before you dive in, ask the florist:

- Are there particular colors you would like me to use?

- May I use any flowers in stock, or would you prefer me to use specific ones?

- What is the total value of this arrangement?

- Are there any special requests for this arrangement?

- Does the shop have any signature touches you would like me to include?

- When would you like me to be finished by?

4.5 Interviews

Think of your interview as an opportunity to show your talents, to let your prospective employer get to know you, and to learn more about the place you hope to work for. You will have the most success if you are relaxed, cheerful and confident about your abilities.

When a flower shop owner or manager calls you to set up an interview, it's a good idea to ask if you should bring anything. Bring your portfolio anyway, even if they don't tell you to bring anything. Also ask if you will have an opportunity to demonstrate your flower arranging skills. If you are being interviewed for a position as a designer, this will be part of the interview process at some point, though it is possible it won't be at the initial interview.

If you will be demonstrating your skills, find out how many arrangements you will need to make. Plan to spend at least 30 minutes for an initial interview, and also for each arrangement you're expected to demonstrate. Asking about this kind of thing shows your efficiency and ability to plan in advance — two qualities which are important in the florist business. And it gives you a chance to prepare yourself.

4.5.1 What Florists are Looking For

While there are various types of positions in flower shops, certain traits characterize a good candidate for any position in this industry. You can learn basic information, such as flower and plant names or how to operate computer systems while on the job, but attitudes can't be taught as easily. This means you can land an entry-level job in a flower shop with no previous experience in the industry. A fast learner with a good attitude will often have an edge over a more experienced but less pleasant person.

A cheerful willingness to work is important. When flower shops get busy, you will be working hard, doing things quickly, and possibly even working overtime. Your positive attitude will help you through these times. Efficiency is important, both in the design room and on the sales floor. An ability to meet deadlines is crucial — demonstrate this by showing up several minutes early for your interview. An ability to solve problems in a creative, appropriate manner is also essential.

A pleasant, friendly attitude is important in positions that spend much time with the public. Customer service is a crucial part of any flower shop's success, and your friendliness coupled with an ability to sell will make you a good candidate in this area.

Creativity and an eye for color and design are important traits for a floral designer, and a commitment to doing quality work and working together as part of the flower shop's team is essential for everyone.

4.5.2 How to Prepare

Before your interview, spend some time thinking about what your role at the flower shop might be. Think of ways you would handle a variety of situations and needs. For example, how would you handle a busy shop, a wire order for something not in stock, or a fussy customer? Imagine what it would be like to be in those situations, and figure out how you would most appropriately address them.

In addition, brush up on your knowledge of flower varieties. Take note of what flowers are in season, and think about the types of arrangements they could be used in. Brush up on plant varieties and their needs. One way to do this is to visit Sierra Flower Finder, which allows you to look at photos and information on over 2,500 varieties of flowers. It is located at **http://sierraflowerfinder.com/default.asp**.

You should also find out as much as you can about the flower shop you're hoping to work for. Think about its layout and display areas, and how you might make displays in them. Consider its main customer traffic — is it in a shopping mall, or an upscale neighborhood? Anticipate the needs of its probable customers. Take note of its location, and consider the likely kinds of arrangements it might do.

For example, if it is near several funeral homes, it probably does a lot of funeral arrangements. Is it near a hospital? It will likely do a lot of business in smaller arrangements in vases or containers, items suitable for patients with limited space to display flowers. Keep this information in mind.

Think about how you'd fit into the flower shop's team. This could be fairly clear, if you know you're being interviewed for a specific position. But if you're being interviewed for a general position in which you'll likely do a bit of everything, think about how you'll get along with the other workers already there.

4.5.3 What to Wear

Take your cues from the clothing the other florists were wearing when you went in to drop off your resume or application. If you mailed your resume, try to visit the shop before your interview (good for getting an overall impression of the store, too). A good rule of thumb is to dress up just one notch from the store's employees.

A clean, tidy pair of slacks and a buttoned shirt (under a sweater, if you like) is appropriate for both men and women. A tie or business suit is not likely to be necessary. If you really want to show your creativity through your clothing, consider a flower-patterned shirt or a single piece of flower-themed jewelry.

For some interesting information about appropriate dress for florists, go to **www.myteleflora.com/DesignEducation/Index.aspx**, click on "Floral Articles," and search for the article titled "Clothes Encounter."

4.5.4 How to Make a Great Impression

Show up on time. Better yet, show up a few minutes early. Introduce yourself with a handshake and a smile.

Be positive, confident and relaxed. Think of it as a conversation, not an interview. Come with a list of questions you would like to have answered about the flower shop's business. Many interviewers make time in an interview to answer a potential employee's questions. By having questions on hand, you appear professional, knowledgeable, and interested in the business. Some questions to ask:

- When are the busiest times each week?

- What is your main customer base?

- What are this store's most popular items?

- How will my role contribute to the shop's overall success?

- What is your business philosophy?

- Ask about anything that makes you curious, as long as it's focused on the flower shop at hand — don't ask the florist to comment on a competitor, for example.

- Don't be afraid to ask, "When do you expect to reach a decision?" or "When might I expect to hear from you?"

CareerJournal, an online publication of the *Wall Street Journal*, offers a range of excellent articles about the interview process. Visit

www.online.wsj.com/careers to find out more.

4.5.5 Interview Questions

The main focus of an interview is to allow the owner or manager to find out more about you, the person they're considering hiring.

You will probably be asked a range of questions that are meant to find out about your previous experience, your abilities, and your approach to the industry in general. Answer honestly. If you don't know the answer to something, say, "That's a good question. Can we come back to that in a few minutes?" That'll give you time to relax and think of an answer.

Some questions you may be asked:

- Why do you want to work in this store/industry?

- What is your previous experience with flowers?

- What educational programs have you taken?

- Describe the best arrangement you've ever made. What was it for? How did you make it?

- Tell me about your creative activities.

- What kind of event would you most like to make flower arrangements for, and why? What would you make?

- Can you give me an example of a problem you encountered in a previous position, and how you solved that problem?

- How have you used computers in the course of your work?

- What would you suggest to a customer looking for a gift for a (man/woman/mother/business associate)?

- How would you handle a customer complaint?

- How do you use flowers and plants in your own home?

Keep in mind that personal questions, such as questions about your religion, your marital status and children, and your general health, are not allowed in job interviews. If you are asked any of these, you may politely decline to answer, then steer the conversation back to your experience and abilities. (For example, you might say, "I prefer not to discuss my personal beliefs; however, I have had many compliments for the fresh flower arrangements I make each week for the front of my church.")

4.5.6 Discussing Salary

There are two ways you may be paid: an hourly rate (particularly for part-time work), or with a salary.

Either way, you will have deductions taken from your gross salary for state or provincial income taxes and federal income taxes. In the United States, you may also have deductions made for medical insurance. In Canada, you will also have deductions for the Canada Pension Plan (CPP), Employment Insurance (EI) and sometimes for Medical Services premiums (if your employer offers this).

Hourly rates can be as low as the minimum wage for your state or province (check with your state or provincial government's employment services office), or, depending on your experience level, $10 per hour or more above minimum wage.

In general, as a beginning florist, you can expect to earn a gross wage of between $18,000 and $25,000 annually, but this varies according to region and the size of shop you're working at. Experienced floral designers can expect between $30,000 and $50,000 annually, also depending on where they work. While there are exceptions, large flower shops are likely to be able to pay more than smaller ones.

When you're discussing your salary, it helps to know what the going rate is for similar work being done in your area. A flower shop may have a rate already set, in which case you may ask if that includes benefits.

You may negotiate a rate and benefits with the employer. Benefits could include practical things like medical insurance, or enjoyable things like extra vacation time, flexible hours, and even flowers to take home occasionally.

To find out the salary range you can likely expect in your area, do some research. Salary.com allows you to search for salary ranges based on job description and location. In this case, you'll be searching under retail/wholesale, which offers a "floral designer" category. For example, an experienced floral designer in Seattle, Washington, could expect to make between $34,000 and $52,000 per year.

4.5.7 Following Up

A pleasant note, mailed the same day as your interview, will help keep your name in the mind of the person who interviewed you.

Use their full name, and spell it correctly. Thank them for their time, and state one or two things you enjoyed about meeting with them. If they went out of their way to show you something about their shop (for example, they gave you a tour of the greenhouse), thank them specifically for that. And if you made a sample arrangement or two, mention those. Be sure to include your phone number, and make sure there are no spelling mistakes in your note!

Sample Follow-Up Note

Dear Sonja,

Thank you so much for taking the time to interview me this afternoon. I enjoyed meeting with you and hope you'll agree to have me join the team at Fabulous Florists. I liked the dynamic atmosphere of your shop, and spent a few minutes admiring your back-to-school window display on my way out. I especially appreciated seeing your greenhouse operation — you grow lovely flowers there. And, of course, I hope the vase arrangement I made sells quickly!

I'm eager to make a contribution to your business. Please give me a call at 111-222-3333 as soon as you've had time to make a decision.

Regards,

Tia Hopkiss

5. Starting Your Own Flower Shop

Maybe you've always dreamed of owning a flower shop. Maybe you live in a community where there aren't any flower shops, and you think there should be one. Maybe there is a strong need for floral services in your community, and those needs aren't being adequately met by existing retailers. These are good reasons to start your own flower shop.

Or perhaps you've noticed a local flower shop for sale. You like the work it does, and it's in a location that you know is a good one. You could buy it and operate it, taking advantage of its already established reputation and customer base.

5.1 Options for Starting a Florist Business

Deciding whether to buy an existing flower shop or open a new one is an important decision. An established shop will cost more than starting from scratch, but it comes with customers, inventory, and reputation — which means it's likely to continue with its pre-established success. A new shop typically costs less to start up, and you can tailor it specifically to your own vision. But you will need to spend lots on advertising, gaining clientele, and making a reputation for your business — and new businesses have a much higher risk of failure.

In either case, owning your own shop is a good way to not only make an investment, but to give yourself a job. Starting any business requires an enormous amount of time, money and dedication, and you should be aware that for the first year or two (or more), you might not earn as much money as you would make working in someone else's store.

But floristry is one profession where you can start up on your own and be successful at it. It won't happen overnight, but you will see the results of your hard work eventually.

One florist I know started out with absolutely no experience in the business. She saw a flower shop advertised in the "Businesses for Sale" section of her local newspaper. Despite having never worked in a flower shop before, she secured a small business start-up loan using her house as collateral, bought the business, and didn't look back. Today, she's one of the most successful florists in the area.

5.1.1 Buying an Established Shop

One way to start is to buy an existing flower shop and make it your own. You'll still need a business plan, financing, a lawyer and an accountant, but many of the other decisions – like what to call it and where to locate it – will already be made. In addition, you will acquire any existing equipment, furniture, supplies, clientele, and the established business name. However, you may have to assume any liabilities that come with the shop, such as bills it owes to its suppliers.

If you make what's called a *stock purchase*, it means you are buying everything, from inventory to liabilities. You will be responsible for any debts the shop has incurred. If you make what's called an *asset purchase*, you will only be buying the material part of the shop, and the previous owner will be responsible for any outstanding financial matters.

You can expect to pay anywhere from $20,000 to upwards of $200,000 for an existing flower shop. This usually includes all contents of the shop, and often means taking over an existing lease or rental agreement for the location. Pricing for flower shops is based on the cost of the store's supplies and on a percentage of its total annual sales.

You don't need to have any experience in the floral industry to buy a shop and begin operating it, but you do need to have the energy to devote yourself to learning as you go along. You also need to stick with it. Plan on taking from two to five years to earn back your purchase price.

If you decide this is the route you want to take, you should begin by looking for flower shops for sale in your area. Approach local florists and ask if they would be interested in selling their businesses, or ask if they know of any other florists who are considering retirement. Look in your local newspaper, ask at the Chamber of Commerce, or read local business publications.

Shops for Sale

Another good source of information for listings of flower shops for sale is Business Nation, which lists florists selling their businesses all across the U.S. at **www.businessnation.com/Businesses_for_Sale/ Retail/Florists-Flower_Shops**.

In Canada, Floralynx (**www.floralynx.com**) offers a listing of flower shops for sale in Alberta, British Columbia and Ontario. Flowers Canada also lists flower shops for sale in its "Classifieds" section at **http://flowerscanada.org/content/en/classifields.htm**.

5.1.2 Franchising

If you are eager to start your own flower shop but are concerned about the many facets involved in getting everything set up, you may want to consider franchising.

Franchising happens when an established company allows someone to run a local business using the same company name, logo, products, services, marketing and business systems. The original company is known as the "franchisor" and the company that is granted the right to run its business the same way as the franchisor is known as the "franchisee."

You have probably bought products and services from many franchises. Burger King, Wendy's and many other fast-food outlets are franchises, as is the Starbucks coffee shop chain. In fact, the KaBloom franchise bills itself as "the Starbucks of flowers."

Pros and Cons of Franchising

People who choose to franchise rather than start their own business from scratch often do so because they want to minimize their risk. They see the franchise as a proven business that already has name recognition, products or marketing concepts that are popular among the public. By working with an established system, franchisees hope to avoid costly mistakes and make a profit more quickly.

Franchises are also good for people who want support running their business. Franchisors typically provide training to help franchisees start, market, and run their new business. The franchisee may receive assistance with everything from obtaining supplies to setting up record keeping systems. Many franchisors are continuously working to develop better systems and products, and you can take advantage of those developments.

It is important to keep in mind that a franchisee does not own any of the trademarks or business systems. Also, a franchisee must run their business according to the terms of their agreement with the franchisor. For example, the franchisee may not be permitted to offer a sales promotion or use a supplier that has not been authorized by the franchisor. While some people appreciate having such guidelines to follow, you might find owning a franchise too restrictive if you are an independent person who enjoys taking risks and being spontaneous.

Since someone else is ultimately "in charge," you may be wondering how having a franchise is different than being an employee. In fact, there are significant differences. You have more freedom than an employee — for example, you might choose your own working hours. And you could ultimately earn a lot more money than an employee.

On the other hand, franchisees must pay thousands of dollars up front for the opportunity to work with the business. In addition, you will be required to cover your own operating costs, including the cost of staffing your store to the levels required by the franchisor.

And then there is the possibility that the franchise will not be financially successful. Many websites on the topic of franchising claim more than a 90 percent long-term success rate for franchises. However, a study reported in the *Wall Street Journal* found a 35 percent failure rate for franchises. Your own success will depend on a variety of factors, including your geographical location and the particular franchise you become involved with.

TIP: If you are considering franchising, do your homework and gather all the information you need to make an informed decision. What you receive for your investment varies from franchise to franchise, so make sure you know exactly what you will be buying and that any claims are substantiated.

In addition, some states and provinces have regulations that govern franchises, and you may not be able to buy your chosen franchise in certain areas. Check with your state or province's small business development office (see section 5.2 to learn more about business development centers) to find out what rules apply in your area. Before signing a contract, it is wise to consult with people you trust to give you unbiased and sound advice, such as your accountant or attorney.

Costs

Entrepreneur Magazine describes a franchise fee as a one-time charge paid to the franchisor "for the privilege of using the business concept, attending their training program, and learning the entire business." Other start-up costs may include the products and services you will actually need to run the business, such as flowers and supplies, store fixtures, computer equipment, advertising, etc. For excellent advice on franchises, visit **www.entrepreneur.com/franzone/ allabout/index.html**.

Floral shop franchise fees vary, but can range from $12,500 to more than $200,000. Your initial investment might be $12,500 for the franchise fee, with an additional $25,000 to $35,000 required for various start-up costs. There are a variety of factors involved in determining the initial investment, including:

• The geographic area you will be working in

• The cost of the lease or rental arrangements for the building or space you will occupy

• The particular company you franchise with

In addition to your initial investment, you can expect to pay the franchisor ongoing royalties, generally on a monthly basis. These royalties are usually calculated as a percentage of your gross monthly sales, and typically range from two percent to ten percent; the exact amount will depend on the company you franchise with.

Florist Franchises

Because flower shops require a high level of service with a relatively low profit margin compared to other items sold in franchises, there are not as many flower shop franchises as there are, say, hamburger or coffee chains. The most successful ones have only been operating since the 1990s, though it is possible that their success may spur others to begin comparative franchises.

In this section we focus on several franchises that involve selling fresh flowers. You can find other franchises by doing a search at the International Franchise Association website at **www.franchise.org**. The companies listed here are provided only for your information. They are not recommendations. Only you can decide which franchise, if any, will be best for you. Also note that contact information can change, so visit the company websites for current information.

Just Roses

Website:	**www.jroses.com/franchise.asp**
Address:	Just Roses Franchising, Inc.
	5428 W. Clearwater
	Kennewick, WA 99336
Phone:	877-9-ROSES-9
Email:	info@jroses.com

As its name implies, Just Roses specializes in roses. Customers select roses by the stem or by the dozen, add filler or greens, and may have them placed in vases. Franchise fee is $12,500, plus a required $30,000 to $50,000 in working capital to start with.

KaBloom

Website:	**www.kabloom.com/info/franchising.aspx**
Address:	KaBloom, Ltd.
	200 Wildwood Avenue
	Woburn, MA 01801-2031

Phone:	800-522-5666
Email:	info@kabloom.com

One of the fastest-growing floral franchises, KaBloom offers a unique European-style approach to selling fresh cut flowers and plants. Minimum investment required is $100,000.

Flowerama

Website:	**www.flowerama.com/franchise_opportunities.asp**
Address:	Flowerama Corporate Headquarters
	3165 West Airline Highway
	Waterloo, IA 50703
Phone:	800-728-6004
Email:	info@flowerama.com

Flowerama stores have a high-volume, cash-and-carry approach to floral products, from bouquets to flowering plants. No previous floral experience is required. Minimum investment required is $50,000-$100,000, depending on location.

1-800-Flowers.com

Website:	**http://franchise.1800flowers.com**
Address:	Franchise Administration Department
	One Old Country Road, Suite 500
	Carle Place, NY 11514
Phone:	800-503-9630

1-800-Flowers.com has been around for more than 25 years. In addition to the florist brand they also own Plow & Hearth, HearthSong, Magic Cabin, The Popcorn Factory, GreatFood.com and Conroy's Inc., so they are well-established in a number of gift-related retail sectors. A minimum investment of $150,000 is required.

Grower Direct Fresh Cut Flowers Inc.

Website:	**www.growerdirect.com/franchise/default.html**
Address:	#118, 4220-98 Street
	Edmonton, Alberta T6E 6A1
Phone:	800-567-7258
Email:	franchises@growerdirect.com

Grower Direct specializes in fresh cut flowers in a high-volume, cash-and-carry setting. This is the only Canadian floral franchise that is a member of both FTD and the Canadian Franchise Association. The initial investment ranges from $60,000 to $80,000 including franchise fee, opening inventory, working capital and other set-up costs. This company operates from Manitoba to British Columbia and the Northwest Territories.

Franchising Resources

The Canadian Franchise Association website (**www.cfa.ca**) offers good information to help you learn more about franchising and evaluate franchises. The Small Business Administration has a franchising information section at **www.sba.gov/smallbusinessplanner/start/buyafranchise/index.html**.

5.1.3 Opening a New Flower Shop

Of course, you can always start from scratch and open a brand new flower shop. That way, you can have complete control over every step of the process and make sure that your shop is everything you want it to be. The rest of this chapter will show you how to do just that.

5.2 Getting Started

So you dream about owning and operating your own flower shop. How do you go about turning that dream into the complex reality that is a real florist business? Fortunately, there are many organizations and government offices devoted to helping would-be entrepreneurs get started.

Because rules and laws vary depending on your location, and because financing options vary from bank to bank as well, your wisest option is to get in touch with the business development center nearest you. They'll help you gather all the information and resources you'll need to get started, and walk you through the process of planning, preparing and opening your own business. You'll also need to talk with your financial institution about the various business grants, loans and other services they are able to offer.

Before we begin, here are a few websites that offer helpful information as you start your own business.

The Service Corps Of Retired Executives has volunteers throughout the U.S. who donate time to mentor small businesses free of charge. Their site, located at **www.score.org**, has helpful articles.

The Small Business Administration (**www.sbaonline.sba.gov**) is an excellent resource with advice on business licenses and taxes as well as general information on starting a business. You can also use the website to look up an SBA office near you.

The Canada Business Service Center offers a Business Start-up Assistant which includes information about taxes, financing, incorporation, and other topics. You can also locate a nearby CBSC office through their website (which is at **www.bsa.canadabusiness.ca**) by clicking on "English," then on the "In-Person Services" tab at the top of the page.

Nolo.com publishes legal information presented in plain English. Their Legal Encyclopedia (**www.nolo.com**) is an excellent resource.

Articles on Starting Your Own Business

Starting your own business is a risky, exciting thing to do. It's one of the biggest challenges you can take on, but can also be the most rewarding. Experts suggest that it takes at least a year for a new business to begin to make a profit, which means that if you're just starting out, you should plan to live on your savings or other income (not from the shop) for at least that long while your business is getting off the ground.

You can find some informative articles and checklists at **www.sba.gov/ smallbusinessplanner/index.html** and **www.bsa.canadabusiness.ca**.

5.2.1 Creating A Business Plan

Your business plan explains everything about how you intend to operate your business and make it a success. It is an essential document that will help you clarify your ideas and needs, and will be required by any banks or other organizations that you approach for funding.

If you're fabulously wealthy and have all the money you could want to begin and grow a business, you don't have to consider the possibility of using your business plan to attract funding. You'll still, however, need a plan to serve as your roadmap.

Your original business plan will guide you as you start out and will keep you on course as your business progresses. It is not, however, written in stone. As your business changes and grows, your business plan probably will need some tweaking as well. Perhaps, for instance, the description of your business will change as you expand. Or, your management plan will change when you discover you need to add a wedding consultant to your staff.

A business plan doesn't have to be overly complicated, and there are some good models available to use as guides. Many entrepreneurs use the Small Business Administration's business plan outline as a model. The Canada Business Service Centres (CBSC) also provides a sample business plan.

- *SBA: Business Plan Basics*
  www.sba.gov/smallbusinessplanner/plan/ writeabusinessplan

- *Sample Retail Florist Business Plan*
  (Click on Volume 01, then scroll down to "Retail Florist")
  www.referenceforbusiness.com/business-plans/

Basically, the main body of your business plan will be divided into the four sections listed below:

- a description of your business

- your marketing plan

- your financial management plan

- your management plan

In addition to those parts, your plan should include the following extra material and information:

- an executive summary

- supporting documents

- financial projections

- a cover sheet

- a statement of purpose

- a table of contents

If the prospect of writing a business plan sounds daunting or confusing, hang in there. Let's take a look at what each of these parts includes.

Description of Your Business

A description of your business is just that — a description of the business you plan to start and run. The trick is to mention the unique and special things about your business so that everyone who reads your business plan will know you're onto something really fabulous.

You'll need to state in this section that you'll be operating a retail business. Don't be afraid to get specific about the types of products you'll be providing. You'll want to mention the everyday and holiday arrangements you'll sell, the wedding and funeral flower services, and so on. Don't hesitate to point out why your services are important. The idea is to paint a picture of the business you plan to start.

And you should explain what the legal structure of your business be. Will you have a sole proprietorship, for instance, or perhaps a partnership? (You'll learn more about legal structures a little later on in section 5.2.3.)

Also in this section, you'll need to explain why your business will be profitable, and how your florist shop will be different and better than any others in the area. What do you plan to offer that will have clients beating down your doors?

TIP: When writing your business plan, pay close attention to spelling and grammar, and try to write clearly and concisely. You don't want to make reading the plan a chore.

Describe your business hours. Most flower shops are open from 8:00 or 9:00 a.m. until 4:00 or 5:00 p.m. However, that may change during the holiday season, so be sure to mention that.

Also, you should identify the planned location of your business, the type of space you'll have, and why it's conducive to your business.

Conclude the description of your business by clearly identifying your goals and objectives, and supporting them with information and knowledge you've acquired about being a florist. This is important, because it's here that you're explaining exactly why you're starting this business and what you hope to accomplish with it.

Your Marketing Plan

How well you market your business has a lot to do with the degree of success you'll experience.

The most important elements of a good marketing plan are defining your market and knowing your customers. You don't want to limit yourself to a very narrow market, because that can affect your chances of getting funding and limit the scope of your business once it's underway. (See section 6.1 for more possible markets for your business.) Knowing your customers is important because it allows you to identify their likes and dislikes and tailor your services to accommodate them.

Your marketing plan also must address the areas listed below:

- *Competition:* Businesses – yours included – compete for customers, market share, publicity and so forth. It's smart to know who your competitors are and exactly what they're doing. In order to be able to provide services that are different and better, you need to look carefully at your competitors' products and services, how they're promoting them, and who's buying them.

- *Pricing:* You'll learn more about setting prices later in this chapter, but know that you should address it, at least briefly, in your business plan. This section should consider factors such as competitive pricing, costs of labor and materials, overhead, etc.

- *Advertising and public relations:* Many people think that marketing is all about advertising and public relations. While they are important components of marketing, they are only pieces of the puzzle. You'll need to think about how you'll advertise your business, paying close attention that whatever means of advertising you choose accurately portrays the image you want to convey.

Your Financial Management Plan

Financial management is crucial to running a successful business. Your business plan should describe both your startup costs and your operating costs. The startup budget includes all the costs necessary to get your business up and running. The operating costs are ongoing expenses, such as advertising, utilities, rent and so forth:

- *Startup budget:* Legal and professional fees, licenses and permits, equipment, insurance, supplies, advertising and promotions, accounting expenses, utilities, payroll expenses.

- *Operating budget:* Make a budget for your first three to six months of operation, including expenses such as: containers, giftware, flowers and greens, other supplies necessary for creating arrangements, personnel (even if it's only your salary), insurance, rent, loan payments, advertising and promotions, legal and accounting fees, supplies, utilities, dues and subscriptions, taxes and maintenance.

Your financial management plan also should address the accounting system you plan to use. Many small business owners conduct their own accounting, using software such as QuickBooks, while others hire someone to set up a system.

Your Management Plan

Managing a business, no matter how big or small it is, requires organization and discipline. Your management plan should be carefully thought out and written, and should address issues such as:

- Your background and business experience, and how they'll be beneficial to your florist business

- The members of your management team (even if you'll be the only member)

- Assistance you expect to receive (this can be financial help, consulting and advice or whatever)

- The duties for which you and any employee or employees will be responsible

- Plans for hiring employees, either now or in the future

- A general overview of how your business will be run

In addition to these four major areas, your business plan should include the extras mentioned earlier:

- *A cover sheet:* This identifies your business and explains the purpose of the business plan. Be sure to include your name, the name of the business, and the name of any partners, if applicable; also include your address, phone number, email address and other pertinent information.

- *Table of contents:* This goes just under your cover sheet and tells what's included in your business plan. Use major headings and subheadings to identify the contents.

- *Statement of purpose:* This is important because it summarizes your goals ands objectives. A statement of purpose should sum up your hopes and dreams.

- *Executive summary:* Basically, this is a thumbnail sketch of your business plan. It should summarize everything you've included in the main body of the plan.

- *Financial projections:* This is just an idea of how much money you'll need to start your business and how much you expect to earn. Remember to support your projections with explanations.

- *Supporting documents:* Include your personal tax returns (and business returns, if applicable) for the past three years, a personal financial statement (get a form from your bank) and a copy of a lease or purchase agreement if you're going to be buying or renting retail space.

You'll also need a list of all equipment and supplies you'll be using, and information about the location you're planning to occupy (lease or purchase documents, for example). You'll need your own resume, the resumes of anyone else involved in the business, and a statement of intent from any wholesalers or suppliers you hope to work with. Gathering all this information will take time, and you should plan to spend as long as several months on this part of getting started.

5.2.2 Financing

You have to spend money to make money — certainly you've heard that before, haven't you? Never is it more true than when you're starting a business from the bottom up.

As soon as you have your business plan figured out, you'll need to pay a visit to your bank or credit union. There are numerous financing options, grants to small businesses, and loans that you can apply for. Because these vary from state to state and province to province, however, you will need to check into them locally. When you visit your bank, take the following with you:

- Your business plan

- Your financial information

- Identification for you and any business partners

- Financial information about the business you hope to buy, if ou are buying an existing shop

- Lease or rental information about the location where you hope to open your business

- Records of any collateral you might have, such as the deed to your house or records of mutual funds or other investments

Glossary of Financial Terms

Here are some financial terms you might encounter:

Business term loan	A loan made by a bank to cover a percentage of the purchase price of fixed assets, with the assets being the items that guarantee repayment of the loan.
Debt financing	This is the money you borrow in order to do business. It must be repaid over time, with

	interest — an additional percentage of the total amount.
Employee investment	Employees may invest in a company, in exchange for a share of the profits.
Equity financing	This is the amount of money you have available to put into the business, from personal resources or the resources of your business partners.
Fixed assets	The permanent things a business owns, such as equipment, location, land, etc.
Interest	The amount a bank charges to loan you money — usually a percentage of the total amount of the loan.
Liquid assets	The saleable goods owned by your shop, such as containers, giftware, and perishables.
Personal investment	As the business owner, you are expected to put the largest amount of your own money and resources into the business.
Shareholder investment	A private company can have shareholders who put money into the business in exchange for shares in its ownership, and therefore a share of its profits.
Venture capital	Comes from outside sources who are willing to invest money in a company in the belief that they will see a return on their investment.

5.2.3 Legal Matters

Because laws vary from area to area, it's important to have a business lawyer help you with matters such as contracts, leases, partnership agreements, financing and even corporate structure. They can also help you register your business.

The first legal issue to consider when starting a business is the form of ownership it will have. Basically, there are four forms of ownership: sole propietorships, partnerships, limited liability companies and corporations. Let's have a look at what these terms mean.

Sole Proprietorship

If you decide your business will be a sole proprietorship, the buck stops with you. It doesn't mean that you don't have to deal with other people or that you can ignore rules and laws. It just means that, ultimately, the responsibility for the business lies on your shoulders.

The good news about a sole proprietorship is that you get nearly total control of the business and all the profits. The bad news is that you also get full liability for all business debts and actions.

A sole proprietorship is the easiest business structure to set up. All you need to do is apply for an occupational business license in the municipality where your business will be located. Usually, the license doesn't take long to be processed, and you can begin operations fairly quickly.

If you're in business by yourself, your social security number can serve as your taxpayer identification number. If you have employees, you'll need to request a taxpayer identification number from the Internal Revenue Service. Don't worry — someone will be happy to send you one!

Sole proprietorships are extremely common and popular among small business owners. Obviously, there is much about them that's appealing. Unless you really want a partner or have another reason for setting up another form of ownership, you should take a close look at a sole proprietorship.

Partnership

When two or more people decide to start a business together, they enter into something called a *partnership agreement*. There are two types of partnerships: general partnerships and limited partnerships.

A *general partnership* is when two or more people get together and start a business. They agree how they'll conduct the business and how the profits, risks, liabilities and losses will be distributed between them.

TIP: Partnerships don't have to be divided equally between all the partners. All partners, however, must agree on how the profit, risk, liability and loss will be divided.

A *limited partnership* is when one or more partners invest in the business, but are not involved in the day-to-day operations. Limited partners are investors, which makes them partners, but they have limited say in the hands-on operations.

An advantage of a partnership is that usually they have more financial clout than sole proprietorships. They've usually got more in the way of assets than just one person would. Another advantage is that in an ideal situation, you and your partner will balance out each others' strengths and weaknesses. And working with a partner who you like can be a lot of fun. On the flip side, many a business has turned sour because a partnership has gone bad.

TIP: If you decide to form a partnership, think very carefully about the person you choose as your partner. Make sure you each understand the others expectations and goals.

If you're thinking of forming a partnership, be sure to consult a lawyer and get a partnership agreement that covers all contingencies. The less that's left to chance, the stronger and more stable your partnership will be.

Limited Liability Company

A limited liability company is like a corporation, except it's not incorporated. You'll read more about corporations in a little bit, but the big thing about incorporating your business is that it makes the business legally separate from yourself.

A limited liability company also is legally separate from the person or persons who own it, and offers some protections that a partnership does not. Partners in a limited liability company get the same personal financial protection as those in a corporation. A limited liability company, however, can't sell stock or have shareholders or a board of directors.

Regulations regarding limited liability companies vary from area to area, so you need to do your homework if you're interested in this sort of ownership.

Corporation

When you incorporate a business, you form a corporation that's legally separate from yourself. Instead of the business being in your name, it's registered in the name of the corporation, and the corporation is responsible for all its business activities. Even if you start the business, once it's incorporated, you're considered an employee and a stockholder instead of a personal owner.

The good thing about having your business incorporated is that it limits the liability of each stockholder to the amount of their investment in the business. If the business fails or is found liable in a lawsuit, the corporation is responsible — not the members of the corporation.

Let's say that you and a partner each put up $100,000 to start your florist business. Now, imagine the unimaginable. Something so terrible happens that you find yourselves liable for a half million dollar lawsuit. If your company is a partnership, you're responsible for coming up with a half million dollars. If your company is incorporated, you and your partner can't be held liable for more than the $100,000 you have invested in the business.

While that's clearly an advantage of incorporation, there's a downside to incorporating your business as well. There's a good amount of paperwork and legal work involved, and more people involved than with other forms of ownership.

Many new owners of small companies do not incorporate their businesses and everything works out fine, while others feel that a corporation is the only viable option for their businesses. See the business resource links at the beginning of section 5.2 for more information about incorporating a small business.

Registering Your Business

Regardless of what form of legal structure you choose for your business, you'll need to have it registered, at least at a local level. This is not a difficult task. All it normally entails is filling out some forms and paying an annual license fee. Contact your municipal or county office for more information about registering your business. Or, check out information on business licenses at the links given in the beginning of this section.

Retail businesses that collect sales must be registered with their state's Department of Revenue and get a state identification number. All businesses that have employees need a federal identification number with which to report employee tax withholding information. If you are self employed, you'll pay a self-employment tax to contribute to your Social Security fund. Contact the Internal Revenue Service office in your area for more information.

The Canada Business Services Centre has an article explaining how a lawyer helps you with your business plans. To find it, visit **www.canadabusiness.ca**, click on "English," then on "Starting a Business," then look for "Legal Issues in Starting a Business" under "Fact Sheets."

In the United States, you can find a lawyer who specializes in small business through your local Yellow Pages. Or visit the American Bar Association's referral directory at **www.abanet.org/legalservices/lris/directory**. You can use the site to find a lawyer based on your location. The Canadian Bar Association offers a similar legal referral service on their website at **www.cba.org/CBA/Info/faq/referral.aspx**. The Nolo site mentioned at the beginning of this section also offers free information on legal matters.

Business Licenses

In order to operate your business, you will need a business license from your city, town or municipality. Costs for these vary, and you may need to meet certain local regulations with regards to by-laws or other regulations for your area. Business licenses are usually renewed annually. Contact your municipal government's business license office for details specific to your area. Your small business administration office can help you with this as well.

5.2.4 Choosing a Business Name and Logo

Choosing a Name

You might already have a business name in mind — and if so, it's worth considering strongly. Think about how it will stand up to the test of time, and how it might impact the sale of your business if you should decide to franchise or sell one day.

Tina's Flower Shop sounds great, if you're Tina, or if Tina has a local reputation for making excellent flower arrangements. But what if Fred decides he wants to take over the business someday? It's better to stick with an identifiable name that can grow with your business and carry on afterwards. That way, customers don't need to be confused.

Location Names

These describe the location of your shop, which is an advantage if you want customers to easily find you, or if you want out-of-town florists to be able to identify the neighborhood you serve. But what happens if you move? Uptown Florists is a fine name, until success forces you to move to a bigger location — downtown.

Flowery Names

Buds and Blossoms, Rosebuds, Daisy's Flowers, Bird of Paradise, Petal Pushers, Rustic Petal, Flower Box, Roseville, Simply Roses, Flower Patch — these are all real names of real flower shops. Check in your local Yellow Pages to make sure a name isn't already in use in your general area. Your shop may have the same name as a shop in another city.

Choosing a Logo

In addition to your business name, you may want an identifiable logo for your business.

Your logo should be a small picture or motif that is used on anything to do with your shop as a way for customers and the general public to recognize your business. It can be as simple as a picture of a specific flower, or as complicated as a monogram. Consult a professional graphic designer (check your Yellow Pages) for help with this aspect of your business.

While there will be an initial expense (expect to pay anywhere from $100 to $500) for developing your business logo, it creates a lasting image that much of your ongoing advertising and marketing can rely upon. You can use it on your stationery, your cards, your boxes, your shop uniforms (if you have them) and even on your delivery vehicles — each time sending the message that your shop is a distinct and professional business. You can even order a business logo online, at places like:

- *The Perfect Logo*
  www.theperfectlogo.com

- *Online Logo*
  www.onlinelogo.com/index.html

- *Logo Design Guru*
  www.logodesignguru.com

5.2.5 Choosing a Location

If you are purchasing an existing business, the location will already be decided for you. If you are opening a new business, you will need to decide upon a location. Since there are many types of places to do business, the location you choose will, in part, determine the type of business you do.

Shopping mall locations offer benefits such as frequent walk-by traffic, mall promotions and marketing, mall security, a recognizable location and plenty of parking. Drawbacks include extended hours (stores in a shopping mall are usually required to be open whenever the mall is), the relative distance a customer will have to travel to reach your shop once they leave their vehicle, and the need to participate in mall-organized promotions that may or may not fit with your own marketing plan. In addition, rents may be higher than at on-street locations.

Downtown or on-street locations offer easy access to your store, walk-by traffic, and a recognizable location, as well as the ability to set your own hours. Drawbacks include less parking, the possibility of damage or vandalism, and a less-predictable stream of customers.

Office and apartment buildings often have retail space on their main floors. Advantages include a steady clientele from the apartments or offices, in-building security, and parking. Disadvantages include less street-front visibility and potentially higher rents.

Other things to consider when you are looking at potential locations:

- Is it big enough to meet your needs?

- Is it so big that it will be expensive to heat or cool?

- Is it within a block or two of an established flower shop? This can be a hindrance to your out-of-town business.

- Is it near funeral homes, hospitals, or seniors' residences? These are all places that receive many floral orders each day.

- Is it in an area with many homes, which might have a need for lots of flowering plants, green plants, and decorative flowers?

For an excellent article on the question of location, visit **www. myteleflora.com/DesignEducation/Index.aspx**, click on "Floral Articles," and search for the article called "The Complete Guide to Leasing the Perfect Location."

5.2.6 Signage

If you do no other advertising at all (and that wouldn't be a good idea), you'll at least need a sign to identify your business to your customers. It should be large enough to be easily read from the street or sidewalk, and simple enough to be recognized. It should announce your shop's name, and could incorporate your shop's logo or a picture of a flower. Use only a few, easily recognizable words, and keep it simple.

If your location comes with a place to install a sign (such as in a shopping mall), you will probably be able to order an appropriate sign with the help of the mall's management. Professional sign companies offer design and manufacturing — check in your local Yellow Pages under the "Signs — Commercial" category.

Check with your municipality regarding regulations that affect signage. Some places have rules that determine size, placement or look of signs. Make sure your chosen sign meets these standards by taking the design and description to the municipal office.

Visit **www.myteleflora.com/DesignEducation/Index.aspx**, click on "Floral Articles," and search for "Signs: The First Step in Marketing" to find out more about the importance of signs.

5.2.7 Insurance

Choosing the right kind of insurance for your business is important. You'll need to insure your location, your business contents, and even yourself. It's a complicated matter that your local insurance agency can help you with and should help you with. Insurances to ask about include:

- *Liability insurance:* Laws regarding liability change all the time, so be sure you get the latest information regarding them. Nearly all businesses require liability insurance because there are so many types of liability.

- *Property insurance:* This will cover your actual shop. If you rent space, you'll need property insurance only on the equipment you have in your office — the owner of the building normally would pay for insurance on the property.

- *Disability insurance:* If you become sick for an extended period or otherwise disabled, your business could be in jeopardy. Disability insurance would provide at least a portion of your income while you're not able to work.

- *Business interruption insurance:* In the event that your property or equipment is damaged or destroyed, this type of insurance covers ongoing expenses such as rent or taxes until your business gets up and running again.

    TIP: Make sure you have the insurance that you need, but don't let a salesperson talk you into buying all kinds of extra riders and policies that you don't need. Develop a good understanding of what you need, and stand firm when a salesperson tries to talk you into buying more than that.

Also be sure to ask an agent about your auto insurance if you'll be offering delivery to customers, even if you use your own car. If you're liable for damages in an accident that occurs while you're conducting business, your business could be at risk. Ask about special coverage that protects your business in those types of circumstances.

You can find a good explanation of insurance options for small businesses in the United States at **www.sba.gov** (click on "Tools" then on "Publications" then on "Management and Planning Series", and scroll down to 17. Small Business Insurance & Risk Management Guide"). Canadians can find similar information at **www.ibc.ca/en/ Business_Insurance/**.

5.3 Supplies and Equipment

Having the proper equipment and supplies on hand is essential. "Equipment" refers to the tools you use every day. They are your hardware, and do not leave the shop. "Supplies" refers to the material goods that are used to make flower arrangements, and which you will need to replenish on a regular or semi-regular basis, depending on how quickly you use them up.

A knife is considered equipment, while a flower or a vase is considered a supply. You can fill an order without the right equipment, if you need to, but without the right supplies, you have nothing to sell. An established flower shop has an abundance of equipment, supplies, and flower materials, but if you're just starting out, gathering these essentials can account for a large portion of your start-up budget.

Most of the equipment and supplies you'll need are available from floral wholesalers, growers, and the product departments of order-gathering services. By planning in advance and keeping tabs on your stock, you will help ensure that you never lack the materials to fill an order.

You can find a checklist outlining some of the the basic equipment and supplies you'll need on the next page. Some links to suppliers are included in this section. Others can be found at the end of section 5.5.1.

5.3.1 Tools of the Trade

Not enough can be said about having the right tools handy at all times. Nothing is more frustrating or time-wasting than a fruitless search for a pair of scissors that were hiding at the bottom of the garbage bin all the time.

Equipment Checklist

❑ Plenty of fresh cut flowers

❑ A variety of flowering plants

❑ A variety of green foliage plants

❑ A variety of vases (glass and plastic) in round, square, tall, short and globe shapes, as well as slender bud vases meant to hold one or two flowers

❑ A variety of baskets with handles and plastic liners

❑ Plenty of lined or plastic containers (in round, square, bowl, oblong, triangular and other shapes) in which to make arrangements

❑ A good supply of floral foam

❑ Rolls of stem tape and florists' tape

❑ Rolls of ribbon

❑ Hot glue and aerosol glue

❑ Floral dyes and spray paints

❑ A range of buckets in varying sizes

❑ A selection of sharp knives, scissors and secateurs

❑ Stands, plinths, shelves and other display equipment

❑ A cooler, either walk-in or standalone

❑ Plant-care equipment

❑ Stationery for order-taking

❑ A cash register

❑ A debit/credit card machine

❑ A calculator

❑ A computer for sending and receiving orders

❑ A fax machine for sending and receiving orders

❑ A telephone

❑ Pens, pens and more pens

❑ Several large garbage bins

Here are the five cutting tools no florist can live without.

Sharp Knife

Florists use knives that are not unlike kitchen paring knives, though they often have a slight crescent shape to the blade. These are essential for cutting floral foam to the right size, trimming flower stems, and curling ribbon ends, among other uses. These can be bought at garden centers, hobby and craft stores, and floral wholesalers.

Good Secateurs

Also known as shears, secateurs are like scissors meant for cutting heavy stems and slim branches. A good pair will have a wire or metal "shock absorber" device, which makes each cut easier on the hands and which pushes the secateurs open after each cut.

Wire Cutters

Florists use wire for reinforcing stems, tying ribbon bows, and attaching display pieces together. A good pair of wire cutters will ensure the wire is the right length every time, and will keep the secateurs and scissors around them sharp, too.

Scissors

Used for cutting ribbons, curling ribbons, trimming plant leaves, cutting fabric for displays and numerous other uses. A sharp pair of scissors should always be tied to – not placed by – the ribbon station of every flower shop.

Shears

Like heavy-duty scissors, shears are used for cutting large clumps of flower stems – such as the ends of a bouquet of flowers – at once. Usually made of metal, their blades are either smooth or serrated.

Other Tools You Should Have Around

- Hammer
- Screwdrivers
- Pliers
- Hand-held stapler
- Staple gun
- Desk stapler
- Letter opener
- Spray bottles

5.3.2 Essential Equipment

Buckets

Every flower shop needs dozens of buckets. These are used to hold flowers when they first arrive from the supplier and, later, to hold the flowers for display. Usually made of plastic, buckets can be decorative (these are the ones for display use) or functional (for holding flowers in the work area before processing, or for holding water for other uses).

Large buckets are usually up to 24 inches tall and 12 inches at the mouth. Smaller buckets are often about 12 to 18 inches tall, and are flared at the mouth. These can fit on wire display racks and are used to display individual bouquets or types of flowers. Buckets should be rinsed and scrubbed after each use.

Display Equipment

There is a wide range of display equipment, and which equipment gets used depends on each individual flower shop's needs and focus.

For example, a shop in a high-traffic area which gets much of its business from customers buying bouquets of flowers on their way home, will likely have lots of bucket racks. (Bucket racks are large metal racks, sometimes with wheels attached to the bottom, meant to hold a selection of small buckets so many bouquets can be displayed at once.) A shop that specializes in wedding work will probably have metal archways, candelabras, and numerous bouquet stands.

Most shops will have tables or stands for displaying plants, some type of shelving for displaying giftware, and a cooler with shelves upon which arrangements and buckets of flowers can be placed.

Other equipment used for creating displays includes mannequins, mirrors, lengths of fabric, *plinths* (tall, solid stands) and *hanging hooks* (rigid metal S-shapes which can be used to suspend items from a ceiling).

Not all flower shops need all of these items, but some are essential. All of the above items can be purchased at floral wholesalers (see section 5.5 for more information about wholesalers). You can also try looking in your local Yellow Pages under "Retail Display Equipment."

Work Bench

The work bench is an essential part of a florist's work area. You can build one, have one built for you, or just use a sturdy table. It should be at a comfortable height for you to work while standing up (hip height works for most people), and should have all the essential tools – especially knives and pens – close at hand. We'll cover this more in section 5.4.2 on "Organizing your Workspace."

Reach Stick

A reach stick is easily made by firmly attaching a hook (a screw-on coat hook is ideal) to one end of a long broom handle. This makes an essential tool for reaching hanging plants up and down from their hooks, for getting light objects off high shelves, and for saving those who are afraid of heights from having to climb up on a stepladder or step stool.

Stepladder or Step Stool

No reach stick? Climb up the old-fashioned way. Step stools are useful for creating displays, getting things off high shelves, or changing light bulbs.

Garbage Bin

There should be at least one large garbage bin in the work area, plus a smaller one tucked neatly under the sales desk. These should be plastic so they don't leak and are light enough to carry when full. The type meant for outdoor home use is ideal, though lids are not essential.

Mop, Broom, and Dustpan

Inevitably, water will spill. The mop takes care of that. Inevitably, flowers, leaves, petals and soil will end up on the floor. That's what the broom and dustpan will take care of, several times a day. It's part of the reality of a flower shop.

5.3.3 Supplies

Remember, supplies are the items you will be using and depleting every day. It is good practice to keep an ongoing list of supplies that are running low so you will be able to order more from your suppliers as needed.

Your most important supplies will be flowers, which you will buy several times a week. Your other supplies will also come from wholesale suppliers. There are floral wholesalers in most cities, and they can be found by consulting your local Yellow Pages for "Florists — Wholesale." You can also find them online. See section 5.5 ("Wholesalers and Suppliers") for more information on this topic.

Container Fillers

Floral foam is a rigid, porous plastic foam that absorbs and holds water. It is soft enough to take even the most delicate stem being pushed into it, yet it is strong enough to hold the biggest stems firmly in place. It is sold under brand names like Oasis, Fil-fast, Water Brick and

Aquafoam. Dry Foam (brand names include Sahara and Camel) is meant for arranging permanent flowers and does not absorb water.

Floral foam comes in bricks measuring about 12" by 2" by 3", and is sold in cases containing 44 to 48 bricks. The foam can be cut to fit into the desired container. Some types of foam need to be soaked before being used, while others can be installed in the container before water is added. Which type you use depends partly on preference and partly on advance planning. If you are preparing a number of containers for a future date, for example, it is best to use the type that does not require water until just before the flowers are inserted.

Shredded or ground Styrofoam is used for extra stability in vase arrangements or to create a "snowball" effect as the white material shows through the glass vase. This material is sold by the cubic foot.

Glass beads or marbles are sometimes used in vases where the filler material will be visible. They offer a degree of control over the flower stems inserted between them, and give visual interest to the base of the vase arrangement. These are more expensive to use than Styrofoam, so they are reserved for higher-priced arrangements or custom orders.

Frogs are small metal or glass holders into which flower stems are placed. Pin holders are metal frogs that typically have a number of sharp pins sticking out of them, and stems are impaled to hold them in place. Glass frogs, which are much less common, look like old-fashioned paperweights with a series of holes in them. Flower stems are placed into these holes to hold them in place. Because frogs are expensive and heavy, they are not often used by florists for commercial arrangements, but they are sometimes used by customers who enjoy arranging their own cut flowers.

Containers

A number of types of containers are commonly used in flower shops, but really, any container that can hold water and be filled with floral foam makes a good container for flowers. You're limited only by your imagination when it comes to making arrangements in gumboots, teapots and children's beach buckets, but there are some types of containers you're most likely to encounter right away.

Baskets

Florists use plastic-lined wicker baskets to create arrangements with an informal or "country" feeling. These baskets can be as small as a few inches across (such as those carried by a flower girl at a wedding), or they can be two to three feet across, (meant to contain a showy funeral tribute). In every case, they must be lined – either by the manufacturer with a pre-made liner, or by the florist with a plastic container that fits – before being filled with floral foam.

Vases

Florists use vases every day, both for displaying flowers in the store and for arranging flowers for delivery to customers. The most commonly used vases are:

- *Bud vases:* Slender vases, typically 12 to 18 inches high, meant to hold one to three blooms. They are often made of glass, but can be porcelain or plastic.

- *Rose vases:* Typically 12 to 18 inches high, and up to six inches in diameter at the mouth. Usually made of glass, they can come in a variety of shapes, but are usually not much bigger around at any point than they are at the mouth.

- *Arrangement vases:* Usually eight to 12 inches high, and meant for arranging cut flowers. They tend to be narrower at the neck than at the body, and often flare out at the mouth.

Plastic Containers

There are many plastic containers made specially for florists — from round bowls with rectangular bottoms for holding floral foam, to novelty containers shaped like licensed characters, holiday symbols, or other items. Rectangular and oval bowls are used for table centerpieces, while taller containers can be used for arrangements of other types.

Containers vary in size from a few inches across to more than 12 inches in diameter, but all will be deep enough to hold both floral foam and some water. They will be constructed well enough to hold up under the weight of the flowers and water.

Metalware Containers

Often made of aluminum or other lightweight metal, metalware containers have an attractive shine. They are sometimes factory-painted with floral or other motifs and are used for displaying flowering plants. A six-inch diameter metal pot, for example, will easily hold a six-inch plastic pot containing a plant. This provides a quick, easy and attractive way of "dressing" a plant for delivery.

Other metalware can include arrangement containers, wire accessories meant to be incorporated into arrangements (especially Christmas stars, angels, and other motifs), and metal accessories.

Funeral Containers

Most floral arrangements for funerals are prepared in plastic or papier-mâché containers, as the focus is meant to be on the flowers, not the container. The basic plastic container shapes used are the *pedestal* (a bowl on a flared base), the *urn* (a taller bowl on a shorter base), the *basket* (a round or oblong container with a wide, looping handle), and the bowl, or *jardinière* (round, low bowls without bases). The papier-mâché containers, which are made of pressed paper with a water-resistant bottom, follow the same basic shapes.

Specialty funeral pieces are prepared on a variety of plastic foundations, as follows:

- The *saddle* (an oblong, tray-like container with a curved base) is meant for casket arrangements.

- The *floral cage* is a plastic cage with a block of floral foam inside it, with an upright post that allows it to be hung or attached to an easel. This is used for easel sprays. These cages are also available without floral foam inside.

- There is also a *tombstone saddle*, meant for holding arrangements on top of a tombstone, and a *cemetery vase*, which is a plastic vase with a spike at the bottom, meant to be inserted into the earth to hold a bouquet of flowers at graveside.

Other funeral containers include satin pillows in heart, square and cross shapes, with a small plastic well built in so a small arrangement can be attached. There are also shapes (wreaths, crosses, and hearts) made of floral foam which may be attached to easels, placed on a casket, or laid on a gravesite.

Bouquet Holders

Wedding bouquets are often prepared in bouquet holders which look somewhat like ice cream cones. They are small plastic cages that hold a piece of floral foam (the ice cream), and have a plastic handle (the cone) so that the bouquet may be carried. Before they can be used, they must be soaked in water so that the floral foam is saturated. Similar cages, known as pew holders, come attached to plastic hooks. These types are used for ceremony and reception decorations.

Tape

There are three types of tape commonly used in flower shops. First, there's the familiar *cellophane tape* (3M, Scotch) used to secure wrapping paper and cellophane around bouquets of flowers.

There's also *cloth tape*, which is an extremely sticky, cloth reinforced tape, usually about 1/4 inch wide and supplied in rolls. It is used to secure floral foam in containers, create grids on the mouths of vases, and to secure plants in baskets. It comes in white, brown and green, and the color used is chosen to blend in with the materials being used.

Finally, there's *stem tape*, which is a thin, sticky, and slightly stretchy but non-adhesive tape used to wrap around stems for corsages or to hide wires used for reinforcing flower stems. It is used mostly in corsages and wedding bouquets, and it comes in light green, dark green, brown, and white. The color used is chosen to match the color of the flower's natural stem. It is about half an inch wide, and comes in rolls about 3" across.

Glue

There are numerous occasions where glue is used in a flower shop, and the use dictates the type of glue used.

Floral adhesive comes in bottles and is similar to school glue. It is waterproof, fast-drying, and used to attach flowers to bases, leaves to stems, glitter to ribbon and numerous other small applications.

Stem adhesive comes in an aerosol can, and is used when it is important to secure a flower's stem in a block of floral foam.

Hot glue comes in sticks that are inserted into a glue gun, which looks like a water pistol and uses heat to melt the glue and distribute it through a nozzle. It is also available in chips which are melted in a pot (often an old electric frying pan). A glue gun is more efficient for small, precise dabs of glue, or for use on large items that can't be picked up. A glue pot is more efficient for small items that can be dipped into the glue and then stuck in place. Often, florists use hot glue to attach dry floral foam to the inside of containers, rather than securing the foam with tape. Take extra care with all types of hot glue, as it is sticky and hot enough to burn skin.

Spray adhesive is typically used to stick tiny items, such as glitter or flower petals, to a surface. It is sprayed onto the object, which is then either rolled or dipped in the glitter, or has the glitter sprinkled onto it. Use this only in a well-ventilated area.

Wire and Wire Piks

Wire is used for reinforcing flower stems and securing ribbons into bows. Sold in 12-pound boxes of 18-inch lengths, wire comes in a variety of thicknesses, from very fine 28 gauge to sturdy 18 gauge. The higher the number of the gauge, the finer the wire.

Wire piks are small wooden sticks, 2.5" to 6" in length, with a fine wire attached to one end. These are used to create stems for materials such as pine cones.

Decorative Piks

These are pre-made decorations that are used to add extra value or extra interest to an arrangement, plant, or package. Christmas piks usually consist of several pieces of artificial greenery, a few baubles, a blossom or more of artificial flowers, and a few loops of ribbon, all mounted on a central stem.

Other piks are often made of plastic in shapes (such as baby booties or Valentine hearts), messages ("Happy Mother's Day"), or motifs (smiley faces, Easter bunnies, holiday symbols).

Water Piks

These are small plastic tubes meant to be filled with water and capped with a flexible cap. There is a small hole in the cap into which a flower stem is inserted. Also known as *aquapiks* or *watertubes*, they keep individual flowers fresh and in water until they are delivered to the recipient.

Dyes and Paints

Dyes are colors added to the water in which flowers are held. As the flower absorbs water, it takes on the color of the dye. These are not used often by individual flower shops, but flower suppliers may dye flowers for special occasions (such as green for St. Patrick's day) or special uses (such as blue for baby arrangements). It is a matter of taste as to whether you use dyed flowers.

In a flower shop, paint means aerosol cans, but these are now produced without the hazardous CFCs (chlorofluorocarbons) that were once used in this type of paint. Paint is used to tint flowers, baskets, containers, and even ribbons. Special effects can be created with glitter spray, lace spray and shimmer spray (which gives a clear, iridescent look).

Care Tags

These are 2" by 4" cards with a loop at one end, printed with information about the item they are meant to be attached to. They are commonly used on flowering plants ("How to care for your Azalea," for example) and offer advice on the plant's light and moisture preferences and other tips for successful care.

Enclosure Cards, Envelopes, and Cardettes

Customers who wish to send a message along with their flowers can write it on an enclosure card. Or, if they are ordering the flowers by phone or from out of town, you can write it for them (in your best handwriting, of course!).

These cards are usually printed with messages (Happy Birthday; Get Well Soon; etc.) and/or illustrations. There is enough room on them to write a brief message. Many flower shops stamp their shop name, address and phone number on the reverse of the cards, for the recipient's reference.

These cards are inserted into 2" by 3" envelopes, upon which the name, address and phone number of the recipient is written. The card and envelope are secured to a bouquet or package with cellophane tape, or inserted into a flower arrangement with a cardette — a plastic holder with a long stem (usually 9", 12" or 18") and three prongs to hold the card.

Ribbon

Ribbon comes on spools in a wide range of materials, colors, patterns, and widths. It can be made of satin, plastic satin, tulle, velvet, chiffon, nylon, paper, cotton, mesh, lace, and can even have metallic finishes. It is printed with motifs (such as Halloween bats) or woven with patterns or plaids. Usually, one side is printed or shiny, while the other is unprinted and matte.

Boxes

Cut flowers are often delivered in long, narrow, thin cardboard boxes with lids that are occasionally printed with the flower shop's logo.

These come in 18", 24", 30" and 36" lengths, are shipped and stored flat and folded into shape as needed. They are often lined with sheets of waxed tissue paper.

Plastic boxes are also used for the same purpose, though they are more expensive. For example, a 30" cardboard box costs less than a dollar wholesale, while a plastic one of the same length costs $1.50.

Corsages are also delivered in plastic corsage boxes or in cellophane bags tied with ribbons.

Waxed Tissue Paper

Sold in 24" by 36" sheets, waxed tissue is used to line delivery boxes, to pad fruit baskets, to wrap individual pieces of fruit, and sometimes to wrap giftware. It comes in green, white, pastel colors and occasionally prints.

Pins, Wristlets, Combs, and Stems

Any florist doing a lot of wedding flowers will have a constant need for these items. Corsage pins are 2" long and tipped with a pearlized bead. Boutonniere pins are slightly shorter and tipped with either black or white beads.

Wristlets are small circles of elastic or plastic fitted with a metal prong to which a corsage can be attached, making it into a wrist corsage.

Combs are plain plastic hair accessories to which flowers may be glued or wired to create floral hairpieces. Hair clips may also be used for this purpose.

Stems are used to create stems for individual blossoms so that they can be incorporated into corsages and bouquets. Chenille stems (the pipe cleaners of old) come in a variety of colors, while tinsel stems are shiny silver and gold. Stephanotis stems, or extender stems, are padded with absorbent material at one end and are used for the fragrant white stephanotis blossoms often used in wedding bouquets.

Foil, Cellophane, Wrapping Paper, and Sleeves

Florists use colored foil to cover the pots of flowering and green plants to make an attractive presentation. Foil comes in rolls and is torn, not cut, to the right length. (See section 2.5.9 on "How to Dress a Plant" for more about how to do this.) Foil is available in a wide range of colors, and the color to be used is chosen to match or complement a plant's flowers.

Cellophane is a sturdy plastic film that is used to wrap fruit baskets, presentation bouquets, and occasionally giftware. It is dispensed from a large roll, and is sliced (with a knife or scissors) to the desired size. It is usually clear, but can also be tinted a variety of colors.

Wrapping paper is also dispensed from a large roll and is torn against the cutting blade of the dispenser to the desired size. It is used to wrap bouquets of cut flowers and to wrap plants to protect them from cold weather. It comes in solid colors, colorful prints and even with a florist's logo printed on it.

Sleeves are wide V-shaped tubes made of cellophane or other sturdy plastic film. They are used to quickly wrap cash-and-carry bouquets, or to protect plants from cold weather during delivery. The bouquet or plant is slid into the sleeve from the wide end, and the narrow end is taped or tied, if needed, to secure the sleeve.

5.3.4 Business Equipment

Telephones

Florists depend on their telephones, both for incoming and outgoing orders, to ensure their supplies will arrive on time and to communicate with customers. While it's hard to know what kind of phone system will be best if you haven't even opened your business yet, keep in mind that you can always upgrade your system if you find that you're busier than it can handle.

Check with your local telephone company's business services department for the particular packages that are available to you. Some features you will probably want:

- Multiple lines (especially if you don't want to tie up your main line all day by being connected to the Internet)

- Voicemail

- Call forwarding (so you can have after-hours calls transferred to your home)

- Caller ID (to make sure you have the correct phone number for a customer)

- A toll-free number (especially if you hope to fill lots of orders from out of town)

- A competitive long-distance rate plan

Fax Machine

When you set up your phone lines, you will have the option of a dedicated fax line. This is a wise investment, as it prevents your phone line from being tied up with faxes.

You may purchase or rent a fax machine. Pay a visit to your nearest office supplies outlet to find out about the different types available.

Once you have your business registered and your business license in hand, you will also be able to purchase office equipment at wholesale prices.

Computer

As mentioned above, you will want to have a second phone line for Internet access so that your phone isn't tied up all day. However, you may also wish to consider cable or DSL access through a local company as an alternative.

You can use a computer to track your orders, process your cash transactions, and keep accounting and inventory records, as well as send and receive orders. There are several software packages that help with this kind of thing:

- *Mercury Advantage*
  www.ftdi.com/mercurytechnology/mercuryadvantage.htm

- *Dove Point of Sale System*
  (Click on the "Dove POS" link near the bottom of the page)
  www.myteleflora.com

- *Visual Ticket*
  www.floralsystems.com

As with phone lines, you can always upgrade your computer systems to match your growing business, but to begin with, consult your local computer store, where the experts will help you choose and set up a system that meets your basic needs.

If you plan to update your own website or use this computer for e-mail orders, you should also have a virus-scanning program that automatically updates itself. Norton and McAfee are two popular anti-virus programs.

Cash Register

As with fax machines, you can find out about the different types of cash registers available by paying a visit to your local business equipment retailer or wholesaler. Some cash registers are standalone — that is, they are not connected to any online service, and you must process credit and debit card transactions separately. Some are online, which means you will have to have a dedicated phone line or Internet connection for them. Others can be connected to your shop's computer system to allow for up-to-date accounting.

If you're starting out, it makes sense to keep your system as simple as possible. You can always upgrade later, but investing in an expensive, possibly too-elaborate system from the very beginning can tie up money you could be using for other purposes.

Some common brand names of cash registers are Sharp, NCR, TEC, Casio and Samsung. To learn more about cash registers available for sale, try the Cash Register Store at **http://cashregisterstore.com**.

Credit/Debit Card Machine

When you set up your store's bank account with a visit to your bank's business services representative, you'll have the option of leasing a credit/debit card machine in conjunction with your account. Your bank will offer technical support for this piece of equipment, and will help you make sure it's working properly.

If your store is a member of FTD or Teleflora (see section 6.3 for membership information), you may use their card processing services. You can read more about them here:

- *FTD Cash-Flo System*
  www.ftdi.com/cashflo/default.htm

- *Teleflora Credit Card Processing Service*
  (Click the "Credit Card Processing" link near the bottom of the page)
  www.myteleflora.com

5.3.5 Furniture and Fixtures

You are going to need furniture and fixtures for your workroom, office and sales floor. In general, furniture refers to something that is not attached to the floor or wall, while a fixture refers to something attached that is not easily moved. In either case, these will need to be purchased or built and installed before you open.

The Workroom

Workbench

There should be enough room for one designer to work comfortably at a workbench — allow no less than 3' by 3' per workstation. This should be placed in the workroom area of the shop, which is usually an out-of-the way part of the store close to the sink.

Sink

The sink is an essential fixture. The sink should be wide enough and deep enough to hold at least one large flower bucket, and preferably bigger. Hot and cold running water, of course, are essential. The sink is always part of the workroom.

Storage Shelves

This depends on the size of your store and workroom, but plan on having separate shelves to store vases, containers, floral foam, and decorative piks.

Storage Drawers

These are useful for small, less frequently used items such as corsage makings, un-inflated balloons, etc.

The Sales Floor

Sales Desk

This is where florists take care of customers, so it should be fully and neatly stocked with order-taking and customer service supplies at all times. Your sales desk should have a place for the cash register and credit/debit card machine, plus storage for pens and order-taking stationery.

Display Shelves or Stands

The number and size of shelves depends on your shop layout, but plan on having separate display areas for, at the very least:

- green plants

- giftware

- flowering plants

- seasonal specials

Cooler

Your cooler is a large, refrigerated display unit fitted with interior display shelves for displaying arrangements and storing flowers. It has glass doors to display the contents inside.

Coolers may be as small as a refrigerator, or as large as a room (these are called walk-in coolers). You may have one cooler for display purposes and another for storage, or you may have one large cooler for everything. Keep in mind that if you use just one cooler, it must be kept immaculately tidy and should be close to the sales floor because it functions as a working display.

You can find coolers for sale or lease in your local Yellow Pages, under "Refrigeration — Commercial." Also, the following companies sell coolers especially for florists:

- *Barr, Inc.*
  www.barrinc.com
  Phone: 888-661-0871

- *Bush Refrigeration*
  www.bushrefrigeration.com
  Phone: 800-220-2874

- *Flot-Aire*
  www.flotaire.com
  Phone: 800-729-5964

- *MEI*
  ww.mei-systems.com
  Phone: 800-352-7220

- *SRC Refrigeration*
  www.src.us
  Phone: 800-521-0398

- *WDP Refrigeration, Inc.*
  www.walkinrefrigeration.com
  Phone: 800-980-0950

The Office

Office Desk

This is where your order-sending computer and printer will sit, where you'll do your accounting, and where you will probably take some phone calls. There should be electrical outlets and phone outlets nearby, a place to connect your computer modem, and space for your fax machine. Plus, there should be a relatively comfortable chair for sitting in while you're there.

Bookshelves

Bookshelves are also a good idea for your office, as they provide a place to store magazines, manuals, and reference books.

File Cabinets

File cabinets offer you an organized place to keep important documents such as invoices, past orders, and personnel files.

5.4 Store Layout and Maintenance

Congratulations! You've outlined your business plan, chosen your location, and your startup cash is in hand. You're ready to set up your own flower shop. Plan to take no less than a month getting set up, and ideally allow yourself as much time as you can to get your shop in perfect shape — with everything in place — for your big opening day.

5.4.1 Décor

Bare walls and floors aren't very welcoming, but a coat of paint can make a huge difference. If the space you are using for your flower shop was previously used for a different type of business, you will need to consider how to adapt it for your own use. If it is a new space, and empty of any décor at all, you'll need to make the same decisions.

Consider the image you want to present in your shop. Is it cozy, contemporary, casual, or classic? Choose colors for the walls accordingly. Keep in mind that muted colors work better as a backdrop for flowers.

Flooring is another consideration. It should be easy to keep clean, not prone to being extremely slippery when wet, and attractive. It should also be able to withstand traffic and moisture.

Hiring an interior designer or decorator is a wise investment at this stage, although you can do it yourself if you prefer.

5.4.2 Organizing Your Workspace

At a flower shop, the entire space is your workspace. But dividing the shop into areas specific to different tasks will make your work go much more smoothly. Work areas are typically private, staff-only areas not seen by the public. Even so, they should be well organized. Public areas should be naturally inviting, attractive and well organized.

Here are ways to organize some parts of the flower shop that you will be spending most of your time in.

Workstations

There should be one workstation per designer. In addition, there should be workstations devoted to specific tasks, such as wrapping, processing, and dressing plants. A design workstation should always have the following equipment and supplies:

- Knives

- Cutting tools

- Pens

- Floral foam

- A water source (watering can or overhead water delivery system)

- Elastic bands

- Garbage bin beneath or nearby

- Clip or box to hold incoming orders to be filled; spike or box to hold outgoing finished orders

Flowers and Plants

In a flower shop, you can expect to sort flowers and plants based on the following categories:

- *Variety:* Flowers of similar varieties should be kept together.

- *Color*: Flowers of similar colors within one variety should be kept together.

- *Temperature needs*: Flowers that need cool temperatures would be grouped in the cooler, for example, while flowers that can withstand warmer temperatures would be grouped on the sales floor.

- *Light needs*: Green plants with similar requirements would be grouped together to take advantage of varying amounts of natural lighting.

You can expect to sort any other materials based on these categories:

- Seasons/Holidays

- Medium (such as glass, wicker, plastic)

- Color

- Type (dried flowers, artificial flowers, etc.)

- Size

- Usage (floral arrangement supplies, display supplies, painting supplies)

The Cooler

The cooler is the refrigerated area in which fresh cut flowers are stored. Typically, there will be several shelves as well as the floor of the cooler on which to place items. Place buckets of tall cut flowers on the lowest level of the cooler. Shorter cut flowers may be placed on shelves, while the uppermost shelves are usually reserved for pre-made arrangements of flowers for display and sale.

Keep a thermometer inside the cooler to ensure the temperature is correct — between 40 and 50 degrees Fahrenheit (4 to 10 degrees Celsius). Also make sure to keep them clean by sweeping and mopping the cooler floor and washing the glass windows and doors once a week, or more often if needed.

Storage Areas

It is helpful to use as much spare space as possible for storage. Frequently used supplies should be kept together according to their purpose. Corsage-making supplies should all be kept together, for instance, as should balloon bouquet supplies. Keep them in clearly-labeled boxes, bins or drawers.

Store frequently used containers and vases on shelves directly below or near the workstations. Baskets may be strung on lengths of string and hung from hooks on the ceiling. Keep out-of-season supplies in dated and labeled boxes in a back room, attic or other storage space. These boxes should be kept on shelves to avoid possible crushing.

Office

Most flower shops have an office area in which the store's company and business records are kept, the computer and fax machine are housed, the incoming and outgoing orders are tracked, and the day's accounting is completed. This area would normally have:

- a desk
- pads of paper
- plenty of pens and pencils
- a stapler
- envelopes for sending out bills and payments
- stamps
- a calculator

- a file cabinet for storing receipts and invoices

- computer and fax paper

- a fax machine

- a computer

And you can expect to sort paperwork based on the following:

- *Orders to be transmitted:* If you can't transmit an order immediately, file it in a "to be transmitted" file.

- *Orders sent:* Once orders are transmitted, draw a line across them and put them in the "sent" file.

- *Orders to be prepared:* Follow the day, time, type formula. That is, sort by the day of delivery, then the time (AM or PM), then the type of order (vase arrangement, container arrangement, cut flowers, plant, etc.).

- *Bills sent:* If your flower shop bills customers for work, send their invoice as soon as the work has been delivered. Keep a record of the bill on file until their payment comes in.

- *Payments received:* Once payment is received, place the bill in the "received" file.

- *Invoices to be checked:* You'll need to compare invoices from wholesalers with your monthly statements.

- *Statements and invoices to be paid:* When a bill arrives or you receive your monthly statement from a wholesaler or supplier, put it in a "to be paid" file.

- *Statements and invoices paid:* Once you've paid the bills in the previous file, move them to a "paid" file.

- *Deliveries made:* Keep a record of all outgoing deliveries, and compare it with the delivery driver's record of deliveries made to ensure all deliveries are completed.

The Sales Desk

The sales desk is where you will meet with customers to take their orders and assist them with their purchases. As such, it should be well-stocked with supplies and neatly organized to present an un-cluttered, efficient image. A well-equipped sales desk has the following:

- A cash register

- A credit/debit card machine

- A telephone

- Pens

- Order-taking stationery

- Stapler

- Enclosure cards and envelopes

- A calculator

5.4.3 Front Window

Your store's front window is the place where you can announce your weekly specials, draw attention to a seasonal holiday, or simply have fun with the creative freedom a large, publicly-viewed space allows.

The front window at your store may be as modest as a kitchen window, or as enormous as a department store's holiday window. Regardless, there are some principles that apply no matter what the size.

It is said that you have approximately three to six seconds to catch a customer's eye with your window. So your message has to be strong, clear, and big. It should reinforce your store's image — whether it's contemporary or classic, eclectic or artistic.

Setting up a store window is basically a matter of setting up a display that will be seen from the outside only. It should be big, bold, and exciting. Its message, above all, should be: "Come inside!"

Proportion

Scale is important. If you are working with a large window, you will be able to use large objects and props much more easily than you will if your window is small. If your window is small, customers will probably be coming closer to view it.

Think of the display window at your favorite jewelry store, for example. It's probably small and jewel-like itself. That kind of window allows you to use miniatures, to showcase one tiny, perfect item that would be lost in a department-store-sized window.

Simplicity

An extremely filled window, with numerous items, can be effective if it is someplace where customers have the time to linger and look. But it is more effective to make a simple statement that will be noticed from far off, and will entice customers to come closer for a better look. When in doubt, leave it out.

Harmony

All the items in a window display should contribute to the overall effect and be arranged in a pleasing manner. Whether it's symmetrically or asymmetrically, they should be carefully placed to ensure they are visible, facing the right direction, and are free of any flaws that would take away from the overall effect.

Focal Point

The focal point is the part of the display where you want your viewers' eyes to be drawn for the most amount of time. It can be created by placing one singular well-lit object in the center, or by arranging the items in the window in rows or lines so that they lead viewers' eyes to a certain spot.

Color

Choose two or three colors, at most, for your front window display. Think of it as you would about painting the outside of a house: many different colors create a visual jumble. Large masses of single colors, on the other hand, make a clear statement. Refer to the chapter on color and design for more ideas and advice.

Props

Gather your props in advance, to avoid having to run back and forth for just the right item. Anything you are considering using should be near the place where you're setting up the display. You can use any kind of prop in a window display, as long as it fits easily into the space available.

5.4.4 Creating In-Store Displays

In-store displays can be categorized in several ways. Point-of-purchase displays offer products for impulse buys, while front window displays entice customers in with tantalizing merchandise or by reminding them an important occasion is on its way. Other in-store displays focus on particular products offered for sale, such as seasonal merchandise, giftware or a particular plant variety.

Props

Props are essential for creating eye-catching in-store displays. For the most part, props are large items that add to a theme. An overstuffed armchair could be a prop for a Father's Day display, for example. Or a ladder could be a prop for a decorating-themed display.

Almost anything you can imagine can be a prop, as in-store displays are one way to really let your creativity shine. All of the following can be brought in (from home, from garage sales, from co-operative fellow businesses) to serve as display props:

- Chairs and tables

- Old bicycles

- Weathered doors

- Ladders

- Tree branches

- Musical instruments

- Lamps

- Wheelbarrows

- Garden tools

- Garden ornaments of all types (birdbaths, gnomes, birdfeeders, etc.)

Gathering props and accessories is an ongoing task. Open your imagination to potential props around you, and soon you'll begin to see the possibilities in everything.

Making displays using found props is one approach, but if you are interested in making something truly unique, you can build your own props. That's one area where you can really let your creative, crafty side shine. Making props doesn't have to be complicated or expensive, and most flower shops already have a stockpile of cardboard, foam-core, and other materials with which you can build your ideas into reality.

Need giant pencils for a back-to-school display? Make them from cardboard tubes and paper cones with floral foam erasers. Spray paint the tubes a bright yellow, color the ends black with felt marker, and they're ready to go in your display window or to hang above your sales desk. Giant flowers can be made with circles of foam-core, with cardboard petals covered in bright florists' foil and glued around the circle.

Gingerbread houses are easy to make. Follow a gingerbread house pattern, but enlarge it by placing it on the cardboard you're using and tracing a wide edge around it. Cut it out with box cutters, assemble it the same way you would a gingerbread house, using hot glue instead of frosting, and decorate it with "candies" made of pieces of spray-painted Styrofoam.

Setting Up Displays

Displays vary depending on the material you want to use, the props involved, and the space you have available. Here's how to make a sample in-store display that assumes you will be using a small area, a table, a table covering, a backdrop and up to 12 items (say, vases or small flowering plants):

1. Gather the plants or giftware you want to display.

2. Decide on where the display will be. Is it meant to influence an impulse purchase of lower-cost items? Or is it meant to catch the eye to draw customers further into the store? Choose a location where customers will be able to linger for a moment to admire the merchandise.

3. Set up the framework on which the display will be made, whether it's a shelf, a table, a stand or series of stands.

4. Cover the surface with a cloth or other covering, if you are using one.

5. Set up any backdrop you may be using. A screen, poster, framed picture, or drape of fabric makes a good backdrop. You might want to use simple, large letters to make words. This can be done in any medium, or even commercially prepared at a graphics company.

6. Arrange your display items neatly. Interesting configurations – like pyramids, checkerboard patterns, or circles – make for a more effective display than randomly placed objects. Try several combinations to see what works best for the items you're using.

7. Check your display from time to time, to replenish sold items and to ensure it remains in order.

Points to remember for all display areas:

- Keep floors and surfaces clean

- Keep merchandise clean

- Make sure lights are working and are directed to shine on merchandise

- Prices need to be clearly marked

- Leave no extraneous material left in display

- Regularly check any plants used and remove dead flowers or leaves

Point of Purchase

Point of purchase refers to displays that offer numerous items of a single variety, usually set up in a convenient area of the store to encourage customers to make impulse purchases. Think of the racks of film or magazines near your grocery store check-outs. These are point of purchase displays. In a flower shop, point of purchase displays are especially good for giftware, small plants, or cash-and-carry bouquets.

A point of purchase display can be as simple as placing the items for sale on a table, adding a sign to announce the price, and leaving it at that. Or, it can be more elaborate, with signs, vases of flowers, or attention-getting items. Order-gathering services will often provide point of purchase display materials, such as posters, shelf-hangers (small signs meant to hang from a store shelf) and brochures.

Cooler

Besides functioning as a working storage area, the cooler provides a place to display pre-made arrangements and bouquets for customers to buy on the spot. At the very least, your cooler should always have the following, fresh, priced and ready to go:

- A single or double rose bud vase

- A mixed vase arrangement

- A container arrangement

- A branded arrangement, such as the FTD Get Well arrangement

- A seasonal arrangement ready for the next coming holiday

Lighting Your Display

While some displays – like Christmas trees – will have lights built in, others will need spot or track lighting to make them stand out. You should have a general source of light, such as an overhead light, to make the display visible. You should also have accent lights, such as spotlights, to focus attention on a particular part of the display.

Your store will probably be equipped with spotlights – either attached to the ceiling or to the upper parts of the display areas – that you can adjust to shine on displays. If not, you can install clip lights or floor lights to provide accent lights for your display.

Choose your lighting to illuminate the display and enhance its mood. You can place colored gels (pieces of thin, transparent colored plastic) over the light to change the color of the lighting, or you can use dim lights to achieve a specific effect. You can also use table lamps, floor lamps and artificial candles to add to the mood of a display.

5.4.5 Special Occasions

You may want to decorate your entire store to help customers get in the mood for special occasions. Halloween, Christmas, and Valentine's Day are three holidays that lend themselves well to splashy décor.

Plan your overall display theme at least a month in advance. Include plans for front window, in-store displays, the sales desk and other decorations.

No less than three weeks before the holiday, begin installing your special occasion décor. Start with the front window, then move on to in-store displays and decorations. Maintain a theme throughout — if you are going with a Victorian Christmas theme, for example, don't set up a shiny aluminum tree in the window.

Likewise, if you are going for a contemporary Valentine's look, don't cover every surface of the store with lace doilies. Instead, plan your design to create a unified look that will give customers a sense of unity and harmony. You can do this by:

- Gathering accessories and decorations that all reflect your chosen theme

- Building accessories that you need but don't have

- Building a theme around accessories you already have on hand (if you have a lot of antique furniture available, for example, you could do an "old-fashioned Christmas" theme)

Christmas Trees

Christmas trees have evolved in the past few hundred years from a few sprigs of evergreen on doors or in houses to fully-decorated extravaganzas. There are as many Christmas tree themes as there are people to decorate them, but it is appropriate for a flower shop to focus on a floral theme for the trees in its display area. Floral theme tree decoration ideas:

- Tiny poinsettias in pots

- Hydrangea blossoms, dried and painted gold or silver, or left natural

- Red roses in water tubes

- Garlands of flower petals made by stringing half-dried petals with a needle and thread

- Pomanders of potpourri made by spraying Styrofoam spheres with floral adhesive and rolling them in potpourri

- Ribbons tied in tiny bows

- Dried flowers glued onto branches

- Ornaments for sale in the store, used liberally on the tree (customers are able to "shop" from the tree)

Florists usually use artificial trees for holiday décor, as they must be on display for a month or more.

Installing Christmas Trees

Here are the steps you should follow to set up a Christmas tree display in your store:

1. Choose where the tree will be displayed.

2. Set it up fully.

3. Inspect it to ensure all branches are in good condition.

4. Starting at the top, unwind a string of lights, tucking it around the trunk and out along each branch. A good ratio is to use one string of lights per foot of tree height.

5. If you are using garlands, start at the bottom, at the back of the tree. Unwind the garland into swags, or wide "U" shapes, between prominent branches. Work back and forth until you reach the top.

6. Add fillers. These can be fruit, bunches of tulle fabric, big ribbon bows, hydrangea blossoms, artificial poinsettia blossoms,or even large ornaments, and are tucked in close to the trunk to add depth.

7. Add ornaments. Forty ornaments per foot of tree height allows for a full look, but this is where your own design sense comes into play. Put the larger ornaments closer to the trunk, and the smaller ones further out on the branches.

Many florists will have more than one tree on display during the holidays. Theme trees are best for large groupings. Themes can be as simple as a single color of ornaments and lights, or can focus on all one type of decoration, such as angels, teddy bears, Santas, fruit or kitchenwares.

5.4.6 Shop Maintenance

Now that you have your own store, learning how to take care of the shop is essential. A clean store attracts customers; plus, an organized store is able to meet deadlines and serve customers in a timely and calm fashion. Taking care of the flowers and plants ensures that your supplies will remain fresher longer, creating happy customers and saving you money.

Shop maintenance can be divided into a number of categories and actual areas within the physical confines of the shop, but one thing is certain: There is some type of shop maintenance to be done virtually every day. Windows and counters must be kept clean. Plants must be watered and maintained, flowers need to be groomed, giftware arranged, and the whole store kept clean and tidy.

The Importance of Cleaning Up

When your mother told you to tidy up your room before you went to bed, she was following a sound principle. No matter what your personal comfort level is with regards to cleanliness, order and general tidiness, it is essential that flower shops be kept clean and tidy. Why? Because a clean store means a healthy environment that helps flowers and plants last longer.

The old maxim of "a place for everything and everything in its place" makes a lot of sense – and saves a lot of time – when it's 11:00 a.m. and you're filling ten orders that must be delivered by noon. If you can't find your knife, and that nice bunch of lilies you were going to use is being squashed under a bundle of greens, you'll lose time and product. And both of those cost money.

Fortunately, a little organizing goes a long way. And a little cleaning whenever there's a spare moment helps your organizing stay organized. Here are some of the messy trouble spots:

Counters

Counters should be cleared as needed. Designing makes for a lot of leaves, stem ends and petals tossed here and there, and it is important to clear these off regularly in order to have a clean workspace.

Floors

Floors, especially in the workroom or design area, inevitably get covered in leaves, stems, dirt, bits of ribbon and other garbage. They should be swept at least twice a day (and more during busy times) to remove these potentially slippery and therefore hazardous materials. Floors in your sales area should be kept free of hazards – electrical cords, puddles from spilled buckets or watering cans, loose carpet or flooring, slippery plant material – in order to ensure customer safety.

Garbage Bins

Garbage bins should be emptied daily, or more often if needed. Most retail spaces will have an outdoor dumpster or other receptacle into which trash may be emptied. Some florists choose to compost their plant material, and only dispose of non-combustible items. This can reduce the amount of waste going to landfills or other facilities, but the stems and leaves of flowers are often not healthy to include in compost, as they may contain pesticide residues.

Flower Care

As discussed in the section on individual flower processing, it is important to regularly maintain the flowers in your stock. Flowers should be stored in buckets or vases filled with water and floral preservative. They should be re-cut and groomed to remove any blemished petals at least once every three days, or more often as needed for particular varieties. When re-cutting, empty the old water down a drain and scrub the bucket or vase with hot water and a scrubbing brush. Rinse and refill with lukewarm water and a fresh dose of floral preservative.

Buckets should be scrubbed clean with a mild bleach solution at least once a week. Filler flowers and greens should be re-cut and placed in fresh lukewarm water with clean buckets at least once a week, or more often if the water gets smelly. This is because the organic compounds (such as ethylene gas) that are created by rotting plant material can cause cut flowers to wilt prematurely.

Plant Care

Regular maintenance of green and flowering plants is essential for keeping them in saleable condition. Set up a schedule for plant care, perhaps twice a week. On these days, check all the plants in your stock for the following:

- *Moisture:* Test by pressing a finger into the soil at the top of the pot. If no soil sticks to your finger, add water from a watering can.

- *Brown or damaged leaves:* If there are brown edges, brown leaves or otherwise damaged leaves, remove them. If this means the plant will be significantly reduced by doing so, remove the plant from the sales floor.

- *Spent blooms*: Flowering plants will bloom longer if they are "deadheaded" — that is, have their finished blooms removed as soon as they are no longer at their peak. Remove them by cutting them off with a pair of scissors or secateurs, or by hand. Short-stemmed flowers like azaleas should be removed at the calyx, while long-stemmed flowers, like cyclamen or gerbera daisies, should be cut off the base of the flower stem.

- *Insects*: If you notice any small red spots, white patchy spots, grey powder, tiny webs, small green bugs or small flies around a plant, remove that plant from the sales floor immediately. Treat it with insecticidal soap (one popular brand is made by Safer) according to the manufacturer's instructions, and keep it quarantined away from other plants until it is free of insects. Monitor other plants for similar symptoms. If you have a wide-scale insect problem, you may need to take more drastic measures, such as quarantining and spraying all your plants with insecticidal soap.

Plant Stress Prevention

Before you have to face an outbreak of insects or a wide scale quarantine of your plants, prevent it. Regularly remove dead leaves. Make sure plants aren't stressed by too much heat or cold (don't keep your plant stock in an extremely sunny window or by a door that opens frequently to the outside, causing cold drafts to hit the plants). Regularly water and maintain them.

Feed your plants with commercially available fertilizers designed for green or flowering plants. There are several types — some come in tablets, others in spikes, and still others are drops you add to the water. What you choose depends largely on your own preference.

Once every week or two, place all small plants in wide saucers filled with water and let them soak up water from the bottom. If this is not practical, try to add water until the water runs from the bottom of the plant pots. Let plants thoroughly soak and dry out between watering — it is better than keeping them evenly soggy or watering them with just a few drops every day.

Display Maintenance

In-store displays need to be changed once every week or two to keep them fresh and interesting for repeat customers. Window displays may be changed every two to three weeks, but the more often they are changed, the more interest they will generate.

In addition to changing the items that are on display, you should check to make sure the display tables or stands are clean and in good condition. Glass should be cleaned, and dust and fallen leaves or petals should be removed. Vacuum or sweep the floor of the display area if needed. Make sure all lights are working, and if not, replace them.

Tool and Supply Upkeep

You won't need to sharpen your knives every day, or even every week, but if you notice they're getting dull, it's time to take them to a knife sharpening shop or sharpen them yourself. If you choose to sharpen them yourself, you can buy a whetstone or other knife-sharpening device to make this task quick and easy. The same goes for scissors, secateurs and other cutting implements. If they're dull, you're more likely to get injured.

Cash register tape and credit/debit card machine tape should be replaced as needed. When you start to see stripes or streaks of colored ink on the tape, that means the roll is about to run out. Follow the machine's instruction book to replace these items.

5.5 Wholesalers and Suppliers

Customers will inevitably ask you, "Where do all these beautiful flowers and products come from?" The answer you give will probably be as varied as the products themselves.

Tropical flowers are grown in Hawaii, Mexico, California, South America and parts of Asia and Africa. Dutch flowers like tulips, lilies, irises and daffodils are grown in Holland, of course, and in greenhouses all over North America. Roses and carnations may come from Colombia, Ecuador, Australia, Chile, California, or the greenhouse right around the corner.

Giftware is made all over the world, often in countries like China, Taiwan and Mexico. And how all these lovely things get to you and your customers is the story of the wholesale florist industry, which deserves an entire book of its own.

Basically, the producer or grower makes the product, which is then shipped to a central distribution port. Miami, Florida, is the hub of most floral imports in North America. Allsmeer, Holland, is where most flowers go before being shipped on to European countries. From these central hubs, the flowers are shipped to distributors in large cities throughout North America and Europe. The distributors sell the flowers to wholesalers and sometimes individual florists, usually at a Dutch-style auction where the flowers are bought in large lots.

From there, the wholesalers will take the flowers to their warehouses, sort them to fill individual flower shops' orders, and deliver them to the flower shops. It can take as long as a week to 10 days from when the flowers are cut in South America to when they arrive at a flower shop in North America.

Most flower shops have an ongoing relationship with one or more wholesale florists, usually the ones that serve their city or geographic area. There are hard goods (vases, floral foam, artificial flowers, etc.) wholesalers, flower wholesalers, Internet wholesalers, auction wholesalers, and growers.

To buy from wholesalers, you need to prove that you are in business and intend to re-sell the products to retail customers. You'll need to provide your flower shop's business license, business card or checks, sales tax number, and GST number (if in Canada).

Wholesale prices are lower than retail prices, but you must buy larger quantities of each item. You might buy a dozen vases of one variety at $5 each, and re-sell each one for $10 each. A typical mark-up (the price difference between the price you pay at the wholesaler, and the price your customer pays you) is 100 percent for hard goods like vases, containers and giftware, and 200 to 400 percent for perishables like plants and flowers.

Buying supplies is where much of your start-up capital will be spent, and you should expect to spend at least $5,000 to $7,000. Knowing how much to order is a tricky business, however. Your wholesaler representative will be your best help, as they will be able to suggest the amount of supplies that other florists go through in a typical week. Start small. It's better to make frequent trips to the wholesalers for small amounts than to over-invest in supplies (especially perishables like fresh flowers) to begin with.

5.5.1 Types of Wholesalers and Producers

Growers

Growers are the original producers. They grow enormous quantities of flowers, plants and greens for sale to floral wholesalers, or directly to florists. They may grow their wares in pots or soil-less hydroponic solutions in vast greenhouses (some covering many acres), or in the ground in fields. They harvest their flowers before they're completely in bloom to ensure the flowers will endure shipment and last as long as possible once they reach the consumer.

Growers may be small-scale greenhouses located in agricultural areas, or they may be enormous companies that own growing facilities in countries like Colombia and Ecuador. For example, Americaflor Ltd., the floral branch of Dole, is the largest flower growing company in the world, and most of the carnations sold in North America come from its fields in Central America.

Regardless of where they're located, most growers have a processing facility where flowers are sorted by color and variety, and bundled into bunches of 10 or 20 or more stems. These bunches are packed either in large buckets of water (called "wet-ship") or in boxes ("dry-ship") for shipment, then stored in large, room-sized coolers before being shipped off by truck or plane.

TIP: Depending on where the grower is located, and where the flower shop is located, it could be one day to a week between when the flowers were cut and when they are processed by the florist. For this reason, it is important to process and condition flowers immediately upon their arrival at the flower shop.

It is possible to buy direct from local or smaller-scale growers, but some require a bulk or minimum order that may be larger than you need. If so, you can co-operate with another flower shop to share the shipment (to both of your advantage), or save such large orders only for busy times. You may need to pay a shipment fee for orders sent directly from a grower. The cost will be based on shipping method (by air or surface) and weight.

A Note About Pesticides

Some consumers, and therefore some florists, are concerned about the use of pesticides and herbicides in the commercial flower growing industry. There are regulations in the United States and Canada as to what chemicals may be used in commercial greenhouses, and these chemicals must be applied according to strict procedures.

However, other countries are not bound by these regulations. Flower growers in other countries, especially in warmer climates, are faced with numerous tropical insects that like eating their crops. To combat these pests, growers use chemicals that may be of concern, whether for their potential effect on consumers, on greenhouse workers, or on the groundwater in the immediate area of the growing facility.

Florists wanting to assure their customers that their flowers are pesticide-free may choose only to buy flowers produced in certified pesticide-free facilities. (Some growers use natural pest-killers, like ladybugs or organic substances that inhibit insect growth.) Or they may opt to use locally grown flowers only, to ensure that their flowers were grown under their state or province's pesticide rules. The advantage to doing so is they are able to assure their customers that no pesticides were used on their flowers. The disadvantage is they may not be able to get all types of flowers at all times of year.

Mom and Pop Growers

Small-scale, or "mom and pop," growers often specialize in one or two varieties of flowers, and sell their wares only in-season, often directly to flower shops. You can find these types of growers through local agricultural organizations, or they'll come to you when they've got product to sell.

Harvester

Harvesters or pickers collect plant material in the wild. For example, individuals or companies may harvest products like salal or cedar in privately owned parts of rainforests in the Pacific Northwest. They may sell directly to flower shops or wholesalers, or to brokers who ship their products to other wholesalers and distributors.

Wholesalers

Fresh flower wholesalers usually buy their materials from large distributors or through flower auctions, and resell them to individual flower shops. They have large warehouses with enormous coolers to keep flowers fresh, and may receive new shipments daily or several times a week. They sell flowers by the bundle (usually ten, twenty or twenty-four stems), and allow florists to choose particular colors or varieties to meet their needs.

Many fresh flower wholesalers also stock green and flowering plants they've purchased from growers or plant nurseries. These are sold in plastic pots grouped together in flats — low cardboard or plastic boxes that hold six, twelve, or eighteen individual plants. Plants are measured and priced by their pot diameter: two-inch, four-inch, six-inch, etc.

For example, a flat of twelve green plants in four-inch pots might sell for $12, or $1 per plant. The florist would then price the plants between $2 and $3 each. Wholesalers also sell larger plants, in 18-inch or 24-inch pots, wrapped in long paper or plastic sleeves to protect their leaves. These are usually sold individually.

You can quickly and easily find a fresh flower wholesaler in your area by checking your local Yellow Pages under "Florists — Wholesale." You can also visit the Floral and Gift Market website at **www. fgmarket.com/Fresh-Flowers** or **www.fgmarket.com/Fresh-Greens-and-Foliage**. The site provides a searchable database of hundreds of North American flower and greenery wholesalers and growers.

Hard goods wholesalers specialize in non-perishable products like vases, containers, giftware and supplies. Some have a central warehouse where individual florists can go to choose the products they need, while others publish a print or online catalog of their wares for order by mail, phone or Internet.

In the United States, Best Buy Floral is one hard goods wholesaler that offers a wide range of products. You can check their website out at **www.bestbuyfloral.com**.

WaterDale Inc. is one of the largest hard goods wholesalers in North America, serving florists across Canada. Visit their website at **www. waterdale.com** and check out their online catalog.

5.5.2 Choosing Materials

When you go to a wholesaler, or are visited by a wholesaler's truck (as sometimes happens), it's easy to be overwhelmed by the vast number of choices. Staying focused on what you need, and what you think you can sell, will help you avoid costly overbuying.

Keep a List

What are you running low on? What kinds of flowers are selling well right now? Are there any particular flowers you need for special orders or weddings? These are the items that should be on your list.

Picking Flowers

You are choosing the best materials to work with and to sell to your customers. At the wholesaler, it pays to be picky.

Concentrate on choosing one type of flower at a time — get the roses you need, then the carnations, then the mums, and so on. Finish up with any special requests that you need to fulfill. Wholesalers will allow you to pick and choose the bundles of flowers that you'll be buying, so take advantage of this. Always choose the firmest, largest, most flawless flowers.

Check the buds. Buds that are still closed but show some color are preferable to ones that are so tightly closed that they are entirely green, or ones that are wide open.

Check the leaves. They should be healthy and sturdy looking — this indicates a well-hydrated flower.

Check the water in the transport buckets, if they're used. It shouldn't be stinky or discolored. If it is, move on to another bucket.

Choose the biggest, most symmetrical plants. Green plants should have strong, sturdy leaves with no yellowing or browning, and definitely no evidence of insects or injury. Choose flowering plants with the largest number of buds, and unless you have a special request or display planned, keep in mind that it is better to have a selection of colors of one variety of flowering plant than numerous plants of the same color.

Hard Goods

With hard goods, you will probably have a running shopping list of items you need. Because you will need to pay for shipping costs on any hard goods bought online or over the phone, it makes sense to limit your orders until you have a good number of items on your list.

Ordering once or twice a month makes more sense than ordering numerous small things as you run out. Better yet, make sure you don't run out — keep track of what supplies have run below the halfway point and add them to your ongoing shopping list for replacement before they're all used up.

Hard goods are less likely to be flawed than perishables, but there is still the chance that they could be damaged in shipment. If this happens, let the wholesaler know, and they will usually replace the item without charge.

5.5.3 Advance Orders

If you've never ordered flowers for a special holiday before, you'll find it surprising when your regular wholesalers start sending you price lists as much as six to eight weeks beforehand. "How do I know how many poinsettias to order?" you might think. "It's barely Halloween!"

But there are advantages to placing advance orders, and the main one is that you'll be getting a guaranteed price for the items you need. If a wholesaler offers poinsettias at $5 per plant in advance orders, for example, you can order as many as you think you'll need at that price, and know how much you'll be paying. If you don't order them in advance, you could end up paying as much as two or three times that amount when the holiday comes around and poinsettias are in high demand.

The first time you place an order for a holiday, it can be a bit of a guessing game. If you advance order 48 poinsettia plants, for example, and only sell 10 of them, you'll be stuck with 38 plants that nobody wants after the holidays. Conversely, if you order 48 plants and end up with orders for 80 of them, you'll have to buy the extra 32 at the higher market rates closer to the holiday (thereby making less profit) or miss out on some sales.

There's no magic formula for the first time around. Go with what you think is reasonable, err on the side of caution, and keep close records of what sells and what is left over afterwards. At the very least, keep copies of your wholesale invoices and sales records. You can also spend some time with a pen and notebook on the day after the holiday, recording the items that are left over.

Once you've gone through a year of florist holidays, you can begin to hone your advance ordering skills. When it comes time to place your advance order, look at your carefully recorded notes from the last year. Plan on selling the same amount this year, unless there are unusual circumstances.

Wire Service Promotions

Wire services such as FTD and Teleflora develop, market, and promote special bouquets for florist holidays. They often come in unusual or keepsake containers which are ordered through the wire services' member service centers.

These are called branded or codified arrangements, and all members of a wire service are expected to stock at least one, if not all, of these holiday specials. They are ordered by the case (24) or half-case (12), and are designed to look the same regardless of where they are produced — so that a customer in New York can see a copy of the exact arrangement that their friend in Seattle will receive.

When the wire services promote these special arrangements to florists, they include the recipe — the number of stems of each type of flower needed for the arrangement. By calculating the number of special arrangements you plan to sell, and multiplying that by the number of each type of flower the arrangements will need, you'll get a base number of each type of flower to order.

For example, say a Christmas arrangement recipe calls for three red carnations, four stems of white chrysanthemum, a cluster of red holiday balls and a sprig of holly, plus three stems of cedar and two stems of pine. Let's say you have to fill 12 containers with this arrangement. That means you can plan on ordering at least 36 carnations, 48 stems of white mums, 12 clusters of red holiday balls, 12 sprigs of holly, 36 stems of cedar and 24 stems of pine.

Of course, that's a bare minimum. You'll no doubt use that many flowers, but you also need to account for flowers that break, that aren't in satisfactory condition, and that are otherwise unusable. So plan on at least one and one-half times the amount you think you'll need.

Leftovers can always be used in other arrangements or made into cash-and-carry bouquets. But if you don't have enough red carnations to start with, you'll find that the laws of supply and demand ensure they're much more expensive come holiday time. In the week before major florist holidays at the flower auction, lots of buyers bidding on the small number of flowers that haven't been sold in advance ensures that market prices will remain high.

Unusual circumstances, such as weather, a holiday falling on a Sunday, and other unforeseen factors can affect the number of flowers you sell. It's a volatile business, but that's part of the fun.

5.5.4 Standing Orders

Because flower prices can change from week to week and even day to day, one way you can get the same price on the same flowers week after week is to have a standing order with your regular wholesaler.

By placing one order for the same product every week, you can ensure the same price is guaranteed year-round, even at holidays (unless the wholesaler lets you know otherwise, in advance). The advantage is that you know you'll be getting at least your standard two bundles of roses at their year-round price, even when it's Valentine's Day. And you can count on having certain flowers in stock at all times.

The disadvantage, of course, is that you have the same flowers at all times, and so even if you don't sell a single yellow rose in a week, you'll be getting another two bundles of yellow roses when your standing order comes in. (And then, of course, it's time for a sale on yellow roses so that you can make some money on them before they wilt.)

5.5.5 Coordination with Wholesalers for Special Orders

Every wholesaler will have an office contact person for florists to call with special requests, and it is also this person's job to inform florists of what's available and what's on special that week.

If you have a special request for a particular product, such as white tulips for a September wedding, when tulips aren't ordinarily available, the wholesale contact will find out the best price for the special request. Tulips may be available in September, for example, but they'll need to be shipped in from Holland and will cost three times as much as they would in March when they're available from a local grower.

Your wholesale contact person is there to make sure your shop's special requests are met and that any standing orders are fulfilled. In addition, they keep records of previous years' sales for each flower shop they serve so they can help with purchasing decisions for the current year.

5.5.6 Invoices

Whether you pick up your flower order from a wholesaler's warehouse, choose it from their truck, or have it delivered to your shop, the wholesaler will give you an invoice to go along with your order.

You need the invoice for two reasons. First, it ensures that you have received and accounted for everything you ordered. Second, it helps you determine your own flower shop's price structure for the items you're about to make available for sale. See section 5.7 for advice on setting prices.

Smaller floral supply companies want you to pay your invoice immediately, while larger companies bill flower shops by sending a monthly statement. It is the shop's responsibility to pay the wholesaler the amount listed on the statement before the end of the next month, or by another date determined by the flower shop and wholesaler (often 15 or 30 days). If there have been any returns to the wholesaler, these amounts are credited on the monthly statement.

5.5.7 Returns to Wholesalers

If the flowers or plants you have received from a wholesaler are not satisfactory, it is possible to return them. Some wholesalers take returns within 24 hours; others don't take them at all. When you are initially starting a relationship with a wholesaler, it is essential to ask about their returns policy.

Hard goods wholesalers will usually accept returns on undamaged goods, but may charge a restocking fee (ten percent of the wholesale cost is not uncommon). For damaged goods, they may credit you for the amount of the item on your next statement, or give you a replacement item for free.

Returns are just part of doing business with perishable products. Expect your wholesaler to accommodate you, just as your customers expect you to accommodate them.

5.6 Finding Help

You're doing well at your business, and the money's finally starting to roll in. Congratulations! You're on your way to success. Unfortunately, you're also on your way to burnout — you haven't had a vacation in more than a year! It's time to look at hiring some staff.

Remember in chapter 4 when we discussed finding a job in a flower shop? Well, the shoe is on the other foot now, and you are the owner or manager looking for the ideal employee to help you run your shop smoothly, efficiently and profitably.

What to look for? Who to hire? What to pay? How to get the perfect person in place? While most of these questions can be answered by referring to section 4.5.1, there are some things you'll need to consider as an employer. How many staff members do you need? Should they work part-time or full-time? What are your responsibilities as an employer? Read on to find out.

5.6.1 Determining Your Staff Requirements

There are several levels on which you can hire staff members, and each has its advantages and disadvantages.

Full-time staff members provide stability, a sense of loyalty, and a consistency that you can't achieve with part-timers and casual help. You make a significant investment with full-time staff members, in that you will be responsible for training them, possibly providing benefits for them and in paying income taxes and other necessary costs for them. You might want to pay them a salary, which covers all their wages, regardless of how many hours they work, or pay them an hourly wage, which must be kept track of to ensure fairness on both sides.

Part-time staff members (those who work less than 24 hours per week) are less costly, in that you do not typically cover their benefits. They are also more flexible, in that they may be scheduled to work just in your store's busiest times, such as weekday mornings. They might also be available for more full-time work at holidays, and as such provide a good source of already-trained workers for the busiest times of the year.

Often, students, seniors, and stay-at-home parents enjoy part-time work, as it allows them some income while not demanding as much of them as a full-time job might. However, you may find that they require more training, as they are less likely to have pursued a career in the floral industry.

Casual or on-call staff can also fill an important niche in your business. A talented designer who is working for a garden center or another non-competing business might be interested in earning extra money when your store is busiest, or when you need a vacation. Also, a family member might want to earn extra money at holidays by filling in at the store or making deliveries.

Determining the appropriate level of staffing that you need should be simple, and it is — especially if you remember that it's always easiest to start small. Begin by hiring someone on a casual or part-time basis, with the understanding that the work might turn to full-time if it seems to be needed. It is better to start someone off with fewer hours and add more later than to start someone full-time and then discover that you can't afford to employ them any more.

Keep in mind that the more experienced a worker is, the higher wage they are able to command. If you find someone you want to hire, but they ask for a higher wage than you are prepared to pay, you must negotiate with them to find a pay rate and benefits package that is mutually agreeable — or look for someone else.

5.6.2 Hiring Appropriately

The florist business, as you now know, requires a wide range of skills and talents. Finding a staff member who is perfectly suited (and as good at the business as you are!) is a task that will be easier if you don't set out to look for perfection, but rather, keep your mind open to the possibilities in each candidate.

Keep in mind that even though someone might not have worked at a flower shop before, they could still be a good candidate for a position in your shop. Look for retail experience, or other experience in customer service. Former waiters and waitresses usually have a good background in dealing with customer needs, and in selling products that are even more temporary than flowers.

Former nurses and teachers are also good potential candidates, as they have experience in helping people and in educating them about unfamiliar things. Anyone who has worked in a garden center or for a landscaper will have a good understanding of plant care and will probably have a good knowledge of plant varieties.

A good floral designer will probably have worked in a flower shop before or will have studied floral design at a college or trade school. But you can also teach floral design to someone who has a background in art, crafts, or any other field that requires them to work with their hands.

Ideally, you want someone who is a willing worker, someone who can participate in your shop as a member of a team. Especially if you have a small shop and only one or two workers, you will need to hire someone that you can get along with and enjoy working with on a daily basis. In this case, attitude counts for more than experience — after all, it's your shop, and you will want to enjoy the company of your co-workers/staff members.

For an interesting article about hiring staff, visit **www.myteleflora. com/DesignEducation/Index.aspx**, click on "Floral Arcticles," and read "A Staff to Lean On."

5.6.3 Paying Staff

Naturally, you'll need to pay your staff. Ask your accountant to set up a payroll for your store and maintain it for you. That way, you can be assured that you are making the correct amount of deductions for taxes and other benefits.

Employees are paid either weekly, bi-weekly, or on the 15th and last day of each month. You should have sufficient funds in your business checking account to ensure payroll checks will be covered. You may offer employees direct deposit paychecks (in which their pay is deposited into their bank accounts) or regular checks (which they may take to the bank themselves).

See the websites listed at the beginning of section 5.2 for more information on payroll and payroll taxes.

5.6.4 Meeting Staff Needs

As an employer, you have certain obligations to your staff. You will need to pay their wages. You will need to pay taxes on their behalf and contribute to worker's compensation, pension plans, and insurance plans. You will need to allow for vacation time off, as required by your state, provincial, or national employment standards.

You also have an obligation to be fair, consistent, and open as an employer. If you have more than one staff member, you should treat them all equally, without affording special privileges to one employee that you don't allow to the others.

You have a responsibility to give feedback to your staff, both positive and negative. If they are doing a good job, tell them so. If they are doing something you don't like or don't want them to do, explain what they are doing, why it isn't desirable, and how you would prefer they do it. By keeping these kinds of discussions neutral and in the spirit of smooth store operations, you will be able to maintain a positive working relationship with your staff members.

Motivating your staff to sell more, produce more, and take on new responsibilities is an ongoing part of being a flower shop owner and manager. You can do so by providing opportunities for growth. Ask them to make the big wedding bouquet this time, or arrange for them to attend a business motivation seminar during work hours.

You can also treat interesting additional responsibilities, such as installing the front window display, as a reward for good work. Or you can provide cash or time bonuses for work well done, but these aren't always the most effective method of motivation. Sometimes a well-placed compliment actually means more than anything else you can give, because it shows you care about your staff members as individuals.

For a good article about employee motivation and bonuses, go to **www.myteleflora.com/DesignEducation/Index.aspx**, click on "Floral Articles," and search for "When Money Isn't Everything."

5.7 Setting Prices

There are several pricing structures at work in any flower shop:

- Pricing for perishable goods, which is meant to cover costs for easily damaged, fragile goods

- Pricing for hard goods; that is, the materials and containers that are not likely to go bad or be easily damaged (like vases or baskets).

- Price of labor, which varies from shop to shop and arrangement to arrangement. It is typically factored as a percentage of the total retail cost of the materials (flowers, greens and hard goods).

- Occasional charges for rental, such as with large flower-covered archways used in weddings. A client would rent the archway structure itself, and pay for the cost of the flowers, labor, and setup.

Following is an explanation of the basic pricing structures.

5.7.1 Mark-Up of Perishable and Hard Goods

Florists sell flowers, which are fragile and perishable. As such, they need to cover the costs of these items quickly to ensure a profit, even if something happens to damage the perishable goods. For this reason, perishable goods are priced differently than non-perishables or giftware.

The mark-up is the amount by which a price is increased over the wholesale cost (the price the florist pays their supplier) in order to determine its retail price (the price the customer pays the florist).

Basic Rules for Mark-Up

Below are the basic rules of thumb for marking up the different items you will sell in your shop:

- *Fresh flowers:* Mark up by 200 to 400 percent, depending on the flower and relative availability. A flower that cost $1 wholesale would therefore sell for $3 to $5 retail.

- *Plants:* Mark up by 200 to 300 percent. A plant costing $10 wholesale would be sold for $30 to $40 retail.

- *Giftware:* Mark up by 100 to 150 percent. An item costing $10 wholesale would be sold for $20 to $25 retail.

- *Artificial flowers:* Mark up by 200 percent over wholesale cost. A stem of artificial flowers that cost $1 wholesale would sell for $3 retail.

TIP: It is customary for giftware and plants to be sold at a price that is a few pennies below the full amount. For example, instead of $10, an item would go for $9.99 (or $9.98, or $9.95). Which amount you choose isn't as important as consistently using the same ending for all items in your store — don't mix .99 and .95 endings.

5.7.2 Mark-Up for Labor

Most arrangements are priced by adding up the retail cost of the materials used, then dividing by a percentage to determine the total price of the arrangement including labor. Thirty percent is a common percentage for labor costs in North America, though some shops charge more or less.

To determine the price of an arrangement with a 30 percent labor cost, first add up the cost of your materials at their retail price. Then, multiply that amount by .3 and add it to the original amount. That will give you the total retail price of the arrangement.

For example, if the cost of your materials is $20, multiply that by .3 to get $6, then add it to the original $20 to get $26. You can then round to the nearest .99, which would make the total price $25.99.

Because wedding arrangements and corsages both tend to be more labor-intensive, it is customary to charge as much as 50 percent for labor. The same formula can be used, substituting .5 for 0.3. Therefore, you factor the cost by adding up the retail cost of the materials, multiplying that amount by .5, and adding back the original figure to equal the total price.

For simpler arrangements that still require some work, such as basket gardens or cash-and-carry bouquets, it is more common to charge about 20 percent for labor.

5.7.3 Rental Costs

Most clients who want archways, candelabra, or other special, large structures adorned with flowers will not want to purchase them. In these cases, your shop may rent these items, typically for a percentage of the items' retail cost.

If an archway costs $500 to purchase, for example, you might choose to rent it to a client for use on their wedding day for 10 percent of its retail cost, or $50. In this case, they would pay a deposit or give a credit card number to guarantee the rental, and of course pay for the flowers adorning the archway.

5.7.4 Setup Fees

Occasionally you will be required to set up large arrangements for clients. You need to determine what you will charge for these cases. Your rates should be inclusive of setup time, fuel costs to get to the location where the setup will take place, and the number of people required.

A good starting point is to charge $50 per hour, per person required for the setup. But you may choose to charge more or less, depending on the complexity of the job. Placing an arrangement at the head of a table is less complicated than installing a flower-covered archway, so you could feel comfortable charging more (perhaps $75 an hour) for the latter.

5.7.5 Reducing Prices for Less-Than-Fresh Flowers

Rather than cut the price of flowers to sell them quickly when the blooms are past their prime, it is preferable to sell only the best, most perfect flowers, and dispose of the ones that are no longer perfect.

There are two reasons why. First, if you sell flowers at a lower price, customers will get accustomed to that price and be reluctant to buy flowers at their full value. Second, customers will be trained to believe that flowers only last a few short days, and will be reluctant to buy them as often, believing them not to be of lasting value.

It is far preferable to throw out slightly less-than-fresh flowers, or, if you prefer, to surprise regular customers with a take-home gift (be sure to let them know they are getting "leftovers"). You can also give them to staff, take them home yourself, or donate them to hospitals, nursing homes, or other organizations that might enjoy the flowers for the few more days they will last.

With regards to hard goods, especially as seasonal merchandise, you can discount your pre-holiday prices by as much as 40 percent and still make a profit. Customers will like it, and you will still make a small amount of money. Or, you can simply put your seasonal merchandise into storage, and bring it out again to sell at full price again next year.

5.7.6 Sample Price List

Prices for flowers and even hard goods vary according to region, season, supply and demand. A rose in Miami, Florida, in summer will not be the same price as a rose in Saint Paul, Minnesota, in winter. As such, this price list is given merely as an example.

Sample Price List

Fresh Flowers

Item:	*Cost:*
Roses	$ 5.00 /stem;
	$ 50.00 /dozen
Carnations	$ 1.50 /stem;
	$ 20.00 /dozen
Tulips	$ 2.98 /bunch of 5
Daffodils	$ 2.98 /bunch of 5
Iris	$ 2.98 /bunch of 3
Gerbera Daisies	$ 1.95 /stem
Bird of Paradise	$ 7.00 /stem
Oriental lilies	$ 6.50 /stem
Tiger lilies	$ 2.50 /stem
Gladiolus	$ 2.50 /stem
Chrysanthemums	$ 2.00 /stem
Anthuriums	$ 3.95 /stem
Sunflower	$ 5.00 /stem
Liatris	$ 1.50 /stem
Alstroemeria	$ 2.50 /stem
Freesia	$ 2.00 /stem
Nerine	$ 1.50 /stem
Stocks	$ 2.50 /stem
Snapdragons	$ 2.50 /stem

Hard Goods

Item:	*Cost:*
"PB-100" plastic bowl	$ 1.00
"PB-101" double plastic tray	$ 2.00
6-inch wicker basket	$ 4.00
10-inch wicker basket	$ 6.00
Floral foam	$ 1.50 /brick
Glass bud vase	$ 3.00
Glass 6-inch tall vase	$ 4.00
Glass 8-inch tall vase	$ 6.00
Glass 10-inch tall vase	$ 10.00
Specialty vases	$ 18.00 – $ 26.00

Plants

Item:	Cost:
Green tropical plants	
4-inch pots	$ 3.00 – $ 5.00
6-inch pots	$ 9.00 – $ 15.00
8-inch pots	$ 15.00 – $ 30.00
10-inch pots	$ 40.00 – $ 60.00
Cacti, 4-inch pot	$ 5.00 – $ 10.00
Flowering plants	
Azalea, 6- or 8-inch pot	$ 35.00 – $ 45.00
Begonia, 6-inch pot	$ 15.00 – $ 25.00
Chrysanthemum, 6-inch pot	$ 15.00 – $ 25.00
Gerbera, 6- or 8-inch pot	$ 15.00 – $ 30.00
Hydrangea, 6- or 8-inch pot	$ 25.00 – $ 40.00
Kalanchoe, 6-inch pot	$ 15.00 – $ 25.00
Lilies, 6-inch pot	$ 15.00 – $ 30.00
Zygocactus, 6-inch pot	$ 25.00 – $ 35.00

Other Items

Item:	Cost:
Balloons	
Latex	$ 1.50 each (w/ ribbon)
Mylar	$ 4.95 each (w/ ribbon)
Stuffed Toys	
Small	$ 7.00 – $ 10.00
Medium	$ 15.00 – $ 20.00
Large	$ 25.00 – $ 75.00
Candles	
Tapers (18" and longer)	$ 2.50 – $ 3.50
Pillars	$ 9.00 – $ 20.00
Cards	
Greeting cards	$ 3.00 – $ 4.50
Enclosure cards	Complimentary with purchase; 45 cents otherwise

The prices in the list appear courtesy of Daisy Chain Florists (**www. daisychainflorists.com**).

5.8 Delivery

A bouquet of flowers, delivered to a thrilled recipient, is one of the mainstay images of the floral industry. The ability to deliver flowers anywhere in the world is what FTD built an entire industry on (even styling their logo after Mercury, the winged messenger of the Roman gods), and delivery is a service every florist must offer in order to be a member of a wire service like FTD or Teleflora.

Customers expect florists to deliver flowers, pay for florists to deliver flowers, and depend on florists to deliver flowers. As a florist, it's up to you to make sure people get their flowers when and where they want them. There are several ways that can happen. You can deliver them yourself, or with an in-house driver whose duty it is to take deliveries where they should go. You can contract with a delivery service. Or you can use a combination of options, depending on your immediate and ongoing needs.

Delivery Fees

Most flower shops charge between $3 and $25 per delivery, depending on where the flowers are to be delivered (determined by mileage from the flower shop). A higher fee may be charged for out-of-area deliveries, priority deliveries, or after-hours deliveries. Whether or not a florist decides to provide special request delivery service depends on what type of delivery service they have readily available.

5.8.1 Types of Delivery Service

Determining your delivery needs is the first step in deciding what type of delivery service is best for your shop.

Are you working at a shop that sends out numerous small orders to one or two parts of town? Or do you send one or two orders far and wide each day? Your local geographic area will partly determine your delivery needs, too. A small town surrounded by rural homes will have different needs than a large city filled with apartment buildings.

You can determine your delivery needs by tracking, for 100 deliveries, the following statistics:

- Number of deliveries made per day, on average

- Areas most often served

- Other factors, such as same-day and evening delivery requests

Once you know how many deliveries you typically send, and where they go, you can look at small-scale and large-scale delivery options.

If you only have the occasional delivery, the smallest-scale option is to send it via taxi or courier or to have a staff member make deliveries in the company vehicle. Perhaps you have more deliveries going out than is feasible for one person to do in a day. Maybe the geographic area you must cover will require more driving and fuel expenses than is worthwhile. If this is the case, it makes more sense to use a contracted delivery service or delivery pool, or have a full-time staff member to make deliveries.

Types of Delivery Options

Here is a breakdown of the advantages and disadvantages of commonly used delivery options.

Taxi Companies

Instead of transporting passengers, taxi companies are also willing to transport objects such as flower arrangements. They may quote a price on pickup, based on the distance to be traveled, plus a base rate. That amount is paid in cash to the driver, on pickup of the delivery.

Advantages:	Available on-call, any time of day or night. Can take deliveries quickly and efficiently.
Disadvantages:	Drivers may not know how to transport flower arrangements safely. Can be expensive if the delivery is far away. Florist must pay cash up front. Signatures for delivery should be requested.

Courier Services

A courier service typically offers deliveries within a local area with little notice. Fees may vary depending on the weight or size of an order, and where it is being sent to, but are based on a per-delivery basis. They may be paid cash on pickup, or a florist may settle their courier accounts on a regular (weekly or monthly) basis.

Advantages:	Available on-call. Drivers tend to be aware of requirements of transporting flower arrangements. Drivers have a good knowledge of the delivery area. Will keep recipient's signature on file, and usually won't deliver an order unless recipient is there to sign for it.
Disadvantages:	Can be expensive. Not likely to be prepared for large numbers of deliveries (such as at holidays).

Delivery Pools

Drivers from participating flower shops bring all the day's deliveries to a central location and divide them all based on which part of the city each driver serves. Payment is typically made by a tag system, in which participating florists buy two-part tags in advance, and attach one to each outgoing delivery.

The driver who completes the delivery keeps the tag, and returns it to the pool coordinator, who pays them a portion of the initial fee for the tag and keeps a small portion (perhaps 20 percent) for their own expenses (like renting the warehouse where the pool drivers exchange their deliveries, for example).

Advantages:	Environmentally friendly, because each driver's vehicle covers their territory more efficiently. Effective way to provide more efficient service. Allows florists to maximize the work of hourly drivers.
Disadvantages:	Florists who deliver more orders than they send out may feel like they are subsidizing others. One pickup per day may be insufficient.

Contracted Delivery Services

An independent contractor or delivery company offers its delivery services, through one or more drivers, with its own vehicles. It usually picks up at regular intervals, and is paid per delivery. The drivers keep track of the deliveries made, and the florist pays the delivery company on a regular (weekly or monthly) basis.

Advantages:	Regularly scheduled daily pickup times. Specialized knowledge of how to handle floral arrangements. The delivery service is responsible for hiring its own drivers.
Disadvantages:	Paid per delivery, even if two items go to the same address (such as an apartment building or hospital). Not likely to take last-minute or special delivery orders. May have so many deliveries in a day they have to leave the arrangements at doorsteps. May follow prescribed routes, which could delay delivery.

In-House Delivery Services

An in-house delivery service means that one or more staff members are devoted to making deliveries, maintaining delivery vehicles and other shop maintenance as needed. Usually paid hourly ($7-$8 per hour is a typical rate).

Advantages:	As a member of the flower shop staff, the delivery driver is available at a moment's notice. Familiar with handling techniques. Paid an hourly rate. Can participate in a delivery pool.
Disadvantages:	Must be paid whether or not deliveries are being done. Store must maintain and insure one or more delivery vehicles.

5.8.2 Responsibilities of Delivery Service

A delivery service is responsible for:

• Delivering floral products in a timely, efficient way.

- Keeping complete records of all deliveries.

- Submitting invoices (bills for payment) on a regular basis to the flower shop contracting them.

- Having adequate drivers and capacity to deliver all arrangements they're given to deliver, no matter the season or occasion.

- Insuring, fueling and maintaining their own vans.

- Carrying hang tags to put on the doors of recipients who are not home, to indicate a delivery was attempted and to tell the recipient where their flowers can be found (i.e. left with a neighbor; on the back porch; in the garage; returned to the flower shop).

- Determining the appropriate place to leave flowers when a recipient is not home.

- Returning any arrangement damaged in transit to the flower shop for repair before delivering it to the recipient.

- Redelivering repaired arrangement at no extra charge.

If a delivery is not made and the driver is determined to be at fault, the driver's employer (the delivery company or the flower shop) must replace the flowers and ensure the recipient receives them.

If a delivery is not made because the flower shop is at fault (they've written the wrong address on the delivery label, for example), the flower shop must pay for another delivery fee.

5.8.3 Glossary of Delivery Terms

Delivery terms you should know:

Bad address   An address that can't be found, or is wrong.

Delivery fee   The amount charged the customer for delivery. Can be anywhere from $3 to $25 and up.

Delivery zone   A geographic area served by a delivery company.

Driver   The person driving the delivery vehicle; may also load the delivery vehicle and carry arrangements to the recipients' doors.

Fleet   A group of vehicles owned by one company, group or individual. May be painted to match, may display the store's logo, and is usually insured as part of a group, which allows for a slightly better rate.

Local deliveries   All floral products that go out of the shop to be delivered in a nearby geographic area.

Out-of-area deliveries   Deliveries that are not prepared by the flower shop or delivered by their drivers, but rather are transmitted to another flower shop for preparation and delivery.

Pickup   When a driver picks up arrangements for delivery.

Same-day cutoff   The time of day at which all orders for same-day delivery must be received.

Swamper   The person whose job is only to carry arrangements (from shop to vehicle, from vehicle to recipient).

Timed delivery   An order that must arrive at a certain time of day.

Tracking   The process of keeping track of where deliveries are at any given time.

Waybill   An invoice that is reproduced several times (usually by carbon copy) and used by the delivery or courier company to track the order, by the florist to keep track of billing, and by the customer as a receipt.

5.8.4 Responsibilities of In-House Drivers

If your store employs an in-house driver, they will be expected to deliver all the store's orders in a timely, efficient manner by prioritizing deliveries. If there are special requests for deliveries, such as the need to phone first, they will accommodate these requests in a polite way.

They will be responsible for maintaining the delivery vehicle, including fuel, oil, and taking it to the service station when needed. In addition, they will need to keep a thorough record of all deliveries made, and follow through on deliveries in cases where the recipient is not home or the address is wrong.

They should have a clean driving record, good driving habits, and a pleasant and cheerful manner.

About Uniforms

Uniforms are not absolutely essential, but in an era when people are concerned about the identity of strangers knocking at their door, there are some advantages to having all delivery drivers wear some kind of identifying clothing:

- Offers a professional appearance

- It's recognizable, to alleviate any recipient anxiety

- Creates visibility for your shop name and logo

- Encourages others to be more helpful to delivery drivers (for example, when asking for directions)

- Can be adapted for a seasonal theme – for example, tuxedos at Mother's Day and Valentine's Day, Santa hats at Christmas, bunny ears at Easter – to create a lasting impression.

A uniform can be as simple as a baseball cap, shirt or jacket with your shop's name and logo or the logo of a wire service, or as elaborate as a full suit in your shop's colors. Delivery services often ask their drivers to dress in a company shirt or jacket, and their vehicles are usually marked with the delivery service's name.

Think about how recognizable a UPS driver, in their brown uniform and truck, is to most people. When a UPS driver arrives, people are not afraid to open the door. This is because the company is clearly identified and recognizable.

In most cases, individual drivers are responsible for washing and pressing their uniforms, but the delivery company or flower shop purchases them for the drivers. If drivers do not wear some kind of identifying clothing, they should still be sure to have a clean, tidy appearance.

5.8.5 Delivery Vehicles

In a pinch, your own car may serve as a delivery vehicle, but this should not be the rule, as private car insurance does not permit this kind of commercial activity. If you have an in-house driver, you will also need an in-house delivery vehicle.

Panel vans or minivans, usually equipped with shelves or other means of stabilizing arrangements in transit, are the most commonly used because they offer the largest amount of cargo room. These vehicles are insured by the florist, and the insurance policy may have provisions for varying drivers, damage to contents, and third-party liability. It is important to insure delivery vehicles as commercial vehicles.

When choosing or considering a delivery vehicle, take into account the following:

- Fuel efficiency

- Size – is it big enough to meet your needs?

- Is it customizable, so you can install shelves or racks or other container holding devices?

- Is it air conditioned? If you are in a warm region, this is essential.

- Does it have adequate heating? If you are in a cold region, this is essential.

- What will the cost of insurance be?

- Does it require a special license to drive?

- Does it have all-weather tires? (May be regionally important.)

The Seminole Floral Delivery System is one way of ensuring arrangements are transported securely. Made up of interlocking plastic mats with holes and adjustable brackets, the Seminole system will hold any flower container and keep it from tipping over in your vehicle. You can find information at **www.seminoleds.com/main.html** or phone 800-638-3378.

5.9 Record Keeping and Financial Matters

5.9.1 Record Keeping

Depending on your flower shop's accounting and sales tracking methods, you may have all sales records recorded automatically by inventory control software (usually each item will be bar-coded and scanned in at the cash register), or you may need to complete a daily list of the items sold. If you do need to maintain a list, here are the things you will need to keep track of:

- Total amount of cash sales

- Total amount of sales paid with a check

- Total amount of debit card sales

- Total amount of credit card sales

- Total amount of billed sales

- Amount of outgoing wire service orders

- Amount of delivery fees charged to in-store customers

- Amount of cut flower sales

- Amount of plant sales

- Amount of arrangement sales

- Amount of giftware sales

- Amount of state or provincial sales tax charged

- Amount of GST charged (if in Canada)

- Amount of payouts from the till (i.e. for petty cash purchases, cash on pickup deliveries or other store-related purposes)

After counting out a float – a small amount of cash to use as change for the next day's sales ($100 is a reasonable amount) – you should also record the amount of cash you have left over. This amount will be deposited directly into your shop's bank account at the end of the day.

Record all of these amounts, either on daily account sheets or in a ledger book with columns for each amount. These records will be used for your banking and accounting needs.

Wire Orders

You will only have to worry about wire orders if you belong to an order-gathering service or a wire service (discussed in more detail in section 6.3). For record-keeping purposes, however, just remember that it is important to record the order number of each incoming and outgoing wire order to make sure you haven't missed an order and to ensure you're being paid for each one.

If you use a software program provided by the wire service, you won't need to keep records by hand, as the software does it for you. However, when you receive your itemized statement from the wire service, you should check your records against each item on the statement to ensure you're being paid for every incoming order.

Deliveries

Whether you have an in-house or contracted delivery service, it is a good habit to keep records of all deliveries that leave your shop. Keep a list each day of the recipient's name, phone number and address, and indicate on the list whether the order originated in town or from a wire service. Doing so will help you find the order information faster if there is a question or concern about a delivery.

Sales Records

For all orders that you take in the shop (by phone or from walk-in customers), you must keep a record of each transaction. Order-taking stationery makes three copies — one for the customer, one for the workroom, and one for your records. File the ones for your records by month, and put them aside in a safe place at the end of each year. You need to keep these records, plus all cash register tapes and other sales records (such as incoming wire orders) for seven years, in case of audit by the Internal Revenue Service or Revenue Canada.

Staff Records

If you are the flower shop's owner or manager, and you employ people other than yourself in the company, you will also need to keep a record of the hours your staff members work. Record the time they arrive and leave, and the amount of time they take for lunch. If they work extra hours, you will need to record this, too, in order to pay them for any overtime. You will need this information when you or your accountant calculates their weekly or bi-weekly pay.

If they are salaried employees, you will still need to keep track of time spent on the job, in order to ensure they are not working more time than is necessary, and to determine their efficiency on the job.

You may also want to keep personnel files for the purpose of recording staff achievements or concerns. In these, you should keep information as to the staff member's date of hire, their salary or pay rates, and their social insurance/social security numbers, as well as their home address and phone number. Record the date on each piece of information you include. Progress review documents should be signed by you and the staff member in question. Other information, such as a record of bonuses or raises, should also be included in these files.

If you are daunted by the prospect of keeping this kind of record, hire an accountant or bookkeeper to take care of it for you. These positions are not typically staff positions at a flower shop, but rather individuals who the shop has contracted to do this type of work. As such, you can ensure your bills stay as low as possible by keeping complete records and providing them when asked.

5.9.2 Financial Matters

Of course, you're in this business because you want to make money, aren't you? Keeping track of the money that comes in, and the money that goes out, is essential. Ideally, you want to have more money coming in than going out. What's left over is called your profit, and the more there is of that, the happier you'll be.

That's a simple explanation. But the truth is, financial matters are complex, because there are many rules about expenses, taxes, and deductions, and those rules vary depending on which state or province you are in.

Your best investment, when it comes to managing your finances, is to hire a professional accountant. For a fee, they will help you set up a plan for your daily bookkeeping (monitoring and recording the amount of money that comes in and goes out on a daily basis), keep track of your wire service income and expenses, ensure your taxes are completed in a timely and accurate fashion, and even manage your payroll.

Taxes

You are required to charge state or provincial tax on all taxable purchases, and in Canada, you are required to charge GST on many goods and services as well. Your state or provincial government's small business office will help you with this, and will explain how to go about making your regular payments of tax collected to the state, provincial, and federal agencies that require them.

You will also need to deduct income tax from your employee's paychecks, and pay that amount to your state, provincial and federal government. And of course you'll need to pay income tax for yourself.

In the United States, the Small Business Administration offers information about taxes at **www.sba.gov/smallbusinessplanner/manage/paytaxes/index.html**. In Canada, the Small Business Start-Up Assistant page has information about taxes, based on your province, at **http://bsa.canadabusiness.ca** (click on "English" then look for the "Taxation and Business Number" link).

Getting Paid

When customers pay in cash, you've got a simple situation of having money to deposit straight into your bank account. Any other time, however, you've got a more complicated situation.

Much of your business will be conducted with credit and debit cards. Debit cards are the most similar to cash, in that they transfer your customer's funds from their account to yours. Credit card companies typically pay you monthly, by check, so you will need to wait for any income from them.

Wire services pay you at regular intervals (weekly, bi-weekly or monthly, depending on the service). You also need to pay them at the same intervals.

All of the above are regular, predictable payments. Less predictable are customers that have in-store accounts, corporate clients, and others who pay on an occasional basis. These customers need to be asked to pay their bills as soon as possible — upon receipt of the bill is ideal. The longer they go without paying you, the longer you need to wait to pay your bills. When more than 15 days has passed between their account being due and you still not receiving payment, a polite phone call is often all it takes.

As for you, you will also need to earn some money. You should count this as a business expense, and not as part of the shop's profits. You should pay yourself the same amount you would pay someone else to manage your shop. Your accountant will help you set up a payment plan whereby you, too, can draw a salary.

To learn more about keeping a positive cash flow, visit **www. myteleflora.com/DesignEducation/Index.aspx**, click on "Floral Articles," and read the article called "Ensuring Positive Cash Flow." The article called "Customer Billing," available from the same website, is also a good read.

6. Getting and Keeping Customers

Any business owner knows that customers are the most important part of their business. Without them, the business would have little reason to exist. If you went by statistics alone, you might imagine that all flower shops are booming businesses. Of the millions of dollars spent on flowers each year in the United States and Canada, there should be enough to go around to give every flower shop a piece of the pie. But some flower shops do better than others at getting and keeping customers.

Of course, you want to have one of the shops that not only attracts flower-buying customers once, but keeps them coming back. It is especially important to make sure the goods and services offered by your shop stand out above the rest.

6.1 Choose Your Target Markets

You would ideally like to have enormous amounts of business from everywhere. But if you try to be all things to all customers, especially when you're just starting out, you run the risk of not focusing enough on the most profitable sections of your business, and possibly losing out on the money they have to offer.

In addition, trying to advertise your services to all the possible customers out there is expensive. Experts at Teleflora suggest spending 10 percent of your advertising budget on the general public, 30 percent on potential customers in your target market, and the rest – a full 60 percent – on advertising to your already existing customers in order to maintain loyalty and increase sales.

There are, naturally, advantages to all types of customers. But certain things appeal more to some types of customers than others. Knowing what works with each group will help you match what you do best with the type of customers you're trying to attract.

Each of the groups mentioned below can be considered a "niche." Targeting one or more of these will ensure you have a firm customer base, which creates a solid financial base for your store. For an article about niche marketing, go to **www.myteleflora.com/Design Education/Index.aspx**, click on "Floral Articles," and read "On Becoming a Niche Marketer."

6.1.1 Walk-In Customers

You're most likely to attract walk-in customers if you're in a location where there's lots of pedestrian traffic — a shopping mall or busy city street, for example. These kinds of customers are often drawn in by attractive window displays, tempting merchandise displayed just inside the store, the promise of a sale, or lower-priced, cash-and-carry items displayed outside the store.

Walk-in customers are often "looky-loos" who are simply curious about your shop — these are the people you can reach with low-priced impulse purchases, a friendly sales staff, and lots of variety.

Your enthusiasm and knowledge about flower varieties and design styles will help your customers feel as though they are in capable hands. Here's what you need to do to achieve a successful in-store sale.

Ways to Attract Walk-In Customers

Here are some possible ways to attract walk-in customers:

- Unique plant varieties in small keepsake containers.

- Cash-and-carry bouquets at various price points.

- Balloons.

- Small vase arrangements meant for desks or tables.

- Seasonal merchandise.

- Unusual giftware priced below $50.

Greet the customer as soon as they walk into the shop. Ask an open-ended question rather than a closed-ended question (i.e. "How can I help you today?" instead of "Can I help you?") An open-ended question can be answered with a "Just looking, thanks," but human politeness dictates that it can't be met with a flat-out "No thanks."

If the customer is "just looking," offer them something to look at, while telling them about it. For example, you could say, "Look at these gorgeous roses. We just got them in today, and they're a new color variety, called 'Ravel.' They've got a lovely scent."

Let the customer smell the flowers and admire them. Tell them something that reminds them the roses are for sale: "They're on at a great price today, just $25 for a vase arrangement that would be perfect on a desk or counter."

If the customer seems interested, offer information about other flowers available. Ask questions about their flower needs ("Do you have a particular place you like to keep flowers?" or "What occasions do you have coming up that these beautiful roses would work for?"). If they're not interested, let them know you'll be available when they are. Tell them where they can find you if they have any questions.

Watch the customer as they notice items of interest. If they are admiring something, offer information about it. For example, "Isn't that a stunning plant? It's called an azalea, and it'll stay in full bloom for at least another week or two. You know, those are great transplanted into the garden — they come back year after year."

When the customer appears ready to make a choice, help them say yes by giving them a choice that assumes a sale. For instance:

- "Shall I wrap those up for you, or would you prefer them arranged for an additional fee?"

- "Would you like to take that with you, or shall I have it delivered?"

- "Will you be sending the flowering plant or would your friend prefer the arrangement?"

If the flowers are to be delivered, take down the recipient's name, address and phone number, and ring in the sale.

While you are taking care of the cash register and credit/debit machine, ask the customer to fill out an enclosure card to send along with the purchase. Give them a pen and an envelope so they can tuck the card in without it being seen.

Give the customer their receipt, smile and thank them. Remind them of any upcoming holidays, sales or special events that they might want to take advantage of.

6.1.2 Phone Customers

Most phone customers are likely to have their first encounter with your store through a Yellow Pages or newspaper advertisement. They may be looking for a florist because of a particular need or because they've been enticed by an advertised special or arrangement.

When a customer calls to place an order, they are at a disadvantage because they can't see the flowers in front of them. They know they want flowers, but they may not have a good idea of what you have available, or what those flowers look like. The key to a successful telephone sale is to use descriptive language, evocative phrases, and precise descriptions when you tell customers about the various options available. Some descriptive words and phrases to use:

- Colorful

- Fragrant

- Bright, intense colors

- Hot colors

- Cool colors

- Soft pastel colors

- Long-lasting

- Cheerful

- Classic

- Contemporary

- High-style

- Feminine

- Bold

- Spring-like

Instead of naming specific flowers to be included in an arrangement, it is simpler to offer color choices, arrangement styles and price ranges.

You can use the following descriptive words to help describe the arrangement you will make in each price range:

Price	Descriptive Words
$25-$30	*Cute, modest, delicate, small, dainty*
$35-$50	*Standard, popular, pleasing*
$60-$75	*Lovely, beautiful, nice*
$80-$100	*Showy, substantial, impressive*
$125-$150	*Stunning, fantastic, gorgeous*
$175-$250	*Spectacular, breathtaking, outstanding*

You may also indicate size by measurement ("An arrangement about two feet high and one foot wide") or by description ("A big armload of cut flowers").

Just as for in-store sales, asking the customer questions to determine their needs will help them make their choice.

How to Sell Over the Phone

Answer the phone after no more than two rings. Greet the caller with the shop name and your first name: "Good afternoon, Fabulous Florists. Lisa speaking."

Listen to determine the reason for the call. The customer might say: "Yes, I'd like to send flowers to my mom." Respond in the affirmative, and get the customer's information immediately: "Sure, I can do that for you. May I have your name, please? And your phone number?"

Write down their information accurately on an order form. Read it back to the customer, using their name: "That's 555-9999. Is that right, Ms. Christensen?"

Move on to determining the customer's needs. Ask about the occasion, and suggest possible options: "I can send a gorgeous bouquet of bright cut flowers, a classic arrangement she could use to decorate for her birthday dinner, or a long-lasting flowering plant she could have for a while."

Explain price ranges, using the earlier list of descriptive words. When the customer makes a choice, affirm it: "A colorful bouquet of cut flowers will certainly brighten her day, and she can have the fun of arranging them to suit her house perfectly."

Find out the recipient's name, address and phone number. Also ask for any special instructions: "Would you like us to phone first to make sure she's home, or should it be a surprise? When is her birthday? Would you like them there in the morning, or would the afternoon be better for her?" Write the delivery date and time on the order form.

Explain the delivery fee, and give the total cost. Determine the payment method: "Shall I put this on your Visa or MasterCard?" Write down the credit card number, repeating it back to the customer. Ask for the card's expiration date and write that down.

Ways to Attract Phone Customers

Here are some possible ways to attract phone customers:

- Newspaper advertisements offering pictures of arrangements (especially seasonal specials).

- Radio advertisements that offer a bonus, like free delivery or a discount, on orders placed within a certain amount of time (starting from when the advertisement runs).

- Television advertisements that display the shop's phone number along with images of a special arrangement.

- A website that shows pictures of the shop's work.

- A toll-free number.

Find out what message to write on the enclosure card: "There will be a card going along with the flowers. What would you like to say on it?"

Write down the message on the order form and read it back to the customer: "Happy Birthday, Mom. I love you, from Wanda June."

Thank the customer by name, and assure them their order will be taken care of: "I'm sure your mother will be thrilled with her flowers, Ms. Christensen. I'll make sure they are absolutely beautiful. Thank you for your order."

Let the customer be the one to hang up first.

6.1.3 Hotels and Restaurants

Hotels and restaurants need flowers for their dining room tables, their reception areas, and any special events they may hold. Large hotels will often have regular contracts with florists to provide lobby and reception area arrangements. These contracts come up for renewal from time to time, and you can "bid" on the new contract by providing the hotel's purchasing manager with a price list, sample arrangements, and any other information they may specifically request.

Ways to Attract Hotel and Restaurant Clients

Here are some possible ways to attract hotel and restaurant clients:

- Provide detailed price lists.

- Aim to beat the competitor's prices, or if not, explain how your products will be superior, longer-lasting, or otherwise better.

- Include a sample with any bid or response to a request for proposals.

- Attend events at the hotel or restaurant, take note of the existing flowers, and, in your proposal, identify specific ways your arrangements will be better.

Hotel purchasing managers are easy to contact — just call the hotel's main number and ask for them. Introduce yourself and your shop, and find out whether the hotel has a contract with a florist. If they don't, find out who you should address a proposal to and send it right away. If they do, find out when the contract comes up for renewal.

Restaurants may have a similar bidding process for ongoing contracts. Whenever you're in a restaurant that uses flowers on its tables or in its reception area, find out who makes them and, if you can, how often they are refreshed. Take note of any shortcomings — for example, that the bud vases on the tables look a little old.

Leave your business card with the manager, perhaps with a note written on the back — something like, "Need even more beautiful table flowers? I can arrange it. Call me this Tuesday."

Follow up with a phone call or even a delivery of the type of bud vase you would be able to provide for the restaurant's tables. Include a price list and, again, your business card.

Sample Proposal

Fabulous Florists
1234 Main Street
Prettytown, PA 33333-8888
111-222-3333

July 14, 2008

Attn: Jane Goodwyn, Purchasing Agent
Amazing Luxury Resort
4321 Main Street,
Prettytown, PA 33333-9999

Dear Ms. Goodwyn,

Thank you for taking the time to speak with me yesterday regarding Amazing Luxury Resort's floral needs. Further to our telephone conversation, I am including the following proposal. I am certain that Fabulous Florists' trademark mix of quality, creativity, and value will meet your needs to the fullest extent.

You indicated a need for flowers in your front foyer, resort restaurant, and guest rooms. Here are the prices based on those areas; I am more than happy to fulfill additional requests or special needs on a per-arrangement basis, at a uniform discount of 20 percent off the retail price.

Front Foyer

Item:	*Price:*
Large arrangement in freestanding planter, completely replaced weekly	$200/week
Vase arrangement for reception desk, replaced weekly	$50/week

Resort Restaurant

Item:	*Price:*
One-sided arrangement for maitre d's station, replaced weekly	$100/week

| Twenty bud vase fillers for guest tables, flowers replaced as needed | $5 each, $5/replacement |

Guest Rooms

Item:	Price:
Take-home arrangement for premium service guests	$50/arrangement
20 permanent arrangements of artificial flowers for guest lavatories, assorted colors. (Repair sessions done by Fabulous Florists every six months, if needed)	$50/arrangement, $100/repair session

Fabulous Florists will be responsible for delivery of arrangements to Amazing Luxury Resort and for placement of the large foyer arrangement. Amazing Luxury Resort staff will ensure placement of all other arrangements.

If repairs or replacements are needed to individual flowers during the week that the flowers are on display, Fabulous Florists will repair and replace the flowers up to the value of $100. This does not apply to take-home guest room arrangements or where otherwise specified.

I trust that these prices will meet your budget and that we will be able to begin our working relationship in time for your annual general meeting on February 18.

I have included a sample arrangement of the type your premium guests would be taking home.

If you have any questions, please do not hesitate to contact me at 888-555-1111. I look forward to speaking with you soon.

Sincerely,

Tia Hopkiss
Owner/Manager
Fabulous Florists

Here is a sample service agreement, which you and your client will both need to sign once your proposal is accepted.

Sample Service Agreement

February 15, 2008

Service Agreement between:

Fabulous Florists
1234 Main Street
Prettytown, PA 33333-8888

And:

Amazing Luxury Resort. Inc.
4321 Main Street
Prettytown, PA 33333-9999

This agreement is understood to be applicable to all services provided by Fabulous Florists to Amazing Luxury Resorts Inc. until February 15, 2009, at which time this agreement will be renewed or terminated at the agreement of both parties.

Under this agreement, Fabulous Florists will:

- Provide and install one large foyer arrangement @ $200 weekly.

- Provide and install one front desk vase arrangement @ $50 weekly.

- Provide one arrangement for maitre d's station at Resort Restaurant @ $100 weekly.

- Provide 20 bud vase fillers @ $5 weekly.

- Provide take-home arrangements for premium service guests, on as-needed basis, to be delivered to hotel as required.

- Provide touch-up maintenance to all arrangements in public areas of the resort, on an as-needed basis.

- Deliver and install flowers by 2:00 p.m. every Friday, except where otherwise noted.

- Provide any other arrangements required by guests or staff of Amazing Luxury Resorts at a regular discount of 20 percent, before taxes.

- Provide an itemized invoice to Amazing Luxury Resorts on the 15th and last day of each month.

Under this agreement, Amazing Luxury Resorts will:

- Provide at least 24 hours' notice for all premium service guestroom arrangements.

- Notify Fabulous Florists if any replacement flowers are needed for an arrangement in a public area, indicating which arrangement they are needed for.

- Agree to use Fabulous Florists exclusively for all its floral needs, including but not limited to special events, employee bonuses and seasonal decorations.

- Pay its invoices promptly by check, no later than five days after receipt.

Both parties agree to give at least four (4) weeks' notice of the termination of this agreement if the termination is for any reason other than reaching the expiration date of the agreement.

Signed by:

_____   _____
Tia Hopkiss,   Jane Goodwyn,
owner/manager   purchasing manager
Fabulous Florists   Amazing Luxury Resorts

6.1.4 Corporations

Corporations often need flowers for business functions and for decorating their reception areas, and some also need an ongoing account for sending flowers to customers.

You can attract this kind of business by making a note of the corporate headquarters located in your area (any business counts as a corporation, but for the best results, target ones likely to have more than 50 employees). Contact the purchasing manager for the company, and say that you are interested in becoming their company's florist. Ask about their floral needs:

- Do they have an employee incentive program?

- Do they like to thank customers for their business?

- Do they send flowers to recognize clients' special days or holidays?

Offer to send a sample and information package to them. Make a sample arrangement of the type you anticipate they might need most. In your information package, include a full list of the types of arrangements you offer, and include a price range form. Photographs or brochures are also helpful.

Write a cover letter that explains why you want to work with the company, and what kinds of benefits you would offer in exchange for being their exclusive florist.

A ten percent discount on all orders? Free delivery? Fresh flowers for its reception area for every ten orders sent? Any of these are possibilities. The minor cost of providing these benefits is meant to be outweighed by the income you will make serving a steady clientele.

In order to determine a client's needs and requirements, you're going to have to ask lots of questions. A casual – but scheduled – meeting is a good way to get to know the client and their particular desires. It's a good idea to meet with most clients in your store, especially if you have particular flowers or arrangements that they want to see.

Ways to Attract Corporate Clients

Here are some possible ways to attract corporate clients:

- Send information and sample packages.

- Network with corporate executives.

- Join a business networking group.

The advantage of such in-store consultations is that you are able to show the range of your products, offer examples of specific flowers, and have all of your design resources (such as ribbons, accessories, and containers) at your immediate disposal.

Other times, you will meet with your clients at their office or event location. In these instances, be sure to arrive on time, and keep the consultation under half an hour (unless circumstances dictate otherwise). Bring a tape measure to get accurate measurements of any place that will have floral decorations.

Also bring a camera to snap quick photographs of the areas you will be making arrangements for. By taking photographs, you will be able to create designs that will better fit with their settings, and accurately plan the flowers you will need to bring, should the space and size of the arrangements needed require you to create the arrangements on-site. Bring a notebook to record measurements, color preferences and any technical requirements. Here are some questions to ask your clients:

- What is the impression you are hoping to create?

- What is your budget range?

- How long should these arrangements last?

- How often are you planning to replace these arrangements (if they are to be replaced)?

- Are there any special flowers or colors you would like included?

- Do you have containers you would like me to use, or will I supply the containers?

- Do you prefer seasonal flowers or exotic flowers?

- What time of day will the flowers need to be delivered/arranged (if on-site arrangement is required)?

- How many events are the flowers meant to serve?

- Would they like flowers in the arrangement to be refreshed periodically between new arrangements, or will each arrangement be replaced completely?

For an example of how a florist turned one corporate account into many, visit **www.myteleflora.com/DesignEducation/Index.aspx**, click on "Floral Articles," and search for the article called "Corporate Accounts."

6.1.5 Government

Depending on where you are, city, state, or provincial governments might be a source for customers.

Just as with corporate clients, you should prepare samples and information packages. Contact the government body you're targeting and ask for the name of the person responsible for making purchasing decisions. Ideally, you want to let them know that they can earn certain benefits by using your shop for all their flower needs — whether it's a discount on all orders, free delivery, or another benefit that you feel you are able to offer.

Occasionally, government offices or corporations publish a Request for Proposals (RFP) to get a new vendor for their floral needs. You can find out about these by visiting government websites or checking the business pages of your daily newspaper.

Typically, an RFP will ask potential vendors for specific information, in a specific order. They might want to know about your product availability, prices, delivery systems, and on-line ordering capabilities, for example. Read the RFP information carefully, and then answer their questions with as much detail as you can, in the order they are asked.

Ways to Attract City Government Clients

Here are some possible ways to attract city government clients:

- Attend city council meetings

- Join the chamber of commerce in your area

- Sponsor community events

- Donate to charity groups connected with the city

Include supporting materials, such as a copy of your portfolio, photographs of recent work, reference letters from satisfied customers, and a sample arrangement delivered along with your information package.

These types of contracts are typically for a large amount of work over a fixed period of time, such as one year or more. Be sure, before you answer an RFP, that you will be able to handle the amount of work it might entail. Also find out what the terms of payment are — some could require you to carry all the costs for six months or more before getting paid for the first time. Make sure you have the financial resources to see the work through.

Overall, doing this kind of work can be rewarding and a good source of steady income, but it is not frequent or certain enough to count on as a large part of your business.

6.1.6 Hospitals

There are several ways you can use hospitals as a source of customers. One, of course, is to be conveniently located near a hospital. If you are so fortunate, you can capitalize on your location by reminding people on their way to visit someone in the hospital that you have the perfect gift. A sign outside your store indicating "Hospital flowers" or "Cheer someone up with flowers" will go a long way toward increasing this kind of traffic.

If you are not near a hospital, you can still gain a share of the market. If you have your own delivery vehicles, for example, you could offer free delivery for all hospital orders. Since your driver only needs to make one trip no matter how many arrangements they take, this is a bonus to your customers with a minimal cost to you.

Or you could arrange to provide cash-and-carry bouquets and small arrangements for sale in the hospital's gift shop. Contact the gift shop's administrator and ask about their current flower supply system, if any.

Find out what their needs are. Vase arrangements? Cut flowers? Small flowering plants? You could provide these on a consignment basis (that is, they pay you only for the ones they sell), or simply sell the flowers to the gift shop at a slightly lower rate and leave it up to them to sell them at whatever price they choose.

> **TIP:** Some hospitals have regulations about the kinds of flowers they will permit. Call the hospital and find out what its rules are. For example, some don't permit strongly scented flowers, while others don't allow latex balloons because some people are allergic to them. In addition, it is wise to find out the maximum size arrangement that patients are allowed to have in their room, and make your designs accordingly.

6.1.7 Funeral Homes

Get to know the funeral directors in your area. Pay a visit to their businesses, and find out their specific needs with regards to delivery and size of arrangements. Get a floor plan of the chapel or service area. Leave a stack of your business cards, and perhaps a stack of brochures about your funeral work as well (you can order these from the wire services you belong to, or print your own — see section 6.2.2 for more information).

You might also want to do the same with local clergy members in case any of their congregation is in need of funeral arrangements. That way, they can easily offer information to family members.

If you are located close to one or more funeral homes, you can also attract out-of-town funeral orders by making a note of that fact on your website or in your wire service directory listing. Be specific about which ones you are close to.

You can read an excellent article about the relationship between funeral directors and florists at **www.myteleflora.com/DesignEducation/ Index.aspx**. Click on "Floral Articles" and search for the article called "Funeral Home Deliveries."

> **TIP:** Some florists pay a commission to funeral directors for any referrals they receive from them. While this is not desirable, it has become the custom in some areas. If this is the case in your area, find out how much commission you will be asked to pay and decide if it's worth your while for the amount of business you could expect.

6.1.8 Online Customers

Online customers may be anywhere in the world. They will find your shop through your website, and may place orders either via e-mail, online ordering, or by calling your toll-free telephone number.

You'll attract online customers with a website that shows lots of clear photographs of your arrangements, plainly marked prices, and some specific indication about your delivery area (i.e., Downtown Atlanta; Greater Toronto). Because there are many online florists, you'll want to make sure your website stands out and is among the first to appear when a potential customer does a web search (see section 6.2.2 on websites).

When potential clients e-mail you, it's up to you to respond promptly, as this particular mode of communication has allowed people to expect a fast response.

When you reply to an e-mail enquiry, copy the client's initial e-mail (you can set your e-mail preferences to automatically do this for you) and address each of their questions as fully as you can. Be specific about prices, delivery options, and availability of flower varieties.

Ask questions, too, if you need more information from the client. By asking questions, you can create a dialogue and increase the chances that you will end up making a sale.

Ways to Attract Online Customers

Here are some possible ways to attract online customers:

- Have a changing special on the front page of your website, with an "order now" link next to it.

- Advertise your site with banner ads on other websites.

- Offer an e-mail reminder service that reminds the customer when birthdays, anniversaries and other events are coming up.

6.2 Marketing Your Business

As discussed earlier, many florists get a lot of business from walk-in customers. You can learn how to increase your walk-in traffic with the advice provided in the sections on location and window displays. This section offers a variety of other techniques to market your business and attract customers.

If you are new to marketing, you can get an excellent overview of basic business marketing from the Small Business Administration by visiting **www.sba.gov/smallbusinessplanner** and browsing through their marketing section.

6.2.1 Advertising

"Buy now!" "Big sale!" "The perfect gift!" "Shop at our store!" These are all messages you might want to send to the general public, especially if business has been slow lately and you're wondering what you can do to attract more customers. How will customers know that you've got the most exquisite orchid plants in full bloom right now unless you do something to let them know? It's time for an advertisement.

There are many places you can advertise your shop and its services, including the Yellow Pages, newspapers, magazines, radio, television, and the Internet. Experts agree that it is wise to combine two or more of these media, but you will want to consider several factors before you decide for sure which you choose. You'll want to know how much a particular advertisement costs, how often it will appear, and how long it will last (or be in the public eye).

Cost

Your advertising dollars go towards supporting the media organization you're buying an ad from. The more expensive the media, the more expensive its ads are likely to be. A high-school yearbook will be able to offer much lower rates than a daily newspaper, and a college radio station (if it takes ads at all) will be cheaper than the area's hottest new music station. And television ads are the most expensive of all.

To find out how much various ad types cost in your area, call your local media outlets and ask them to send you a rate card. Rate cards list all the advertising options offered by the media outlet, and they often include other useful information such as demographic statistics (age, gender, income level, etc.) about the target audience — the type of viewers, listeners, or readers the outlet tends to reach.

Before you make any decisions, read the rate card and target audience information carefully. Is this the media outlet where most of your customers will hear your message? Sixty percent of your advertising budget should be aimed at existing customers, so keep that in mind when you're looking at the rate cards.

If advertising in a local magazine is really inexpensive, but you know most of your customers prefer to listen to the radio, you might want to try the magazine ad as an experiment to see what kind of new customers you might get from it. On the other hand, if you know your customers read the local daily newspaper, you should plan on doing most of your advertising there, and perhaps even forego the expensive television ad that targets people unlikely to shop at your store.

Frequency

Repetition builds recognition, so the more often people see or hear your ad, the more the message will sink in. A catchy jingle on the radio gets stuck in people's heads. An identifiable image in the newspaper links people's thoughts about flowers with your store's logo or message.

However, you have to pay for each time an ad appears — these are known as insertions. The more frequent your insertions, the less it usually costs per insertion, but you need to agree to a certain number up front to get a good rate (cost per insertion).

Duration

The length of time an advertisement is in the public eye can range from less than a minute (for television or radio) to as long as a month (for magazines) or a year (for the Yellow Pages).

Print media tend to offer the best value when it comes to duration. But you need to consider what any particular ad is trying to sell. There's no point in advertising a one-day special in a magazine that will be around for a month, because there's a good chance customers won't read your ad until after the special is over. Likewise, a one-off radio ad for "plant month" won't be more than a drop in the bucket when you're trying to promote green plant sales for an entire month.

Duration can be a good quality in an ad, but only if it matches the type of thing you're advertising. Longer-lasting ads are best for raising ongoing awareness of your shop and its services. An ad in a wedding magazine, for example, would be a good place to show some of your shop's bouquet designs.

Content

The content of your advertisements, regardless of what type of media they're placed in, is important. Spend some time thinking about items you want to promote, aspects of your store that are particularly unique, and other ideas you want to get across to the public.

Look at your competitors' ads, such as those in the Yellow Pages or other local publications. Don't worry if you have never written or created an advertisement before — you don't need to be able to do that. You just need to know what you want to sell.

To get customers to call, you could offer free in-home or in-office plant consultations. Or you might have a special promotional offer. How about a two-for-one event? If you have lots of merchandise to sell quickly, such as cut flowers, you can offer them two-for-one.

Plan this kind of promotion as a regular weekly event scheduled for the day before you get your new shipment of flowers in, and you'll free up space in your cooler, too.

Or, if you have lots of plants to sell, you could advertise a "trade-in" sale — customers can bring in an old houseplant, no matter what shape it's in, and receive a discount (perhaps up to 50 percent) on a new plant from your store.

Your Sales Representative

Advertising sales representatives work for the media outlets you want to advertise with. They will help you figure out how your ad should be worded, how often you need to have it run, and what size or length of ad will suit your budget. They may show you sample ads – these are called "spec" ads – to show you some possible ideas for how your shop's advertisement could look.

Once you and the sales representative have agreed on an ad campaign – a series of ads that will suit your needs – you will sign a contract, which is an agreement about the terms and conditions of your advertisements with that media outlet.

Before your ad runs, you will be sent a proof, which is a sample of your ad that you must check carefully to make sure there are no mistakes. If there are any, let your sales representative know right away.

After your ad runs, you will be sent a tear sheet – the page of the publication with your ad on it. Keep this for your records. Your sales representative will follow up with you, too, to find out your satisfaction with the ad and to plan future ones. Keep in touch with this person, as they can be one of your best advocates.

Trading Flowers for Ads

Sometimes you will be able to trade advertisements for products. Ask your sales representative about "contra" deals, in which you build up credits towards ads by providing services such as regularly replaced arrangements for the lobby of the media outlet's office. These types of trades are organized on a case-by-case basis, so if one outlet doesn't want to participate, try another.

Keep track of the value of each arrangement you prepare for the media outlet, and keep track of the value of the ads you use. Make sure, every six months or so, that you're on an even footing and aren't owing or being owed more than you're comfortable with.

6.2.2 Promotional Tools

A promotional tool is anything that you use to explain your business to others in order to convince them to use your products and services. These can be simple items such as brochures or postcards, or more complicated items, like entire websites. Ideally, you should have a combination of tools at your disposal. That way you'll be able to reach potential customers, whether they're recipients of flowers from your shop for the first time or corporate accounts eager for something new.

Tools from Florist Associations

Being a member in a floral trade association, such as the Society of American Florists or Flowers Canada, comes with a certain amount of access to promotional goods and services. These organizations sometimes work on marketing campaigns that benefit the floral industry in general, and your membership allows you to get access to their marketing resources. See Chapter 7 to find contact information for national and regional trade associations.

The Flower Promotion Organization runs the "Flowers: Alive with Possibilities" marketing campaign that you may have seen on television or in magazines. Visit **www.flowerpossibilities.com/retail.html** to find out how you, as a retail florist, can order some of the brochures and information this organization has created.

Coupons

Coupons are a good way to track the effectiveness of your print ads, your newsletter, or any direct-mail marketing effort you might make.

You can tell if people are paying attention to the larger advertisement if they bother to cut out the coupon and redeem it. Some experts suggest that only two percent of people who receive coupons use them; others suggest it's much higher. However, offering coupons remains one way to bring people into your shop who wouldn't ordinarily come in, and encourage customers who would have bought something anyway to buy a little bit more.

The coupon offer should be simple, but with high perceived value — a buy one, get one free offer, or perhaps "This coupon good for 40 percent off your entire green plant purchase," or "Redeem this coupon for a free rose with every purchase." Above all, it should require that customers come into your shop to redeem their coupons. The idea is to get them to pay you a visit, see what other lovely things you have for sale, and maybe buy something besides what they came for with the coupon.

For the purposes of measuring advertising effectiveness with coupons, it's a good idea to put a time limit or expiration date on it. Make sure this date is clearly printed on the coupon. It should allow customers enough time to get themselves to your store – maybe a week or two – but not so much time that they forget about the coupon, thinking they can use it well in the future. Tie the coupon to a date that's easy to remember, such as the end of the month.

Brochures

A brochure is a flyer, usually printed on both sides and folded so it can fit into an envelope. It can give a brief package of information about your shop, or focus on a single season or a single occasion — Valentine's flowers, for example, or birthday flowers. Usually, brochures will have big pictures and relatively few words.

Wire services such as FTD and Teleflora regularly print updated professional brochures that their members can buy for a reasonable cost. This is the easiest option, and the one many florists choose simply for the convenience.

You can make your own custom brochures with a digital camera and graphic design software like QuarkXPress or Adobe InDesign. However, this method takes a great deal of money (the software programs alone cost nearly $1,000) and requires desktop publishing experience.

If you don't have the time or equipment to make your own brochures, there are companies that can make them for you (check your Yellow Pages under "printing" or "graphic design"). You'll need to supply the basic information you want to present (usually brief descriptions of arrangements), and pay the designer for their time. Ask the designer to give you a price quote before they begin so you won't be surprised with a large bill.

Then, you'll need to pay for the brochures to be printed. Keep in mind that the more you print, the less the cost is per brochure. However, if you're making them for a specific holiday, they'll have a limited shelf life. It is wise to order fewer, unless you're sure you'll be selling the same products at the same prices next Mother's Day, for example.

Because brochures are usually small enough to tuck into a standard envelope, you can use them as "statement stuffers" – that is, tuck them in along with any bills you might send out to customers or corporate clients – or attach them to the delivery information on outgoing arrangements and plants. They're also handy to have along when you attend trade shows. Carry a few with you to any networking events you attend so that you have a quick and easy way to show people pictures of flower arrangements.

Give-Aways

Give-aways are anything that you give to customers or potential customers in the hope of attracting them to your shop. They should always be printed with your shop name, address, phone number, website and e-mail information.

Simple giveaways can be effectively tied into promotions. For example, you could advertise that anyone bringing in a keychain with your shop's logo can have a buy one, get one for half-price deal on fresh flowers. Or you could tie the key chains into a frequent flower promotion.

Other give-away items include calendars, fridge magnets, pens, coffee cups — you name it. It doesn't matter what you choose, as long as it reflects your shop's aesthetics and overall image. And, of course, give-aways should be cost-effective, so decide on a budget before you start looking into ordering any.

There are numerous companies that can supply you with promotional items. Check the Yellow Pages or do an online search for "advertising specialties" or "promotional products."

Learning from the Competition

One of the first steps in making sure customers will return to your store is to check out your competition and figure out what they do right and wrong. If anyone else sells flowers in your area, pay them a visit and see what they offer.

Are they selling big bundles of flowers for a low price? Do they offer free delivery? Is there an in-house wedding consultant? All of these are reasons why customers might choose the competition over your business.

Look at the competition's weaknesses, too. Are they slow to help walk-in customers? Are their big bundles of flowers only available in limited varieties? Is their return policy too limited? Any of the competition's shortcomings will suggest ways you can do something differently in order to draw customers to your store.

Identify Your Strengths

Make an honest list of everything your flower shop does well. Make another list of places where you could improve your products or services.

Is there a talented designer on staff? Do you have air-conditioned delivery vehicles? Is your shop located next door to a business that you could connect flowers to? What about the products you sell? Are there unique varieties of plants? Unusual giftware? Hard-to-find flowers? All of these can be promoted in order to draw customers into your shop.

Sell Your Strengths

Perhaps you have a talented designer on staff. You could plan to advertise their work by name — "Designs by David," for example, or "European-style arrangements by Flora." Include a tag with each outgoing order telling the customer the arrangement was "Custom-designed for you by David" (or

Flora, or whomever). After a while, customers will be asking for their arrangements by name.

Or maybe you offer high-quality, premium roses. Sure, the competition is selling roses for $10 a dozen, but you know yours will last longer because they've been properly conditioned. Plus, you have three different types of red roses. You could promote your more expensive roses as having superior quality, and offer a 24-hour guarantee or a service such as free gift-wrapping.

Perhaps you have a wide selection of unusual plants. Why not make a window display that showcases some of the more interesting ones? Include signs that identify the plants (you could make it look like a museum display, for example), and draw customers into your shop with the offer of on-call expert advice in plant care for every plant purchased. Customers will appreciate this, even if they don't ever need to call with questions about their new plant.

Match Your Competition

Look at your list of the competition's strengths and weaknesses. In your own shop, do what you can to improve on their weaknesses and match their strengths.

If they offer in-house wedding consultations (and what florist doesn't?), why not offer wedding consultations with the bride in her own home or at the site of her wedding? It doesn't take a lot more effort on your part, but will be seen as a special bonus by your customers.

Perhaps they sell vast quantities of roses at $10 a dozen. Even if you can't match the price they get from buying in bulk, you could offer specials on other flower varieties, or provide free arrangement in a vase with every dozen roses ordered from your shop. It will cost you a few dollars for each vase, but could earn you some business you might otherwise never get.

Your Portfolio

As explained earlier, your portfolio offers a way to show people examples of the types of arrangements you have made in the past. You can have a physical portfolio in the form of a scrapbook or photo album that you can take with you to client meetings and trade shows, and which your customers can browse through while they're in your store. Or you can make a virtual scrapbook by putting images on your website or saving them on a CD-ROM.

CD-ROMs are fairly cost-effective to reproduce, so you can give them to potential clients as part of your information package. If you have a computer capable of burning CD-ROMs, you can make your own. Otherwise, you can have them professionally done for a reasonable cost. Check at your local computer store, or at your photo-finishing store — some offer to put photos onto a CD-ROM for a reasonable price.

In your scrapbook – whichever form it takes – you should include large pictures of the most impressive arrangements you've made, with brief descriptions about the occasions they were for and their price. That way, even if you're not sitting with a customer as they look through your portfolio, they'll still be able to get an idea about the kinds of designs they could expect.

Your Website

Your shop's website is its most visible international presence. Anyone, anywhere, anytime, can potentially see your shop's pictures, prices, and anything else you want to include. It is a powerful promotional tool, and to take best advantage of it, you need to pay some attention to what's on it, how often it's updated, and whether it gets seen.

If your shop is a member of FTD (see section 6.3 for membership information), you will have the option of having a website linked through FTD.com. The advantage of doing so is that all you need to do is supply prices, descriptions, and a photograph of your shop, and FTD does the rest for you, right down to providing secure online ordering.

However, you can also do it yourself. If you are already experienced at creating web pages, or learn quickly, you can design your website yourself using a program such as Microsoft's Front Page or Netscape Composer (free with the Netscape Browser), or you can hire a local web designer. Look in the Yellow Pages under "web design" or call the new media department of your local community college to find a student willing to do it for a reduced rate.

It's desirable to have a domain name (the address of your website) that's as similar to your business name as possible, to make it memorable to your customers and potential customers. If your shop name is Downtown Florist, for example, you might want a domain name like "www.mydowntownflorist.com." You can easily find out if your potential domain name is available by going to a site such as **www.godaddy.com**. If it's available, you can follow the steps outlined on the site to register your domain.

The bigger question is what to put on your website. At the very least, you should have photographs of several different types of arrangements, your business name, address and e-mail address, and your toll-free phone number. Including prices along with the photographs is even better, as is offering an instant-ordering option. Other elements to include on your website:

- Upcoming holiday information

- Order-by deadlines for upcoming holidays

- Seasonal specials

- Your shop hours

- Plant- and flower-care tips

- Staff information, such as brief profiles of your designers

- Your portfolio

TIP: Updating your site regularly is important, because it gives customers a reason to visit again to see what's new.

Of course, you'll also want to make sure people find your website when they search for flowers online. Most people regularly use only a handful of search engines, such as Yahoo, Google, MSN, and AOL. You can submit your website to over a dozen search engines for free at **www.bravenet.com**.

Other Promotional Tools

Here are a few other ideas to promote your flower shop:

- Print and wear T-shirts or baseball hats with your store's name and logo. Give them out to your best customers.

- Paint your shop logo on your car.

- Post your business card on every bulletin board you see.

6.2.3 Trade Shows and Events

Trade Shows

Wedding shows, garden shows, home shows — all of these offer chances to meet new customers and show off the kind of work you do. You can find out about upcoming shows by contacting your local Chamber of Commerce or the facilities where trade shows are held.

Typically, these types of shows are held in large arenas, convention centers or exhibition halls, which may temporarily house dozens or hundreds of booths. Rent a booth, and whatever you put into it is up to you. When you set up, imagine you're setting up a display window — one that people can walk into. Make your space inviting and pleasant. It should reflect your shop's aesthetics and range of merchandise, but also focus on the nature of the show.

If it's a wedding show, you'll want samples of the types of wedding flowers you do. If it's a home show, bring arrangements that could be used in peoples' homes every day. If it's a garden show, focus on your green and flowering plants, or on containers that can be used indoors and outdoors.

Here are some ideas of what to bring to a trade show. (Some of these items, such as tables and chairs, may be supplied free or rented for a small fee from the organization sponsoring the trade show):

- Table with tablecloth

- Chair or chairs

- Large floor arrangements

- Arrangement for your table

- Sample wedding bouquets on stands (if it's a wedding show)

- A portfolio with examples your previous work

- Sample home arrangements such as everyday wreaths, artificial flower arrangements, and planter baskets

- Holders for brochures and business cards

- Giveaway or promotional items such as single stems of flowers with your business card or a coupon attached.

- Small items for sale — ornaments, small vases, or small plants

You can find an article with more than 50 tips on exhibiting at a trade show at **www.espexhibits.com/trade-show-tips.php**.

Promotional Events

Even if there is no trade show planned for your area, you can always hold your own event. A tent sale or sidewalk sale is one tried and true means of promoting your business. To read an article about how to go about doing it, visit **www.myteleflora.com/DesignEducation/ index.aspx**, click on "Floral Articles," and search for the article called "Taking It Outside — Staging Sidewalk Sales Events."

You can do many other things in the name of promoting your store, and you're limited only by your time and imagination. Anything that puts your store name out into the public eye and encourages customers or potential customers to visit your shop is great.

You can participate in a local parade (these are often organized by the local Chamber of Commerce or the municipal government). You can dress up your staff as different types of flowers, or build a flower-covered float like they do every year for the Rose Bowl. You can get some float-building tips from a Rose Bowl Parade winner at **www. valleydecorating.com/howto.html**. Check with your local government or Chamber of Commerce for events that you could use as a floral tie-in, even if you don't have your own float. You could promote your shop as a place to buy green-tinted corsages to wear at the St. Patrick's Day parade, for example.

Donations

Donations are a good way to get your shop's name and products into the public eye. You'll probably be approached for donations by churches, community centers, non-profit or not-for-profit organizations, schools, sports teams, hospitals, and more. They might ask for a cash donation but, more often, will want a product (a plant or arrangement) that they can use as a prize in a raffle or drawing.

You don't, by any means, need to donate to every organization that asks. But ones that offer charitable tax receipts are worth considering, as are causes you believe in. Ones that you know will reach a large number of people are always worth supporting, because you'll have your shop name recognized by a large group of people as a donor. Be sure to ask for acknowledgment in any programs or posters made for the event.

When donating, it is nice to donate a fresh arrangement that will catch the eyes of those who will see it. But consider donating coupons instead – something that will bring people into your store to collect their free arrangement – and possibly encourage them to buy something else besides.

Here are a few other promotional event ideas to get you started. You can adapt them to suit your own tastes or needs:

- Sponsor a "flower count" in the early weeks of spring. Encourage people in your area to count the number of blooms in their yard. Award prizes.

- Decorate Christmas trees for hospitals or seniors' homes (using their tree and decorations, or donating homemade decorations). Beside the tree, put a sign that says "Decorated by (your shop name)."

- Declare an annual "Flower Day" in your community, and give out free flowers to the first 100 people in your store. See if your municipal council will participate by making an official proclamation.

- Hold a community flower-arranging contest, with prizes from your shop.

- Visit local schools, community groups or senior centers to demonstrate flower arranging techniques.

- Hold a "flower tea" in your store a few weeks before Mother's Day. Serve tea and cookies to customers, and give a discount on any Mother's Day order.

- Sponsor a singles' event a few weeks before Valentine's Day.

- Organize a charity event or participate by making a donation.

Networking Events

Flowers are a personal product, in that people buy them for a specific person and for a special reason. Getting out there and meeting customers turns you into a person in their minds, and not just a business.

People like to do business with people they know, and networking is one way to meet more people with whom to do business. Any place where there are people is a potential networking opportunity. Networking can happen in formal or informal settings. A haircut might become a networking opportunity, just as attending a chamber of commerce mixer might also introduce you to new customers.

Go out to every party, social event or business occasion you can. Never miss an opportunity to tell people about your store and the services you offer.

Be sure to always carry a supply of business cards when you go anywhere — you never know when someone might mention an engagement, a new baby, or a new house, for example, and you'll have the chance to offer a personalized floral consultation. For more formal networking, try these:

- Attend community events and talk to as many people as possible. Be sure to give them your business card.

- Join the local Chamber of Commerce and participate in its events.

- Join a business networking group, like Business Network International (**www.bni.com**).

6.2.4 Free Media Publicity

Much of the time, getting into the media involves buying advertising space. But a far better, and free, way of getting into the media is to make the news. Television and radio stations and newspapers are always in need of ideas for stories, and you can help them by suggesting stories their audience might be interested in.

To begin, make a list of remarkable things your store has recently done, or is about to do. Say you're making the flower arrangements for a visiting dignitary. Or your designer has recently achieved special recognition, such as accreditation from a professional association for florists, such as AFID. Let the media know. You can even invite a reporter from the local television station to come and do a story about the vast number of arrangements you have prepared for any given holiday.

News Releases

One way to get publicity is to send a press release (also called a "news release"). It should be on letterhead and contain the specific information about the event. Include the date, your contact number, and the best times to reach you. Fax it to the assignment desk at your local newspaper, radio stations, and television stations. Here are some tips for writing a good press release:

- Make sure the press release is newsworthy. For example, you could write about an upcoming event you'll be making the flower arrangements for.

- Give your press release a strong lead paragraph that answers the six main questions: who, what, where, when, why, and how.

- Include factual information about yourself and your services. Remember, a press release should read like a news story, not an advertisement.

- Keep it short. Aim for a maximum of 500 words.

- Include your contact information at the end of the press release so that reporters and readers can get ahold of you.

Sample News Release

Fabulous Florists
1234 Lovely Street
Prettytown, PA
111-222-3333

February 8, 2008

FOR IMMEDIATE RELEASE:
(If you don't want the story told until a certain time, you can put "Embargoed until" and the date instead)

Fabulous Florists has been chosen to make the flower arrangements for British Prime Minister Gordon Brown's visit to Prettytown on February 19.

Master designer Tia Hopkiss will make twelve table centerpieces for the Prime Minister's dinner at the British-American Club and will also prepare rose boutonnieres for the visiting dignitaries.

"It's an honor to make the arrangements for this event," said Hopkiss. "I hope he likes them."

Members of the media are invited to witness the creation of these arrangements and to find out more about the very specific requirements of the Prime Minister's floral needs. The arrangements will be prepared between noon and 4:00 p.m. on February 19, and delivered to the Club at 5:00 p.m. sharp.

For more information, contact:

Jane Goodwyn, Owner
Fabulous Florists
111-222-3333

Some more suggestions on how to write a press release are available at **www.publicityinsider.com/release.asp**.

Don't assume a reporter will call, but when one does, be as accommodating as possible. Invite them to come to your shop to see the arrangements in question, to meet the designer, and to take pictures of the enormous shipment of flowers you've just received for Valentine's orders.

Know what kind of media you're talking to, because their needs vary. Print reporters will welcome photographs of your shop or arrangements (or they may bring their own photographer). Television reporters love to have beautiful, colorful flowers to show on TV, whereas radio reporters would prefer a few interesting quotes or comments. Visit **www. wellesley.edu/PublicAffairs/tvradiotips.htm** for some additional tips to keep in mind when talking to a reporter.

Regular Appearances

Beyond sending out press releases when events of note take place at your store, you can also get a regular spot on your local community access television station. Contact your nearest one to find out the procedure, as they vary and some require a certain amount of training or orientation.

Another option is to make yourself available to the local television station as a "guest expert." Prepare a portfolio of your work, and offer to come on-air to discuss a specific plant or flower-related topic each week, or once a month.

Suggest a list of topics you could cover, making sure they would be relevant to local viewers. Try topics like "How to make a Christmas wreath," "What to do with your garden flowers," or "Fast and easy ways to decorate for a dinner party" — whatever you feel comfortable talking about.

A week or so after you've sent your package to the television station's lifestyles reporter, follow up with a phone call and an invitation to stop by your shop to see what kinds of things you could discuss. Even if you don't end up as a television regular, you might just meet a new client!

6.3 Out-of-Area Orders

6.3.1 Wire and Order Gathering Services

A wire service is a network of affiliated florists who send orders to each other in order to provide customers with worldwide delivery. An order-gathering service is an independent business that takes orders from consumers through toll-free phone numbers (like 1-800-FLOWERS) or the Internet (like Flowers.com). These businesses then use a wire service to send the orders to affiliated florists, just as independent florists would do.

Florists usually belong to one or more order-gathering services, such as Florists' Transworld Delivery Association (FTD) or Teleflora. These organizations inspect individual flower shops to ensure high standards are met, both in the quality of the product they produce, the ability of the designers working there, and the overall appearance of the flower shop. Florists pay membership fees to belong to these organizations and benefit from them by being part of a network of florists who transmit orders to each other.

These organizations also offer accreditation programs which allow individual florists to pass tests that will make them more recognized in the business. An FTD accredited Master Designer, for example, would be able to use that credential to find work as a designer almost anywhere.

Through their networks of florists affiliated with wire services such as FTD, Interflora, and Teleflora, florists are able to send flowers virtually anywhere in the world. The countries served are listed in the order-gathering services' directories, which are like large phone books with all member florists listed by country, state and city. These directories are also available on searchable CD-ROMs for PC computers.

The store that takes the original order from the customer is called the *sending florist*. The store that fills the order and delivers it to the recipient is called the *filling florist*.

Sometimes, florists will reciprocate orders — that is, send their orders only to the stores that regularly send them orders in return.

To send flowers to another city, a florist first takes an order. They find out where a customer wants to send flowers, and for what occasion. They suggest a reasonable price for the order — a vase arrangement, for example, might cost $25 for a modest one, $45 for an impressive one, or up to $75 for a spectacular one.

They write down the name, address, zip or postal code and phone number of the recipient, and find out what day the flowers should arrive. The customer pays for the order, plus the cost of delivery in the city where the flowers will be delivered (usually anywhere from $5 to $10), and a service fee determined by the florist (again, anywhere from $5 to $10 is typical).

The florist – now known as the sending shop – then looks in their online or book directory of florists belonging to the same order gathering service. (In order to have one of these directories, your shop must belong to one or more wire service or order gathering service.)

After using the directory to find the city in which the flowers will be delivered, the sending florist then uses the recipient's zip or postal code to determine the closest flower shop to the recipient's address — that shop will be the filling or receiving florist.

The sending florist records the filling florist's wire service member number on the order, and transmits the order by Internet, fax, or phone to the filling shop. The sending shop keeps the service fee, and tells the price of the flowers and the price of the delivery to the filling shop.

Through the order-gathering services' clearing house (a central location where accounts are sorted out), the filling florist is credited for the incoming orders, and the sending florist is debited for the outgoing order. At the end of each month, the clearing house sends a check or a bill to each flower shop in its network, depending on whether a florist has filled or sent more orders.

Florists must apply for membership in all of these services. Belonging to one or more order-gathering or wire services is a good way to bring in business from out of town, and assures you will be able to send flower orders to other cities. Wire services usually have high standards and require you to have been in business for a minimum amount of time before you can become a member.

Order-Gathering Service Resources

Order-gathering services offer a variety of benefits and responsibilities, at a variety of rates. Here is a list of some suggested by the Society of American Florists:

Blossoms Network Floral Services

Website: **www.tryblossoms.com**
Address: P.O. Box 1395
Bancroft, Ontario KOL 1C0
Phone: 866-261-5428

FloralSource International

Website: **www.fsiflorists.com**
Address: P.O. Box 810
Eagle Point, Oregon 97524
Phone: 877-231-2478

1-800-FLOWERS

This service focuses on stores in New York, New Jersey, Illinois, Connecticut, Florida, Texas, Arizona, and Nevada.

Website: **www.1800flowers.com/about/index.asp**
Address: One Old Country Road, Suite 500
Carle Place, NY 11514
Phone: 800-503-9630

Wire Service Resources

Wire services have stringent standards for their member flower shops. They offer the benefit of recognition, co-ordinated advertising and marketing campaigns, a network of numerous florists to whom you can send your out-of-area orders, and a professional reputation.

In addition, they create and market specific arrangements for holidays and everyday use. They also offer regular education and accreditation opportunities for their members.

Florists' Transworld Delivery, Inc. (FTD)

Website: **www.ftdi.com/about.htm**
Address: FTD Inc.
              3113 Woodcreek Drive
              Downers Grove, IL 60515
Phone: 630-719-7800
E-mail: ftdmemberservices@ftdi.com

Teleflora

Website: **www.teleflora.com**
Address: Teleflora Membership and Directory Services
              P.O. Box 30130
              Los Angeles, CA 90030-0130
Phone: 800-421-2815

6.3.2 Selection Guides

Selection guides are large catalogs of pictures of flower arrangements prepared by order-gathering services such as FTD, Teleflora and others. They are divided into sections such as:

- *Any occasion*: Birthdays, get well, new baby

- *Seasonal*: Christmas, Valentine's Day, Easter, Mother's Day

- *Roses*: Roses in vases, boxes and arrangements

- *Sympathy*: Funeral tributes

- *Wedding:* Wedding bouquets, corsages and decorations

These selection guides have code numbers and prices marked next to each picture. Usually there are two prices offered: a standard price and a deluxe price. Depending on the flower shop's individual price structure, there could also be a within-the-city price and an out-of-town price. Every flower shop that belongs to an order-gathering service will have the same selection guide. Using the code number printed next to the chosen arrangement ensures the florist filling the order will make what the customer expects.

6.3.3 Orders Within the Country

To send an order within the same country as you're in, you need the following information:

- Recipient's name, address, city, zip or postal code and phone number

- Flowers requested

- Value of the order (in the currency of the country you're in)

- Delivery date

- Message for the card

Search either the order-gathering service's CD-ROM or the print directory for the store closest to the recipient's address. Once you've found the closest shop, check the codes in its listing to ensure the requested product will be available.

On the order form, write down the name of the chosen shop, its wire service membership number (all florists belonging to a wire service have a membership number listed immediately after their shop name in the directory), and its phone number.

6.3.4 International Orders

To send an order to a different country, you need the following information:

- Recipient's name and contact information (address, city, zip or postal code, country and phone number)

- Flowers requested

- Value of the order (in the currency of the country you're in)

- Delivery date

- Message for the card

As in the case of same-country orders, you will need to determine the florist closest to the recipient by searching the print or online directory. As with the previous section, write the filling florist's store name, membership number and phone number on the order form.

Accommodating Regional/International Customs

Flower-giving customs vary from region to region and country to country. In Europe, hand-tied bouquets of flowers are popular. In the United States, arrangements are preferred. In Canada, both arrangements and cut flowers are commonly requested. In addition, different parts of the world have different flowers in season at different times of year.

When you are sending an order to another part of the world, it is wise to specify only a general type of order (cut flowers, arranged flowers, plants, etc., depending on the customer's wish) and a value including the cost of delivery, and leave it up to the filling florist to take care of it from there.

6.3.5 First and Second Choice

For all out-of-area orders, it is important to have a first choice of product – based on the customer's most desired request – and a second choice of product which the customer understands will be sent if the first choice is not available.

If only a first choice is given, a sending florist may specify "no substitutions." If the filling florist does not have the requested product, they must decline the order or forward it to another florist in their area.

If "no substitutions" is not indicated, the filling florist may use similar flowers that add up to the order's intended value. The substitution should be for color first, then type of flowers (i.e., pink roses instead of red roses is preferable to red carnations instead of red roses).

Open Orders

When an order is sent within 24 hours of a major florist holiday (Christmas, Easter, Mother's Day, Valentine's Day), they are often sent as open orders or designer's choice. This means that the filling florist is able to fill the order with whatever is available, to the value specified. The customer understands that they will get their money's worth, but they do not have the freedom to choose what the recipient will receive.

6.3.6 Transmitting an Out-Of-Area Order

To transmit an order, you may use a florist network such as Mercury or Dove (which you gain access to by joining a wire service), you may fax the order, or you may phone the filling florist directly.

If you are using a network, you will follow the instructions that came with the computer software you got when you joined the network. Print out the order and attach the original order form to the printed page. Record the order number onto your incoming/outgoing orders log, and file the order.

If you are faxing the order, you will write or type the order on a piece of paper, including only the following information:

- First choice requested

- Second choice requested

- Total value

- Recipient's name, address and phone number

- Date of delivery

- Message for card

- Your flower shop's name, your florist network membership number, plus your phone number and fax number

If you are phoning the order, you will call the filling shop and announce "I have an FTD/Teleflora order for you." You will then give your shop name, florist network membership number, your phone number and your name.

Write down the name of the person you are speaking to, and then proceed to tell them the following information:

- First choice requested

- Second choice requested

- Total value

- Recipient's name, address and phone number

- Date of delivery

- Message for card

6.3.7   Receiving an Out-Of-Area Order

Phone Orders

When another florist calls with an out of area order, they will announce "I have an FTD/Teleflora order for you." You will need to get the following information:

- Their shop name, city and wire service membership number

- Their shop phone number

- The caller's first name

- Recipient's name

- Delivery date

- First and second request

- Value of order, including delivery

- Message for card

Orders are usually phoned when there is a special request, when the sending florist wants to make sure the requested product or delivery time is available, or when the sending florist doesn't have a computer system to send the order with.

Fax Orders

Usually the florist sending the fax will include all of the information listed above. If they do not, you will need to contact them and ask for the missing information. Orders are not commonly sent by fax, though faxes are occasionally used if there is a specific arrangement style that the sending florist wants to illustrate for the filling florist.

E-Mail Orders

If your flower shop has a website, customers may e-mail you directly with orders, or you may have an electronic order form incorporated into your website. These orders are treated in the same manner as telephone orders.

Wire Service Orders

When a wire service order arrives, it is automatically processed by your Mercury or Dove Network software, and it will automatically print on your computer's printer. You need to record the order number and date it arrived, and process it as described in the following section.

Filling an Order

When an order arrives, the same steps should be followed no matter where it came from:

1. Calculate the amount of the delivery fee, and subtract it from the total order amount.

2. Circle the delivery date so it is instantly noticeable.

3. Write the message on an enclosure card, and place it in an enclosure card envelope.

4. Write the recipient's name, address and phone number on the envelope.

5. Attach the order to the envelope with a paper clip or staple.

6. File the order under the delivery day/date. Some florists use a file system, some use a series of pegs marked with the days of the week, and some use boxes marked with the days of the week. If the order is for more than a week in advance, it would

go into the box marked "advance," which is checked daily for upcoming orders to move into the daily order boxes. See the sidebar on the next page for advice on setting up a filing system.

7. When the order is to be prepared, look at the first choice request and prepare the requested item. If the first choice item is not available, prepare the second choice item.

8. Remove the envelope with its enclosed card from the order form, and attach the envelope to the finished item with tape or a cardette holder.

9. Draw a line across the order form and file it in the box or file where completed orders are stored.

10. Place the finished product in the delivery staging area (the part of the shop where deliveries are kept until the delivery driver removes them).

11. Some florists record their own outgoing deliveries on a log that includes the recipient's name, a brief description of the product, and the delivery date. Others have their delivery driver keep track of this information.

12. If there is a request to phone the recipient to ensure they're home before delivery, keep the order near the phone, and make the call while the driver is at the shop. That way, if the recipient isn't home, the order can be held back until the recipient can be reached.

When taking an out-of-area order, it is customary to charge the customer a service or transmission fee, which is usually anywhere from five to twenty dollars based on the order's destination.

Orders sent within the same state or province will have a lower service fee than those sent internationally. Part of this fee goes to the wire service, which charges a per-order transmission fee. Part may go to the sending shop, for providing the service of taking and sending the order.

Organizing Daily Orders

Here's an easy, low-tech way to organize daily orders:

Prepare a series of boxes, one for each day of the week your shop is open, plus two extras. Label each box with the day of the week it corresponds to (e.g. Monday, Tuesday, etc.). Label one extra box "Today" and the other "Future." When orders arrive, place them (complete with card and delivery envelope attached) in the box that corresponds to the date of delivery. If an order arrives for "Today," put it in that box.

Each day, remove the orders in the box according to the day of the week it is, and put them in the Today box for preparation by the designers. However, if there is an order in the Monday box for a week from Monday, leave it there. If there is an order for sometime next month, put it in the Future box. At the end of each week, check the future box to see if there are any orders that are for delivery in the coming week. Move those to the appropriate boxes.

Consider designating a special box for holidays, particularly ones that have a lot of advance orders. For holidays that require a variety of orders that must be delivered on the same day, it is possible to designate a box for each type of flower order (i.e. Valentine's Cut Flowers, Valentine's Boxed Roses, Valentine's Arrangements). That way, when the busy time comes, individual designers can concentrate on one type of arrangement, a system that makes their work more efficient.

6.4 Getting Paid

Credit and Debit Cards

When a customer pays with a credit card or debit card, the transaction is usually approved and the customer is free to leave with the item. If, however, the card is declined, you must ask for a different payment method.

Tact is welcome in this situation. Apologize to the customer and suggest that they try another card. Say, "I'm sorry, it seems to not be taking your card right now. Would you like to try another one, or would you like to use cash instead?"

You can also contact the card issuing company (the phone number will be printed on the back of the card) for further instructions. They may permit the sale, or they may instruct you to retain the card to be returned to them. Or, they may instruct you to destroy the card on the spot.

Billing

Many florists tend to prefer to bill customers only after they've developed a longstanding relationship with them. They may also bill corporate clients they know they can rely on to pay promptly. Policies about billing vary from flower shop to flower shop. Usually, the terms of the bill require customers to pay as soon as they receive the bill, with interest or a late fee charged after 30 days.

Order-Taking Stationery

There are many varieties of order-taking stationery available, some of which are meant to fit into invoice holders and some of which stand alone. In any case, these are all referred to as customer invoices or order forms. Make three copies of each invoice — one for the customer, one for the workroom, and one for accounting. They are printed with spaces for the florist to write all the information needed to fill the order.

6.5 Gracious Returns and Refunds

With a perishable product such as flowers, it is inevitable that, at some point or another, an order may not meet a customer's expectations. When this happens, it is important to listen to the customer to determine their desired outcome.

Ask what they would like to have happen, and if their request agrees with store policy, agree to it. If not, calmly explain the store's policy and ask them what the best option would be for them.

Sample Customer Invoice

Fabulous Florists
1234 Main Street
Prettytown, PA 33333
(888) 999-1234

Invoice #: 99999
Date: December 15, 2008

Contact Information

Customer name: Jared Hopkiss

Address: 4321 Main Street
Prettytown, PA 33333

Phone: 222-1234

Payment method: ___ Cash   ___ Credit
___ Check   ___ Debit

Order

		Price
First choice:	12 long stem roses, red, in vase	$60.00
Second choice:	12 roses, any color, in vase	$60.00
Delivery fee:		$5.00
Sales tax (at 7%):		$4.55

Total:		$69.55

Other

Notes: Recipient is allergic to baby's breath; please use other filler (likes statice)

Delivery date: December 24, 2008

Special instructions: Call first, if not home leave in porch

Deliver to: Tia Hopkiss
4321 Main Street
Prettytown, PA 33333
(Phone: 222-1234)

Card: "Merry Christmas, Sweetheart. With love, Jared. P.S. Look in your stocking!"

Store policies on returns and refunds vary, and so do the guarantees they offer. Here are a few possibilities:

- *Unconditional guarantee:* Full refund, anytime, for any reason.

- *Conditional guarantee:* Refund offered on flowers as long as certain conditions have been met. Could also apply to individual flowers in an arrangement.

- *24-hour guarantee:* Flowers that do not meet customers' expectations will be replaced, unconditionally, as long as they are returned to the store within 24 hours of delivery.

Replacement Options

If a customer desires a replacement, there are several options. If flowers in an arrangement are unsatisfactory, invite the customer back to the shop to have individual flowers professionally replaced. If the entire arrangement does not meet the customer's needs (a situation which occurs most often with orders sent from another city), they may return it to the shop and choose something else of equal value.

Usually, due to the fragile nature of flowers and their sensitivity to the conditions under which they are kept, this kind of return must happen within 24 hours.

Preventive measures go a long way towards minimizing returns:

- Spray arrangements with Hawaiian Mist, Crowning Glory, or other preservatives before delivery.

- Send cut roses with water piks on the ends of their stems.

- Enclose care instructions and a packet of floral food/preservative with each delivery.

- Package "tippy" arrangements, such as vase arrangements, in shallow cardboard boxes. Wrap doughnuts of crumpled newspaper around the base of the vase inside the box, or anchor the vase between criss-crossed strips of cellophane tape attached to the sides of the box.

- Wrap plants in paper sleeves to prevent damage to leaves or flowers.

- Ensure delivery drivers have adequate space and stabilizers in their vehicles to prevent spills or breakage in transit.

- Avoid promising specific times for delivery. "Morning" or "afternoon" is a realistic expectation, but "Exactly 3:15 this afternoon" is not.

Make sure the original bouquet is returned before a refund or replacement is made. Remember that while you may not agree with a customer's reasons for dissatisfaction, they are justified in their feelings and disappointment. A repeat customer is one whose needs are met promptly, cheerfully and unquestioningly.

6.6 Keeping Customers

Experts say that 60 percent of your advertising dollars should be spent on maintaining your existing customers. It seems like a lot, but it's a wise piece of advice because your existing customers are your best ones. They know the kind of work you do and have a good idea of the options available for using flowers in their daily lives. They probably have your phone number at hand, and may even recommend your store to their friends. That kind of customer is your best ally — but don't be fooled, because even the most loyal customer can be swayed by a competitor with a better deal.

Keeping customers is essential to the ongoing success of your business, and there are many ways you can do so. You can offer rewards, such as flowers or a discount, for frequent purchases. You can keep in touch with customers by mailing them a monthly newsletter, or inviting them to answer a survey about your business. You can even offer a "frequent flower" club membership that encourages them to make frequent purchases.

I watched one florist sell a bonsai plant to a pair of young men who were looking for a gift for their mother. When they walked into the shop, they didn't know anything about bonsai, the ancient Japanese art of miniature trees. They simply knew their mom liked plants. The florist asked questions about the mother's interest to determine the best kind of plant to suggest: Does she have a lot of plants? Do they have flowers on them? Where does she keep them?

It appeared that the mother was an experienced keeper of houseplants, and would like something different. So the florist showed the young men a selection of indoor bonsai and explained how the plants were carefully treated to create dwarf plants. She explained the history of the art form and discussed the differences between indoor and outdoor bonsai.

The young men agreed that their mother would like to try something new, and not only bought a bonsai plant, but a number of accessories to go with it. And next time they need flowers, the florist feels sure they'll return to her shop, because she took the time to explain and share with them — not as a sales pitch, but simply as a way of helping them learn about something new.

This is how customers like to be treated — especially in flower shops, where they may feel intimidated by their lack of knowledge. If they don't know anything about flowers beyond the common conceptions that flowers are delicate, expensive, and don't last long, they're likely to appreciate your explanations about the quality and variety of your flowers. They'll be happy to have the opportunity to make up their own minds, rather than be faced with a strong sales pitch that tells them the $60-a-dozen roses are the only way to go.

Whether they walk into your shop on a whim, phone for a specific purpose, or are considering using your shop for all their corporation's floral needs, your clients are people. It sounds simple, but it's an important principle to keep in mind. Human nature is such that if you treat your customers well, they'll return and bring their friends. Treat them poorly, and they'll complain to everyone they know. The next few sections will help you along the path towards making sure you treat every customer well — so that ultimately they'll buy more and help you make your business more successful.

6.6.1 Promoting Client Loyalty

Customers tend to be more loyal to businesses where they feel like they're known and recognized. Try to learn the names of as many of your regular customers as you can, and greet them by name when they come into your shop. Keep a list of all your customers' names, addresses, phone numbers, and e-mail addresses, and make note of their birthdays, anniversaries, or other special events.

Whenever a customer makes a significant purchase – say, more than $50 or $100 – why not thank them? A quick e-mail message takes you almost no time to send, but it lets your customer know that you appreciate their business.

Offer an e-mail reminder service. A week or so before their family birthdays, anniversaries, or other events, send a quick e-mail letting them know what kinds of flowers are in season, and that you'll be ready to prepare their flowers as soon as they call to place their order.

Send out a monthly newsletter, keeping customers in touch with your shop. Offer flower and plant care tips, talk about what's in season, and give a preview of the types of arrangements that will be available for any upcoming holiday.

Identify your top 50 or top 100 customers on this list by keeping track of the amount they purchase. At least once a year, thank them with a small arrangement or even a single rose with a personal note on the card.

6.6.2 Client Rewards

By rewarding your best customers, you will make them into even better customers, and you will also enlist their goodwill when it comes to passing your business name along to others.

Rewarding your customers doesn't have to be expensive or elaborate, unless you want it to be. Here are some suggestions for ways to remind your customers how much they mean to you:

- Host an evening gathering for your top customers to preview new arrangements. Send out invitations, and encourage them to bring their address books so they can have priority for sending out-of-area orders.

- Offer free transmission for out-of-area orders for your top customers.

- Invite small groups of interested customers to learn basic floral design techniques at your store on an evening when your store isn't open. Offer a modest discount on any flowers they want to buy that evening.

- Offer services such as free plant repotting with every new pot purchased, or free arrangement with any cash and carry bouquet purchased along with a vase.

6.6.3 Frequent Flower Clubs

You know the punch cards you get at your local video store or coffee shop? The ones that give you a free cup of coffee or video rental for every 10 you purchase? They're a simple and inexpensive way of rewarding loyal customers, and those businesses know that. So why not start your own "Frequent Flower" club?

First, decide on how you want to structure your rewards program. You could offer an incentive for every $10 spent in your store, or you could go by the number of purchases made. A typical rewards program will offer a bonus at milestones, such as after $50 or $100 is spent.

Next, decide what kind of reward you want to offer. It should be something that isn't too expensive for you, and it should be something the customer wants. Buying ten bouquets to get the eleventh for free is a good incentive, because you know the customer wants bouquets.

Buying $100 worth of flowers could be good for a 10 percent off coupon on their next purchase, or it could be enough to earn a free delivery, free transmission for out-of-area orders, or another minor but useful incentive. Offer bigger rewards for larger amounts.

To keep track of the purchases, print business-card-sized cards with information about your frequent flower program, and boxes or spaces for you to punch each time a qualifying purchase is made. You can also keep track on your computer system, if you prefer.

When the customer reaches their reward-earning goal, don't just give them the reward and let them go. Give them a new card, and encourage them to start again. If you like, you can even get them started with the first square already punched.

7. Resources

The following is a directory of national and regional professional organizations for the floral industry.

National Associations

American Floral Endowment
P.O. Box 945
Edwardsville, IL 62025
Phone: 618-692-0045
Fax: 618-692-4045
afe@endowment.org
www.endowment.org

**American Institute of
Floral Designers**
720 Light Street
Baltimore, MD 21230
Phone: 410-752-3318
Fax. 410-752-8295
AIFD@assnhqtrs.com
www.aifd.org

**Association of Specialty
Cut Flower Growers**
MPO Box 268
Oberlin, OH 44074
Phone: 440-774-2887
Fax: 440-774-2435
ascfg@oberlin.net
www.ascfg.org

Flowers Canada
99 Fifth Avenue, Suite 305
Ottawa, ON K1S 5P5
Phone: 800-447-5147
flowers@flowerscanada.org
www.flowerscanada.org

FTD Inc.
3113 Woodcreek Drive
Downers Grove, IL 60515
Phone: 800-767-4000
emarketplace@ftdi.com
www.ftdimarketplace.com

Society of American Florists
1601 Duke Street
Alexandria, VA 22314
Phone: 800-336-4743
memberinfo@safnow.org
www.safnow.org

Teleflora
P.O. Box 30130
Los Angeles, CA 90030-0130
Phone: 800-421-2815
www.myteleflora.com

Regional Associations

**Alabama State Florists
Association**
2798 John Hawkins Pkwy,
Ste. 124
Hoover, AL 35244
Phone: 205-989-8001

**Alaska State Florists
Association**
253 Idaho Street
Anchorage, AK 95044
Phone: 907-333-6908

Arizona State Florists Association
850 East Camino Alberca
Tucson, AZ 85718
Phone: 520-742-1409

Arkansas State Florists Association
P. O. Box 500
Plumerville, AR 72127
Phone: 501-690-4819

Ozark Florists Association
1111 Garrison
Fort Smith, AR 72901
Phone: 479-783-5146

California State Floral Association
1521 "I" Street
Sacramento, CA 95814
Phone: 916-448-5266
www.calstatefloral.com

Colorado Greenhouse Growers Association
7475 Dakin Street, Suite 540
Denver, CO 80221-6919
Phone: 800-748-3744

Connecticut Florists Association
590 Main St. Bart Center
Monroe, CT 06468
Phone: 800-352-6946
www.flowersplantsinct.com/cfaindex.htm

Florida State Florists Assocation
1612 South Dixie Highway
Lake Worth, FL 33460
Phone: 561-585-9491

Georgia State Florists Association
789 Roswell St.
Marietta, GA 30060
Phone: 912-524-2386

Idaho State Florists Association
715 North Main St
Pocatello, ID 83204
Phone: 208-232-5476

Illinois State Florists Association
1442 Gallatin Pike North
Madison, TN 37115
Phone: 615-868-8606
www.illinoisflorists.org

State Florists' Association of Indiana
P. O. Box 133
Monrovia, IN 46157
Phone: 317-996-2241

Society of Iowa Florists and Growers
48428 290th Ave
Rolfe, IA 50581
Phone: 712-848-3251

Kansas State Florists Association
112 South Main Street
Greensburg, KS 67054
Phone: 620-723-2603

Kentucky Florists Association
3954 Cane Run Road
Louisville, KY 40211
Phone: 502-778-1666

Louisiana State Florists Association
224 Hodges Rd.
Ruston, LA 71270
Phone: 318-255-2671

Maine State Florists and Growers Association
216-A Maine Street
Brunswick, ME 04011
Phone: 207-729-8895
www.msfga.com

Michigan Floral Association
1152 Haslett Road
Haslett, MI 48840
Phone: 517-575-0110
Fax: 517-575-0115
www.michiganfloral.org

Minnesota State Florists Association
1536 Woodland Drive
Woodbury, MN 55125
Phone: 952-934-4505

Mississippi State Florists Association
403 Highway 11 North
Ellisville, MS 39437
Phone: 601-477-8381

Montana State Florists Association
P. O. Box 1456
Great Falls, MT 59403
Phone: 406-452-6489

Nebraska Florists Society
1900 SW 22nd Street
Lincoln, NE 68522
Phone: 402-421-2613

North Nevada Florists Association
519 Ralston Street
Reno, NV 89503
Phone: 775-323-8951

New Hampshire State Florists Association
21 Roger Road
Goffstown, NH 03045
Phone: 603-627-8828
www.nhsfa.com

New Jersey State Florists' Association
88 Fawnridge Drive West
Long Valley, NJ 07853
Phone: 908-876-1850

New Mexico State Florists Association
P. O. Box 3342
Roswell, NM 88202
Phone: 505-265-1019

New York Florists Association
249 East 149th Street
Bronx, NY 10451
Phone: 718-585-3060

North Carolina State Florists Association
P. O. Box 41368
Raleigh, NC 27629
Phone: 919-876-0687
execman@att.net
www.ncflorist.org

Ohio Florists Association
2130 Stella Court, Ste. 200
Columbus, OH 43215
Phone: 614-487-1117
www.ofa.org

Oklahoma State Florists Association
P. O. Box 614
Drumright, OK 74030
Phone: 888-482-4496

Pennsylvania Floral Industry Association
4305 North Sixth Street, Suite A
Harrisburg, PA 17102
Phone: 800-234-3779
info@pafloral.org
www.pafloral.org

Rhode Island Retail Florists Association
820 Boston Neck Road
North Kingstown, RI 02852
Phone: 401-294-9015

South Carolina Florists Association
1663 Russell Street NE
Orangeburg, SC 29115
Phone: 803-534-3780

Tennessee State Florists Association
P.O. Box 240235
Memphis, TN 38124
Phone: 901-323-4521
www.tnsfa.org

Texas State Florists Association
P. O. Box 140255
Austin, TX 78714
Phone: 512-834-0361
txsfa@aol.com
www.tsfa.org

Central Virginia Florists Association
501 Courthouse Road
Richmond, VA 23236
Phone: 804-378-0700

Wisconsin and Upper Michigan Florists Association
6737 West Washington St, Suite 1420
Milwaukee, WI 53214
Phone: 414-755-6290

World Flower Council
10476 East Cannon Drive
Scottsdale, AZ 85258
Phone: 480-860-0906
dean@worldflowercouncil.org
www.worldflowercouncil.org

More Fabulous Books

Find out how to break into the "fab" job of your dreams with FabJob career guides. Each 2-in-1 set includes a print book and CD-ROM.

Get Paid to Plan Weddings

Imagine having an exciting high paying job that lets you use your creativity to organize the happiest day of people's lives. **FabJob Guide to Become a Wedding Planner** shows you how to:

- Plan a wedding ceremony and reception
- Select reputable vendors and avoid disasters
- Get a wedding planning job with a resort, tourist attraction or other wedding industry employer
- Start a wedding planning business, price your services, and find clients
- Plan your own wedding like a professional wedding planner
- Be certified as a professional wedding planner

Get Paid to Decorate

Imagine having a rewarding high paying job that lets you use your creativity to make homes and businesses beautiful and comfortable. **FabJob Guide to Become an Interior Decorator** shows how to:

- Teach yourself interior decorating (includes step-by-step decorating instructions)
- Get 10-50% discounts on furniture and materials
- Create an impressive portfolio even if you have no previous paid decorating experience
- Get a job with a retailer, home builder or other interior design industry employer
- Start an interior decorating business, price your services, and find clients

Visit www.FabJob.com to order guides today!